Hope Is Cut

In the series *Global Youth*,

edited by Craig Jeffrey and Jane Dyson

Daniel Mains

Hope Is Cut

Youth, Unemployment, and the Future
in Urban Ethiopia

TEMPLE UNIVERSITY PRESS
Philadelphia

TEMPLE UNIVERSITY PRESS
Philadelphia, Pennsylvania 19122
www.temple.edu/tempress

Library of Congress Cataloging-in-Publication Data

Mains, Daniel, 1975–
    Hope is cut : youth, unemployment, and the future in urban Ethiopia / Daniel Mains.
        p. cm. — (Global youth)
    Includes bibliographical references and index.
    ISBN 978-1-4399-0479-4 (cloth : alk. paper) — ISBN 978-1-4399-0481-7 (e-book)
    1. Urban youth—Ethiopia—Social conditions. 2. Urban youth—Employment—Ethiopia.
    3. Urban youth—Ethiopia—Attitudes. 4. Ethiopia—Economic conditions. I. Title.
    II. Series: Global youth.
    HQ799.E82M35 2011
    305.2350963'091732—dc22

                                                                            2011015095

ISBN 978-1-4399-0480-0 (paperback : alk. paper)

Printed in the United States of America

032713P

In memory of Elias Beyene, a great teacher and a wonderful friend who dedicated his life to providing hope for others

Contents

Series Editors' Preface   ix

Acknowledgments   xi

Introduction: Youth, Hope, Stratification, and Time   1

1   The Historical and Cultural Roots of Unemployment
and Stratification in Urban Ethiopia   25

2   Imagining Hopeful Futures through Khat and Film   43

3   "We Live Like Chickens; We Are Just Eating and Sleeping": Progress,
Education, and the Temporal Struggles of Young Men   67

4   Working toward Hope: Youth Unemployment, Occupational
Status, and Values   87

5   Hopeful Exchanges: Reciprocity and Changing Dimensions
of Urban Stratification   113

6   Spatial Fixes to Temporal Problems: Migration, Social
Relationships, and Work   135

Conclusion: Sustaining Hope in the Present and the Future   155

Notes   171

References   179

Index   187

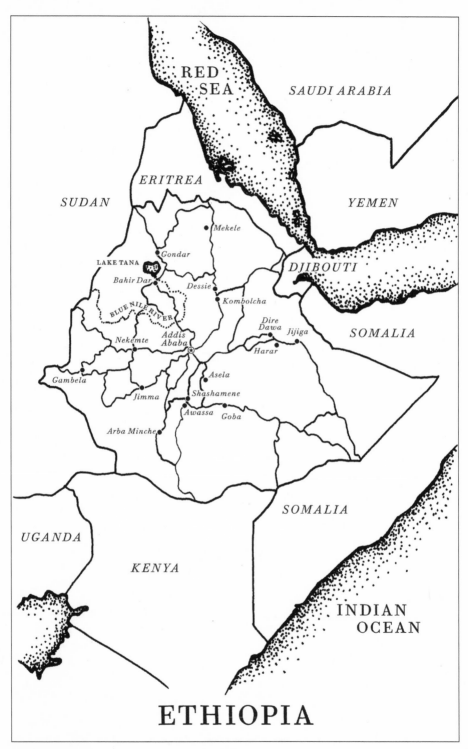

Ethiopia country map. (Courtesy of Walter Baumann.)

Series Editors' Preface

Global social and economic changes are transforming the lives of children and youth. In many parts of the world, the decline of state welfare systems since the 1980s has undermined young people's efforts to obtain social goods associated with "adulthood," such as a stable job, valuable skills, and secure housing. At the same time, economic collapse and the restructuring of labor markets have often forced children and youth to assume responsibility for social reproduction. Ironically, converging socioeconomic crises are occurring at a time when, via the international media, young people are increasingly exposed to images of successful adulthood based on education and professional employment.

Young people are not passive in the face of these changes; they are centrally involved in a range of disparate, and sometimes complexly linked, forms of social and political action. Writing nearly eighty years ago, Karl Mannheim (1972) famously argued that the members of each generation experience a "fresh contact" with their social and natural environment. He emphasized young people's capacity to rethink the institutional structures that they inherit from previous generations. But even Mannheim would be perplexed by the intensity of young people's contemporary assertions, from striking new efforts to fashion youth cultures, to novel types of entrepreneurship, to innovative political mobilization of various hues, of which the recent protests in North Africa and the Middle East are only the most obvious. Perhaps one of the inevitable consequences of this curious combination of young people's subordination and assertion is that people in their teens and twenties have become mythologized in the media. We are now accustomed to reading of young people as heroes and zeroes, innocent and guilty, the problem and the panacea.

The *Global Youth* book series offers a venue for scholars charting the experiences and practices of young people entangled in these global changes. We bring together work that examines youth and aspects of globalization within sociology, anthropology, development studies, geography, and educational studies. We are especially keen to encourage work on youth in areas of the world that are often excluded from mainstream discussions of young people, such as Latin America, Africa, Asia, and Eastern Europe, but we also aim to include studies from Western Europe and North America, as well as books that bridge the global North and global South. The series, which focuses on those between the ages of (roughly) ten and thirty, is also concerned with studies of the different ways people and institutions discuss "youth" as a concept. Books in the series may take the form of novel syntheses of existing research or accounts of innovative substantive research. They may consist of outstanding single-country studies or offer comparative perspectives. What will unite books in the series is their commitment to sharp, critical, highly informed analysis that moves forward not only academic and policy makers' thinking but also public understanding of youth. As is surely fitting, we expect many of the books to be written by early- and mid-career scholars.

Daniel Mains's wonderful anthropology of Ethiopian youth provides a superb start for the series. Mains focuses on the predicament and practices of jobless young people in urban Ethiopia, where youth unemployment runs at 50 percent. Building on long-term ethnography, Mains describes young people's experiences of economic malaise, teasing out how youth in contemporary Ethiopia perceive time and space. He also provides a detailed account of the complex ways in which different young people navigate this uncertain environment—for example, by developing new social networks, joining nongovernmental organizations, or migrating. We are left with a vivid picture of young people's resourcefulness, one that resolutely refuses to fall into the trap of eulogizing or infantilizing the book's subjects. It is an extraordinary achievement and a testament to the continuing importance of ethnography for an understanding of globalization. Mains's study will soon become a landmark in its field. We hope that all the books in the series do the same.

Craig Jeffrey and Jane Dyson
Oxford
February 2011

Acknowledgments

The long process of researching and writing this book has extended across a range of times and places. At each point along the way, people have provided valuable advice and critiques. At Emory University Don Donham, Bruce Knauft, Hudita Mustafa, and Debra Spitulnik patiently advised me through the research and writing processes. Special thanks go to Don Donham, who shares my interest in Ethiopia and was happy to engage in lenthy discussions about historical and cultural particularities. Don was also very generous in hosting a writing group at his home in Oakland, California. Sarah Mathis, Chris Krupa, Tim Murphy, Ayesha Nibbe, Nick D'Avella, and Ramah McKay all participated in that group and provided valuable feedback on early versions of this book.

Walter Baumann is a great friend, and he was very generous with his time in volunteering to make the beautiful maps of Ethiopia and Jimma that appear in the book. Ryan Brown was very helpful in thinking through some of my quantitative data and comparing notes on issues concerning youth and aspirations. I owe thanks to Brandon Kohrt and Dan Hruschka for their humor and their outstanding questions. Ron Barrett provided detailed feedback on the introductory chapter. Material in Chapter 2 was originally published in Daniel Mains, "Chewing and Dreaming: Youth, Imagination, and the Consumption of Khat in Jimma, Southwestern Ethiopia," in *Khat in Ethiopia: Taking the Place of Food*, edited by Ezekiel Gebissa, 29–56 (Trenton, NJ: Red Sea Press, 2010). Ezekiel provided a number of insightful suggestions that influenced the argument developed here. Joanna Davidson offered helpful comments on material in Chapters 5 and 6. Mulugeta Tsehay provided commentary on the Introduction and Chapter 1.

It has been wonderful to develop friendships and research partnerships with other anthropologists working in Ethiopia. Jed Stevenson, Craig Hadley, and Kenneth Maes all read portions of this book and, even more important-ly, spent time with me in Jimma talking through the practical and theoretical struggles of research.

Portions of this book were presented at numerous conferences and were included in various invited presentations. I am grateful to all the people who organized these talks and asked the tough questions that pushed my thinking in different directions.

Funding for my 2003–2005 research was provided by a Fulbright-Hays Doctoral Dissertation Research Abroad Grant and by grants from the Emory University Graduate Fund for Internationalization and the Emory Universi-ty Department of Anthropology. Research conducted in 2008 and 2009 was funded by National Science Foundation grant # 0717608.

Much of the writing and revising for this book took place during a two-year postdoctoral fellowship with the African and African American Studies Program at Washington University in St. Louis. I thank my colleagues in the African and African American Studies Program and the Anthropology Depart-ment for all their support. I am especially grateful to Derek Pardue for organiz-ing a "work in progress" seminar, which generated very useful feedback. I also thank Amina Gauthier, who was a great friend to my family and me during our time in St. Louis.

The final manuscript revisions were completed while I was teaching at Colby College in Waterville, Maine. I have been inspired by the passion for activism and research shared by my colleagues in the Anthropology Depart-ment at Colby: Tom Abowd, Jeff Anderson, Catherine Besteman, Chandra Bhimull, Britt Halvorson, Mary Beth Mills, Maple Razsa, and Winifred Tate.

I thank Craig Jeffrey and Jane Dyson, editors of the Temple University Press series *Global Youth*, for believing in the value of my work. Craig and Jane were very generous with their time, providing feedback on the complete book manuscript. I am grateful to Jennifer Cole and an anonymous reviewer for their detailed and insightful comments on the manuscript. It has been a pleasure to work with Mick Gusinde-Duffy at Temple University Press. Mick has been extremely helpful in guiding me through the publication process. Rebecca Logan and her staff at Newgen North America did a great job with the copyediting.

In Ethiopia I was affiliated with the Institute for Ethiopian Studies at Addis Ababa University. The Cultural Affairs Department at the U.S. Embassy in Addis Ababa provided valuable support from 2003 to 2005.

I am eternally grateful to all the people in Jimma who participate in my ongoing research. I have become good friends with most of the young people who are discussed in this book. I have also developed a number of friendships that are less directly related to my research. Taddesse Habte-Selassie, Elias Beyene, ·Kidist Kereta, Wondwosen Taye, and Teshome Bekele all invited me into their homes and lives. They have been eager to hear about my research and have not hesitated to tell me when they disagree with my conclusions. I do not know of another place in the world where I can return after two years and feel at home the moment I arrive. It is the support of all these friends that inspires this wonderful feeling.

Alise Osis is the one person who has been part of this project at every stage. We have been together in Atlanta, Jimma, San Francisco, St. Louis, and Waterville, and our next stop is Oklahoma. Alise has supported me at each phase of the process, always encouraging me to keep researching and writing. Now our children, Iris and Gus, are also part of the team, and together with Alise they make the journey all the more joyful and interesting.

Introduction

Youth, Hope, Stratification, and Time

I n the mornings and evenings, when the sun does not burn with such an extreme intensity, the street corners of Jimma, Ethiopia, are crowded with unemployed young men. They stand with their hands in their pockets sharing gossip, cracking jokes, and occasionally tossing out a mild insult at a passerby. These young men often joke that the only change in their lives is following the shade from one side of the street to the other with the passing of the sun. In neighborhoods with more commercial activity, the unemployed share the streets with young men working as shoeshines, barbers, bicycle mechanics, minibus touts, and petty traders. These two populations, working and unemployed young men, both negotiate a situation in which their aspirations for the future do not fit with economic realities.

In Ethiopia, it is common to use the Amharic equivalent of the word *hopeless* (*tesfa qoretewal*) to describe the condition of urban youth. Like in other Ethiopian cities, in Jimma, a city of approximately 150,000 located about two hundred miles southwest of Addis Ababa, the unemployment rate for youth with a secondary education is estimated to be close to 50 percent (Serneels 2007). Young men claim that a lack of available work is the most significant barrier to attaining their aspirations. To be hopeless, one must have previously had hope. The Amharic phrase *tesfa qoretewal* expresses this clearly.[1] It literally means "hope is cut." The notion of hope being cut evokes an image of hope existing as a thread linking the present to the future. Hope is necessarily temporal in the sense that it is always fulfilled in the future. Progress is the process of moving toward hope with the passage of time. When hope is cut, one's relationship to the future changes. Progress no longer takes place. The connection to the future is severed, and one's future becomes indistinguishable from the present.

Modernization and development are hopes. They are powerful beliefs in the possibility of reaching a better world by following a specific series of steps that connect future hopes to the present. To some extent, narratives of modernization have structured the hopes of young men in urban Ethiopia. Capitalist and socialist models of industrial modernization that dominated the twentieth century attempted to bring about utopia at both the individual and collective levels (Buck-Morss 2000). The Ethiopian state sought to enact specifically local versions of these models during the latter half of the twentieth century. Revolutionary socialism touched lives in remote areas of the country during the 1970s and 1980s (Donham 1999b), and a slow process of economic liberalization has done the same beginning in the early 1990s (Ellison 2009).

James Ferguson's work (1990, 1999, 2006) represents perhaps the most extensive investigation of issues related to modernity, development, progress, and capitalism in an African context, and I engage with his ideas throughout this book. Ferguson has argued that in a context of economic globalization, narratives of progress and development in Africa have been derailed. During the past thirty years, dropping life expectancies, stagnant economic growth, and crumbling government infrastructures have become common across the continent. The magic of the free market that was intended to bring about modernization through structural adjustment policies has failed. Ferguson (1999) uses the terms *abjection* and *disconnection* to describe the experience of this process. Like the cutting of hope, disconnection implies the loss of something that was previously present.

If Africa has been derailed from a modernist narrative of progress, then this experience is especially acute for young people. Jean and John Comaroff have argued that youth is "the historical offspring of modernity," in the sense that youth represents a stage in an inevitable process of development. The Comaroffs write that youth is the "essential precondition and indefinite postponement of maturity" (2005: 19). The concepts of youth, development, and modernity are based on linear conceptions of time. Just as maturation from child to adult involves attaining a specific set of biological and social markers, becoming modern requires movement along a linear track that permits little variation. In this sense, to be a youth and to aspire to change are in some ways inseparable.

The difficulty of attaining aspirations and taking on the normative responsibilities of adults is a condition that anthropologists have identified among youth across the continent. Young men in Niger cannot access the funds to make bridewealth payments (Masquelier 2005). Youth in Zambia have little chance of finding work and obtaining economic independence (Hansen 2005). In East Africa, young men often experience their inability to take on the responsibilities of adults as crises of masculinity (Silberschmidt 2004; Weiss 2004b). In urban Senegal, underemployed young men pass their time drinking endless rounds of tea and discussing possible futures (Ralph 2008). On the basis of her study in urban Madagascar, Jennifer Cole (2005) has argued that the social category of youth is no longer a transitional stage associated with the transformation from child to adult. When that transformation becomes impossible, then one's existence as a youth has the potential to become indefinite.

In Ethiopia, widespread urban unemployment has meant that the period in which young men exist as neither child nor adult has been extended. Young men I knew in Jimma were approaching age thirty, still living at home with their parents, unable to marry and start a family of their own. The cutting of hope for young men implies a failure to attain the social responsibilities of an adult male. This should not imply, however, that young people lack goals and aspirations. Despite the difficulty of achieving their aspirations, young men in Ethiopia wish to own a house and car, support a family, and become a respected member of the community. While changing economic conditions are acknowledged, the expectation that young people will take on the responsibilities of adults persists. In the eyes of many, to be a youth is to aspire to and dream of a better life. As one mother of an unemployed young man in Jimma put it, "Today's generation is different. They are educated, and they have knowledge about the world. Today they want so many things." Youth are perceived as both being hopeless and possessing unprecedented aspirations. These conditions are mutually constitutive rather than contradictory. It is partially the elevated ambitions of young men that cause hopelessness.

In a context characterized by both economic decline and increasing access to education and international media, this peculiar combination of hopelessness and lofty goals is common among much of the world's growing population of youth (Amit and Dyke n.d.; Jeffrey 2008). Particularly in relation to young men, anthropologists have argued that the contrast between aspiration and opportunity leads to involvement in political unrest and violence (Cruise O'Brien 1996; Diouf 2003; P. Richards 1996). If young men have no chance of obtaining employment and economic independence, then they have little to lose and everything to gain from participating in political movements. Unemployed, educated, young people were the driving force behind the 2011 political uprisings in the Middle East and North Africa. In Ethiopia urban young men are often referred to with the Amharic term *fendata*, which translates roughly as "explosive." Young men's explosions may take a variety of different forms. Students in Addis Ababa were a key force behind the 1974 revolution (Balsvik 1985; Donham 1999b). More recently, following the 2005 national election, political protests erupted into riots among primarily unemployed young men in Addis Ababa. More than ten thousand young men were arrested and detained in camps outside the city.

Eruptions of political violence such as this are certainly important, but they are also episodic. These spectacular events often attract the attention of journalists and academics, and as a result the day-to-day lived realities of youth are ignored. This book examines less visible, but no less important struggles of young men to find work, attain economic independence, and raise a family. These quotidian experiences shed light on why youth have been at the center of recent political turmoil, but they are also important in their own right. At the core of this study is the basic question of what happens when young people are unable to attain their desires for the future. What happens when hope is cut? The struggles of young men to attain their hopes for the future are wrapped up in issues of class, status, and reciprocity, as well as space, time, and modernity. In this chapter I examine some of the connections between the particular case of young men in Jimma, Ethiopia, and broader theoretical questions. First, however, it is necessary to briefly explain the basic dynamics of youth unemployment, both in Ethiopia and in the global South more generally. The "global South" as an analytical category certainly obscures a great deal variation, but I believe it also highlights important similarities between the experiences of youth in different world areas.

Cutting Hope: Youth and Unemployment in the Global South

For urban youth in Ethiopia, the most important barrier to the attainment of aspirations is finding employment. Among young people in urban Ethiopia, unemployment is the norm. Most are first-time job seekers, and the average length of unemployment is between three and four years (Serneels 2007). I sometimes asked youth if there is any shame associated with long-term unemployment. They were usually surprised by this question. They explained that a condition shared by so many people could not be considered shameful. At the same time, young people felt that a lack of work was at the root of their problems. Taking on the social responsibilities of adults depended on finding work. In the absence of work, long-term unemployed young men sometimes spoke of bouts of depression, asking themselves, "Why don't I work? Why do I still live with my family? For how long will this condition continue?" One young man even claimed that he had considered suicide after more than five years of unemployment.

A stark contrast between aspirations for the future and economic opportunity is common among young people throughout much of the world, but it is particularly acute among urban youth in the global South, and as in Ethiopia, unemployment is often a primary barrier to attaining aspirations. The gap between unemployment and youth aspirations has been exacerbated by the spread of formal education that generated expectations among youth and their parents that they will find high-paying, white-collar positions after completing their education. When these jobs are unavailable, young people often choose to remain unemployed rather than take on low-status and low-paying positions. In Ethiopia, unemployment rates are actually highest among those who have completed a secondary education.

Craig Jeffrey (2008: 743–744) divides the youth population in the global South into three broad categories that work well for the Ethiopian case. The first category consists of youth, primarily young men, who have acquired high levels of education and are well positioned to find desirable jobs. In the Ethiopian case, youth who have completed a four-year postsecondary degree are generally able to find secure, well-paid work in the field of their training. The lack of private education in Ethiopia has meant that historically, for the successful few, education has been a means for young people to achieve rapid economic mobility. Beginning in the early 2000s high-quality private primary and secondary schools have opened in urban centers, meaning that the few young people who can afford to attend these expensive institutions are much more likely to advance to the university.

A second category of youth consists of those who do not advance to secondary school. In urban areas these young people often work for little or no pay as domestic workers or manual laborers. In urban Ethiopia, there are a disproportionate number of women in this category. They work for less than a dollar a day in positions with little or no job security. Although I examine the lives of young men working in the informal economy, for the most part the participants in my research had at least some secondary education and therefore fit better within Jeffrey's third category.

Young people with at least a secondary education but no work are increasingly common in Ethiopia and elsewhere in the global South (Cole 2004, 2005; Demerath 2003; Jeffrey, Jeffery, and Jeffery 2008; Weiss 2009). The gap between expectations for the future and economic realities is particularly acute for these young people. Globally, among these youth there is a great deal of diversity in class background (Jeffrey 2008: 744). Despite coming from a wide range of ethnic and religious backgrounds, all but a few of the young men in my study had at least some secondary education. Most of them had finished secondary school and were unable to advance further in their education because of low scores on the national school leaving examination. Nearly all of these young men were born in Jimma, but for the most part, their parents had moved from elsewhere. None of the working young men in my study were from families that could be considered upper or middle class. The unemployed young men, however, ranged from those with wealthy parents and extensive social networks to the sons of single mothers who scrape out a living from baking bread or brewing beer. This difference in family background means that there is a great deal of variation in the long-term life trajectories of the educated unemployed.

A brief visit to one of the spaces within the city where young men gather to pass the time illustrates the diverse backgrounds of unemployed and working young men in Jimma. In the afternoons there was usually a good crowd at Haile's house. Young men sat on stools and benches in the cool shade in front of the house. Haile's family was poor, and his house was simple—a tin roof and floors and walls made of mud mixed with straw. This was the norm in urban Ethiopia, and Haile's friends, even those from wealthier families, were comfortable here. Inside the house, his sisters relaxed doing handcrafts and sometimes making deliciously strong coffee for Haile and his friends. The area around Jimma is said to be the birthplace of coffee, and like much of Ethiopia, in the afternoon it is difficult to find a house where a clay pot of coffee is not being brought to a boil on a small charcoal stove. Coffee, however, was not the only stimulant being consumed. Outside, the young men sat in a semicircle around a pile of branches covered in green leaves. Most but not all of the young men were here to chew *khat*, a mild stimulant. The chewers occasionally grabbed fresh branches from the communal pile. They pulled off the leaves and stuffed them into their mouths, adding to the massive green ball that they were already masticating. Khat was only half of the attraction at Haile's house; young men also came for the *chewata*, literally "play," the joking conversation that is a favorite pastime for Ethiopians of all ages.

Ethnic and religious difference is a major theme in studies of Ethiopia (Donham 1986; Jalata 1993; James et al. 2002; Mains 2004), but among young men in Jimma, a number of different ethnicities and religions were usually present at any gathering.[2] On a typical afternoon at Haile's, young men of Oromo, Amhara, and Dawro descent were all present, although Amharic was always the language used for conversation. The crowd was divided almost evenly between Muslims and Orthodox Christians, but the emphasis on khat chewing meant that fewer Protestant Christians, who usually abstain from all intoxicants, were present. Class divisions often structure where young men pass their time, especially in the afternoons when khat is chewed, but perhaps because of Haile's unusual personality and the location of his mother's home in an economically diverse neighborhood, on most days, the young men I found at Haile's came from very different backgrounds.

Two of the young men I often encountered at Haile's illustrate differences among the unemployed. Habtamu lived across the street from Haile, but his house was completely different. Habtamu's house had tile floors, block walls, and a sturdy compound fence and was surrounded by a number of "service" apartments that were used as rentals or housing for domestic workers. Habtamu's father was a retired policeman, and his family's wealth was a result of three siblings living in the United States. Habtamu's brothers and sisters sent money often, and he was never without cash in his pocket. Mulugeta lived down the street from Haile and Habtamu, just a couple of minutes by foot. Mulugeta's father was a laborer at a government sawmill, and his mother worked in their home. Although his family was probably slightly better off than Haile's, in general their economic situation was the same. Both could generally be assured of having food on the table, but beyond that they had little or no access to significant economic resources. The economic differences between Habtamu and Mulugeta were not apparent at first glance. They both dressed neatly in a way that reflected their aspirations to be employed in a government office. Differences based on family wealth and social connections were, however, quite significant in structuring the economic decisions of young men, and the intersection between class, status, and employment is one of my major areas of exploration.

Constructing Hope: Modern Aspirations, Temporal Problems, and Spatial Solutions

Haile was a master of *chewata*, especially after he had been chewing khat. He was a strange figure in Qottebe Sefer, the neighborhood where I resided for eighteen months while conducting research in Jimma, Ethiopia. I am not sure how old Haile was, but I would guess he was in his midthirties, making him the oldest of the young men who regularly gathered on his porch in the afternoons. Unlike the other young men who generally wore clean button-down shirts or sports jerseys over loose-fitting jeans, Haile cared little for his appearance, and his clothes were often full of holes. I do not know of anyone else who was both as popular and as universally disdained among young men as Haile. It was said that he used to be a hard worker, but now he devoted his life to khat. For Haile mornings were spent under the shade of a tree waiting for a friend to pass who might lend him the money he needed for his daily bundle of khat branches. Afternoons were spent at home chewing. Haile's father was not present, and his mother was very poor. Everyone in the neighborhood agreed that Haile should be married with a family of his own and helping his mother instead of spending his time and money on khat and cigarettes. If Haile was a model that young men sought to avoid, that did not prevent them from visiting him every afternoon. His jokes, stories, and access to a shaded space out of the burning afternoon sun nearly always attracted a small crowd.

Although the young men who visited Haile in the afternoons were often critical of his lifestyle, there was a sense that they were seeing their future lives in him—unemployed, unmarried, and dependent on their parents. Many of these young men were in their late teens or early twenties. They had recently finished secondary school, and they had expected to find a good job or further education. Instead they were passing each day in the same manner as the last, moving ever closer to becoming another Haile.

The talk at Haile's house usually jumped quickly from topic to topic. On one occasion, Haile gave a detailed account of a film he had watched in the morning, offered up an analysis of differences between Ethiopian and American dogs, and then recited a proverb intended to illustrate the relationship between the rich and the poor. Haile and his friends never tired of grilling me about life in the United States. Sometimes they wanted me to confirm things they had seen in films, but most often they wanted to know how I could help them enter the United States. A young man whom I had not met before was present. He proudly showed off a receipt he carried with him that he explained was for the expenses associated with travel to an unspecified "Arab country."

This instigated a long conversation about the relative value of moving to different countries, such as Saudi Arabia, South Africa, Australia, and the United States. Everyone seemed to agree that this young man's family would have seen a far greater return on their investment by sending him elsewhere.

The young men at Haile's noted the calculus of wages versus transportation costs in relation to migration, but more importantly, they said, leaving Ethiopia was the key to experiencing "progress" (*lewt*).[3] Progress was desired above all other things, and progress can be had only outside Ethiopia. Progress, put simply, is improvement over time, but there is more to it than this. Progress occurs gradually, and improvement is divided into stages. These stages are organized in a linear manner, and progress involves movement from one stage to the next. Ideally, the young men felt that life should be a series of incremental improvements, but most saw themselves in the future living with their parents and unable to marry or start a family of their own. As usual, Haile was a dissenting voice. He pointed out that the day-to-day pleasure he received from chewing khat was far more valuable for him than any long-term prosperity he might achieve by saving his money. Other young men generally denigrated Haile's prioritization of the present over the future. They argued that temporary happiness is not comparable to the value of experiencing progress with the passage of time.

Discussions about progress and international migration at Haile's house provide a glimpse into the nature of young men's aspirations for the future. The ambitions of youth are generated within specific times and places. In the Ethiopian case, policies of structural adjustment associated with neoliberal economic restructuring have drastically shifted the context in which young men seek to attain their goals. At the same time, the values that guide the aspirations and economic behavior of youth have changed with urbanization, engagement in education, and exposure to international media. The values of young men in urban Ethiopia are often constructed in relation to a specific notion of what it means to be modern. Particularly in the global South, desires to be modern are often closely related to discourses of development and an acute sense that life is better elsewhere. At the national level, in relation to infrastructural development, the future is often conceived of in terms of passing through stages that the United States and Europe have already left behind. Most Ethiopians are well aware of their nation's status as one of the poorest countries in the world, and many told me their precise ranking on recent development indexes. Young men in Jimma often claimed that Ethiopia is "backward" and that a "bad culture" prevents the progress that is found in other more developed cities and nations.

Beginning in the 1990s, *modernity* has become an important topic of discussion within anthropology. Anthropologists have critiqued linear notions of development and described multiple ways of being modern, using such terms as "parallel," "other," and "alternative" modernities in order to address this diversity (Larkin 1997; Rofel 1999; Knauft 2002a). Donald Donham describes "vernacular modernisms" as "attempts to reorder local society by the application of strategies that have produced wealth, power, or knowledge elsewhere in the world" (1999b: xviii). Descriptions of how people living in different areas produce and engage with these strategic reorderings have proliferated, as anthropologists document the production of vernacular modernism. In response to academic analyses concerning modernity, James Ferguson (2006) has cautioned against allowing a celebration of multiple modernities to distract from issues of economic inequality and the ways that different world areas continue to be less "modern" than others in terms of economic infrastructure, health care, access to education, and the prevalence of famine and disease. He explains that although deconstructing linear models of modernization is useful, this should not obscure the lived realities of being without "modern" education or clean drinking water.

Ferguson's critique is certainly useful, but it is also important to keep in mind the importance that local understandings of being modern continue to have for the construction of values in many world areas. Ferguson is correct that anthropological analyses of alternative modernities are frequently detached from developmentalist hierarchies of status (2006: 188). However, young men's notions of what it means to be modern are based on locally specific modes of evaluation, and this has implications for the construction and attainment of aspirations. For example, the notions of occupational status that cause young men to reject certain types of work are influenced by a desire to be modern, as it is defined locally. In this sense, local modernities are key to young men's economic behavior and the reproduction or subversion of stratification. The prevalence of multiple modernities is partially responsible for shaping the specific dynamics of inequality, both locally and internationally.

In Ethiopia, the history of formal education is particularly bound up with notions of modernity and relations with the West (Zewde[4] 2002b). The expansion of government education as a means of modernization is a point of continuity across the regimes of Haile Selassie (1930–1974), Mengistu Haile Mariam's Marxist Derg (1974–1991), and Meles Zenawi's Ethiopian People's Democratic Revolutionary Front (1991–present). All have agreed that education is essential for the future of the country and devoted significant resources to the construction of schools. A belief in the transformative power of education also exists at a popular level and extends across boundaries of ethnicity, religion, gender, and class. On the basis of the experiences of earlier generations, youth who complete their schooling have specific expectations about their future employment and economic status. The process of education instills youth with a progressive, or developmentalist, sense of time. Hopes for the future are often structured in terms of a linear notion of progress—gradual improvements that follow a particular series of steps. Hope is cut when the realities that youth encounter after graduation differ from their expectations.

Like education, increasing flows of global culture have generated new imaginative possibilities for living through which youth construct aspirations and notions of what it means to be modern (Appadurai 1996). In the African context, cinema provided a link with Europe and the United States during colonialism (Powdermaker 1962; Larkin 2008). More recently, the proliferation of cheap and easily accessed films and international television shows has had an important relationship with changing identities, spatial imagination and aspirations for the future (Fuglesang 1994; Larkin 2008; Masquelier 2009). In Ethiopia young men are the primary consumers of films, some of which are produced locally but most of which come from Hollywood and Bollywood. Conversations about films, such as those that I observed at Haile's house, are often fueled by khat. It is also quite common for the men to chew khat while watching movies. The everyday activities of consuming khat and watching films are intertwined with a particular style of conversation in which possibilities for the future are thoroughly discussed and evaluated. An examination of these day-to-day activities reveals how aspirations are constructed and how youth negotiate the gap between desires for the future and economic realities.

Young men's aspirations and their conceptions of temporal change provide the grounds for an exploration of the relationship between time, space, and neoliberal capitalism. Changing notions of time and progress in relation to industrial capitalism have been well analyzed within the social sciences (Postone 1993; Thompson 1967). It has been argued that under conditions of capitalist production, time is increasingly abstracted and rationalized. Conditions of widespread unemployment among youth in urban Africa provide the opportunity to approach this topic from a new perspective. Struggles with time among urban youth have been documented across the African continent (Hansen 2005; Ralph 2008; Schielke 2008; Weiss 2004a). The heightened aspirations associated with increased access to formal education and global media coupled with severe economic decline causes many young people to be unsatisfied with their day-to-day lives and unable to construct progressive narratives for their future. Young people in places as different as Lusaka, Dakar, Arusha, and rural Egypt speak about "simply sitting," "killing time," and having "too many thoughts." In urban Ethiopia, young men use these same idioms to describe the experience of time as an overabundant and potentially dangerous quantity.

In Ethiopia, solutions to young men's temporal problems are often conceived of in spatial terms. Although they approach the topic from different perspectives, David Harvey (1990) and James Ferguson (2006) have both argued that in a context of late capitalism, spatial strategies are increasingly prioritized over temporal processes. For example, among urban young men in Ethiopia, migration, especially to the United States through the Diversity Visa (DV) lottery, is thought to solve the problem of progressing through time. In this sense, spatial movement takes the place of temporal change. A close analysis of young men's hopes and discursive practices for migration provides insights into the relationship between space and time, but I seek to move beyond only examining space and time in relation to each other. On the basis of the Ethiopian case, I argue that both space and time must be evaluated at least partially in terms of their implications for social relationships. Movements through time and space are important largely because of how they reposition one within relations of exchange, status, and dependency.

Struggling for Hope: Unemployment, Class, and Status

Perhaps because of my interest in unemployment, when I was present, the conversation at Haile's house often turned to work. The consensus was usually that there was no work and therefore there was no progress or change—often stated simply as *"sira yellem, lewt yellem."* Sometimes when I pushed this point, asking about other youth who were working, they claimed that it was impossible to work in Ethiopia because of *yiluññta*. To have *yiluññta* is to experience an intense shame based on what others may say or think about oneself and one's family (see Poluha 2004: 147). The presence of *yiluññta* is like a mosquito faintly whining in the ear. It is a reminder that others are watching and judging. One young unemployed man explained, "We would never work as a porter here. There is *yiluññta* here, and that kind of work is not respected. People will shout orders at you, and you are expected to obey. If we go abroad, we can work without being insulted. We don't care about seeing other countries, but we want to be free to work and help our families." Young men desperately wanted to work and earn an income so that they would not follow the same path as Haile, but they felt that it was almost impossible to do so because of the social pressure associated with *yiluññta*.

Understanding unemployment in Ethiopia requires exploring the balance between accumulating material wealth and prestige. Max Weber's analysis of class and status provides a useful foundation for examining the Ethiopian case. Weber defines a class situation as one in which "a large number of men have in common a specific causal factor influencing their chances in life, insofar as this factor has to do only with the possession of economic goods and the interests involved in earning a living, and furthermore in the condition of the market in commodities of labor" (1978: 43). A Weberian conception of class may include all factors that influence one's economic chances in life including education, occupation, and status. This perspective also takes into account ways of acquiring economic goods that are only indirectly related to production, such as sharing and gifts. In stark contrast to a Marxian conception of class, for Weber class is not necessarily based on relations of production.

Urban youth that I spoke to consistently expressed a desire for government employment. In his study of consumer culture in Kathmandu, Mark Liechty (2003) draws on Weber to argue that with the rise of government work, a middle class emerges in which consumption plays a greater role than one's position in the process of production in defining identity and relations of power. The growth of the middle class is associated with the movement of a large section of the population toward constructing "their social identities more around the goods and property they own[] than the kind of work they [do]" (Liechty 2003: 15). The instability of the middle class's relationship to production means that expressing status through consumption takes on a heightened degree of importance (Liechty 2003: 18). The Ethiopian case illustrates an interesting variation on the dynamics that Liechty describes. Government employment expanded significantly as a source of work in urban Ethiopia during the twentieth century, and this represents a movement away from directly making a living through the production of goods. A Weberian conception of class is valuable in part because it is flexible enough to analyze both unemployed youth who aspire to government employment and self-employed entrepreneurs.

Weber's analysis of occupational status is helpful in understanding the often conflicting aspirations of young men in Jimma. Weber argued that occupational status is an important area of study because the status of the worker is frequently associated with the occupational lifestyle instead of the position in the process of production (1978: 54). Given the very different context in which Weber worked, his insights are surprisingly useful for understanding the Ethiopian case. He explains that "it is very often the case that all rational employment of a gainful kind, especially entrepreneurial activity, is regarded as disqualifying a person from high status" (1978: 52–53). In Ethiopia, urban young men were certainly interested in earning money, but they feared the status implications of taking on available work. On one hand, money is necessary to consume, to attract a girlfriend or wife, and to support one's family. In the sense that it shifts one's position within social relationships from one of dependence to offering support to others, money is necessary for young men to become an adult. On the other hand, discussions of *yiluññta* at Haile's house demonstrate that regardless of earning power, the symbolic dimensions of one's occupation, as a government employee or otherwise, are a key factor for construction of identity.

The relationship between class and status is well developed in the work of Pierre Bourdieu (1977, 1984). Bourdieu introduces the concept of cultural capital to explain the relationship between taste, prestige, and the reproduction of class. Put simply, cultural capital consists of signifiers of class, such as taste in music, fashion, or style of speech. Possessing cultural capital allows individuals to create social networks that provide access to economic capital. For Weber and Bourdieu, status, or distinction, is associated with elites. Economic capital is secured through the possession of cultural capital.

A variety of ethnographic studies support an elaboration of Weber and Bourdieu's work through examinations of disjuncture between class and occupational status (Bourgois 1995; Freeman 2000; Kondo 1990; Paules 1991; Willis 1977). This work presents detailed examinations of how prestige or nonmaterial advantages lead individuals to accept or even seek out occupations in which their class position is compromised. For example, in Paul Willis's (1977) classic study of working-class young men ("the lads") in 1970s England, "the lads" desired factory jobs because this type of work supported the fulfillment of locally valued masculine norms. In other words, working-class jobs generated status within the lads' subculture. Cultural capital did not translate into economic capital; rather, it led working-class young men to take working-class jobs.

An interesting variation on the relationship between status and class has been documented among unemployed young men who move between urban Congo and Paris (Friedman 1994; Gondola 1999; MacGaffey and Bazenguissa-Ganga 2000). These "sapeurs" invested a great deal of time and resources in acquiring signifiers of prestige in the form of high-fashion clothing. Cultural capital is accumulated through clothing, and in contrast to "the lads," this capital is recognized beyond the subculture of La Sape and appreciated globally. The cultural capital of high fashion does not, however, translate into significant economic gain. Although the sapeur becomes a CEO in his dream world, this does not translate into concrete shifts in his class position (Gondola 1999). These studies demonstrate that cultural capital may constitute an intrinsic source of inequality and need not be translated into economic capital.

I build on these studies by examining the construction of hierarchies of class and status as both independent and interrelated sources of inequality. In urban Ethiopia, young men avoid stigma by remaining unemployed, and they earn money by accepting the stigma associated with particular occupations. The experiences of urban youth demonstrate the continued importance of work as a source of identity. In contrast to many recent analyses of contemporary youth cultures that place great emphasis on consumption, a close examination of unemployed young men and those working in the informal economy demonstrates the importance of the symbolic dimensions of work for positioning one within relationships and the formation of young people's identities.

Hopeful Exchanges: Reciprocity, Development, and Emerging Forms of Stratification

The balance between class and status may be partially conceived of as an exchange. Unemployed young men exchange the potential income they could earn through working in stigmatized occupations for the maintenance of prestige. Although this conception does provide some insight, such a simple divide between status and income is quickly complicated by the concrete realities of reciprocity in urban Ethiopia. All young men were embedded in complex networks of reciprocity, but unemployed young men received particularly valuable gifts in the form of cash handouts and invitations for khat, meals, and other small items. In some cases the value of gifts received by unemployed young men actually exceeded the incomes of young men working in the informal economy. The Amharic proverb *"Sew be sew teshome"* demonstrates the importance of social relationships for attaining one's aspirations. The proverb literally means that one person improves by another person and implies that the fulfillment of hope is inseparable from social relationships.

The complexities of gifting were often on display at Haile's house. On more than one occasion, Haile told me that "conversation is public, but khat is private," implying that visitors to his house should bring their own khat. Haile consistently violated his rule, offering handfuls of khat to most of his visitors and often relying on handouts from others to purchase khat. Although asking a friend for a few birr (Ethiopian currency) is common among young men in urban Ethiopia, Haile annoyed his friends and neighbors, including me, with constant requests for handouts. I quickly learned to avoid Haile at certain times of the day if I did not want to make a donation to his khat habit.

The continual flow of gifts and invitations is inseparable from the maintenance of relationships. As anthropologists have observed elsewhere, in the Ethiopian case, it is difficult to say whether relationships are intended to produce gifts or gifts produce relationships. However, it is clear that certain people have greater access to gifts and relationships than others, and this is an important source of stratification in urban Ethiopia.

Strict dichotomies between social relationships and material accumulation are problematic, but there is great utility in exploring how the balance between the two shifts over time. Anthropological analyses of exchange in Africa from the mid-twentieth century generally posited a linear shift from redistributive to market economies that correlates with a prioritization of material accumulation over social relationships. For example, in David Parkin's (1972) classic study of the Giriama, individual accumulators of capital emerge in the context of increasing cash cropping and access to international markets. Although the details of the cases vary considerably, the notion that cultural rules enforcing the redistribution of wealth and investment in social relations are a significant barrier to participation in a market economy was a common theme in twentieth-century anthropological analyses of Africa (Bohannon 1959; Hart 1973, 1988). In these analyses, the underlying tension is between investing in social relationships and the accumulation of privately owned material goods. The first is associated with tradition, and the second is associated with a modern economy that has largely been developed by Western powers.

More recently, anthropologists have interpreted practices as diverse as international migration (Stoller 2002), schooling (Stambach 2000), and conspicuous consumption (De Boeck 1999) within a framework defined by a contrast between investing in social relationships and material accumulation. Although these analyses do not rely on notions of linear economic and cultural change, implicit in them is the assumption that people place a high value on social relationships, and processes associated with capitalism impact this valuation. For example, it has often been argued that witchcraft is a means of enforcing redistributions of wealth, and rectifying imbalances between investments in social relations and personal accumulation (Comaroff and Comaroff 1993; Geschiere 1997). In these analyses, witchcraft and beliefs about inequality and reciprocity are juxtaposed with economic changes associated with neoliberal capitalism. Accusations of witchcraft have increased with rising disparities of wealth that are associated with a free market economy. I argue that such analytical tension between investing in social relationships and material accumulation continues to be useful. I seek to identify the connections and disconnections between people and things and how they have shifted over time in the Ethiopian case.

James Ferguson (1990, 1999, 2006) and Charles Piot (1999) have offered compelling critiques of the notion of a linear temporal relationship between redistributive and capitalist economies. They argue that investing in social relationships often occurs as a result of economic changes associated with capitalism. Connections between shifting economic context and the balance between relationships and individual accumulation are certainly present, but these changes do not occur in a linear manner. Their research indicates that practices of prioritizing relationships over individual gain are often a result of economic changes associated with capitalism.

In the Ethiopian case, there is a great deal of variation in how young men engage in relations of reciprocity. Unemployed and working young men have distinctive ways of balancing the accumulation of social relationships and things. I argue that maintaining analytical tension between investing in people and things is useful. Stratification exists in terms of both accumulation of material goods and social relationships, and their relative importance shifts over time. This does not imply the linear change from redistributive to market economies assumed by earlier analyses. Rather, the relative importance of access to social relationships and material wealth shifts in unexpected directions with political and economic change.

Neoliberalism, Hope, and Social Theory

Abstracting from the specifics of the Ethiopian case, and following the work of Hirokazu Miyazaki, I am interested in the relationship between space, time, hope, and social theory. Miyazaki identifies the question of hope as an important theme in turn-of-the-twenty-first-century social thought. He explains that there is a growing concern among social theorists about a lack of hope for the future. "Facing the collapse of socialist regimes and other apparent manifestations of the effects of so-called globalization, social theorists have deplored their inability to imagine alternatives to capitalism" (Miyazaki 2006: 162). I seek to extend Miyazaki's analysis of the relationship between hope, social theory, and capitalism by examining it in conjunction with the Ethiopian case. In terms of their hopelessness, leftist thinkers appear to be similar to young men in urban Ethiopia. With the fall of socialism and the rise of postmodernism, social theorists lack a narrative to galvanize their critical examinations of escalating global inequality, imperialism, and environmental degradation. It appears that social theory may also be mired in an undesirable present as a result of a loss of hope for the future. Certainly Barack Obama brought "hope" into everyday political discourse through his successful U.S. presidential campaign. However, if anything, Obama's presidency has convinced the political left in the United States of the difficulty of changing national policies associated with neoliberal capitalism.

In interviews that Mary Zournazi (2003) conducted with prominent social theorists concerning the subject of hope, it is repeatedly argued that closer analyses of a new phase of capitalism are necessary to reclaim hope. The recent proliferation of writing on neoliberal capitalism can perhaps be taken as a sign that leftist thinkers are reconstructing narratives of hope. This critique of neoliberalism is particularly visible in the work of David Harvey. As Harvey has consistently advanced his critique of neoliberal capitalism and applied his arguments to global political and economic shifts, anthropologists have also begun to increasingly analyze social processes in relation to neoliberal capitalism.[5] A neoliberal narrative is apparent in the work of anthropologists writing about turn-of-the-twenty-first-century Africa. Africa has been conceptualized within the context of a "neoliberal age" (Weiss 2004a), a "neoliberal world order" (Ferguson 2006), and in relation to a "neoliberal culture" (Comaroff and Comaroff 2000). Care must be taken so that this new narrative does not become antithetical to hope. Although each of the analyses that I cite is highly nuanced and does not promote a totalizing theory of neoliberalism, by categorizing the present as "neoliberal" they still pose the danger of closing off potential avenues of inquiry that may be valuable for hope.

I do not wish to imply that policies associated with neoliberal capitalism have not profoundly changed African economies. My previous discussion should make it clear that critiques of neoliberalism like Ferguson's and Harvey's are an essential foundation for my own work. An inability to compete with the nations of East and South Asia in the manufacture of low-cost commodities, the burden of servicing interest on debt, and policies associated with structural adjustment have all contributed to economic decline in Africa (Arrighi 2002). Harvey (2005) describes neoliberal capitalism as a strategic process of dispossession in which the extremely wealthy are able to exert control over an increasingly greater portion of the world's capital. For Harvey, neoliberalism is characterized less by free flows of capital than by the use of space in order to solidify the dominant position of the ruling class. Ferguson (2006) explains that isolated spaces within Africa are linked to the global economy so that resources may be extracted without interacting with or investing in the continent as a whole.[6] For Africa, the rise of neoliberal capitalism does not imply the creation of a free market economy. Instead, to speak of a "neoliberal Africa" is to describe the economic relationship of Africa to the rest of the world. As Ferguson (2006) demonstrates with his discussion of economic growth in states such as Angola, "neoliberal Africa" is characterized by the use of technology and political institutions to selectively extract resources. This is dispossession in Harvey's sense—public property is appropriated by private interests without providing compensation.

Although Harvey's notion of neoliberalism as dispossession has clear value, such a monolithic analysis glosses over the variable ways in which neoliberal policies interact with local dynamics (Ferguson 2007; Kingfisher and Maskovsky 2008; Kipnis 2008; Mains 2007; Richland 2009).[7] A different approach to neoliberalism emerges out of J. K. Gibson-Graham's work (1996, 2006). She[8] argues that subsuming all economic and cultural activity within the category of "capitalism" inhibits social change. Her argument that capitalism is not a unified structure and coexists with other forms of economic exchange is certainly supported by the evidence from urban Ethiopia and elsewhere. However, Gibson-Graham does not rely entirely on empirical evidence to support her claim. Rather, she appears to be operating on the basis of something like Richard Rorty's pragmatic philosophy in which knowledge is based in hope. The notion of hope as knowledge is also taken up in the work of Miyazaki (2004). A hopeful form of knowledge is one that supports possibilities for imagining and achieving a different and desirable future (Rorty 1999). My interest is in the potential of neoliberal capitalism as an analytical category to function as a hopeful form of knowledge. Does analyzing practices and beliefs in terms of neoliberalism generate hope for the future? For the most part this exploration is an implicit rather than explicit aspect of my analysis. It is not until the concluding chapter that I fully engage with the ideas of Rorty, Gibson-Graham, and Harvey in relation to social theory, knowledge, and capitalism. I argue that an investigation of diverse economic activities such as unemployment, informal entrepreneurial work, and sharing demonstrates the indeterminate nature of young men's lives, and that this indeterminacy is grounds for hope.

Sunsets and Kangaroos: Notes on Research Methodology

There is a hotel on the main road to the Jimma market that has a balcony overlooking the street. The hotel is always empty, and there were some days when I sat alone on that balcony and drank cold beer while I stared down at the city. It was a feeling of detached escape that I occasionally craved.

The evening sun is pleasantly burning into my neck and I am looking out at the road lined with stalls of vendors selling clothes and shoes. The stalls are covered with plastic tarps that have been stretched over frames made from eucalyptus limbs. Men walk by in their gray jackets and thick-soled leather shoes. Sometimes a woman in a white shawl, a barefoot boy, or a young man in a faded T-shirt printed with a giant picture of Leonardo DiCaprio passes by. There is the Teddy Afro pop song that I've heard a thousand times echoing up from the street. A woman is squatting behind a charcoal burner lined with ears of corn. She fans the coals and looks straight ahead. A one-legged man pulls himself down the street on crutches. A boy on a red bicycle pedals up the hill. The asphalt is brown with dirt and is bordered by the piles of clothes and the blue plastic of the shops. Behind that, the trees obscure the tin roofs, and then a ring of green hills surrounds the town. Gradual layers of poverty and beauty fade into each other like a sunset made out of dirt, cloth, and vegetation. From up on the balcony, the details are unclear, and only the abstract layers of color are visible. Everything fits together in a way that somehow feels right. All of the people become points of color within a giant collage that is a place called Jimma.

Most days I submerge myself in the density of these layers and layers of people. On these days I am lost within the sunset, knowing that I am surrounded by much more than I am able to see. As I walk from my house toward the city center, the sun burns into my skull, and a line from an old favorite Lou Reed song echoes through my head: "The city is a funny place, something like a circus or a sewer." It is likely that Lou was singing about 1970s New York, but somehow for me the lyrics evoke the gritty beauty that I associate with Jimma. I cross the bridge over the Aweytu River, fascinated by the occasional bursts of flame amid the refuse that accumulates along the river's banks. Then I am in Mahel Ketema, the center of the city. Walking in the city, it is difficult to see anything beyond the continuous flow of people. Boys play table tennis on the streets, and women wash clothes in front of their houses; every business is a home, and every home is a business. In the afternoon, it is time for khat. Crowds surround the khat vendors who sit behind their piles of branches and leaves. Customers shout and grab, and then stuff a bundle of khat under an arm and hurry away.

I knock on a big wooden door and then enter before anyone answers. I know I am welcome at Abdu's house. In the heat and noise of the city, this square room with twelve-foot ceilings is an oasis. Adbu sits on the floor mats smoking a cigarette and chewing on a giant wad of green leaves. He flashes me a grin and hands me a branch as I take off my shoes and join him on the mat. Other men come and go, and the conversation moves in waves, rising and falling. For some men, Abdu's house is an office, and the single piece of furniture is a chair called "the kangaroo." Like its namesake, the chair has a pouch that seems to magically produce things on demand. Books, files, attachments for Abdu's hookah—they are all inside the kangaroo's pouch. It is a space within a space within a space. As I chew the bitter green leaves, I stop worrying about making sense of it all—the endless places and histories. I stop worrying about abstractions and details. For now I can lose myself in one of the many pockets that exist in Jimma and forget about the lives raging outside.

For me the process of research and writing was a continual movement between the abstraction of the sunset and exploring the various kangaroo pouches that existed within the city. In the chapters that follow, I move back and forth between these two perspectives, but in general I spend more time in the pouches. Particularly as I interrogate the relationship of between broad economic shifts and the experience of young men living in Jimma, Ethiopia, it is necessary to examine the spaces within spaces. There is a tendency to conceive of capitalism as a boundless entity covering the globe, from which the only escape is the obscure, the local, and the hidden. However, as Ferguson

(2006) demonstrates in his discussion of resource extraction in Africa, these pouches often provide the ideal environment for capitalist relations to thrive. Therefore, in investigating local spaces, I do not seek to classify them as capitalist or noncapitalist. Rather, I assume that what I find may have a place within the abstract image of the sunset but that it also has meaning and significance in its own right. Just as Abdu's house was one piece of the complex collage that formed Jimma, it was also a specific space that supported specific types of interactions.

In conducting research I often took the individual as my unit of analysis. In this book I describe different young men and attempt to explain their particular practices and beliefs. In doing so I seek to crawl into that space that we often conceive of as being the most hidden and personal, that space that is thought to exist in our head that contains values and ideas. I used a number of methods for eliciting values, particularly surrounding work and status, and based on these values, I attempt to understand the cultural and economic behavior of young men. I continually contextualize my analysis of the individual within local, national, and global discourses. However, I also assume that each of the participants in my research is in some way unique and can never be fully explained with any theory. My goal as a researcher and writer is to arrange these observations into a meaningful pattern. I do not assume that this pattern exists independently of myself. Just as lines of color that appear in the sky can be called a sunset at only a particular point in the evening, my observations are coherent only within a particular analytical perspective.

This book is based on eighteen months of research conducted in Jimma, Ethiopia, between 2003 and 2005 and additional months of research in 2008 and 2009. I spent much of my time in the field moving through the city and visiting with people at the various sites where they congregated. Residents of Jimma were often curious about my activities. Those who did not know me personally were mystified as to why a foreigner would spend so much time wandering about visiting with young men as they chewed khat, watched films, and worked. It was often assumed that whatever I was doing, it could not be good. In some of the rougher neighborhoods, it was not uncommon for people to shout insults at me after I had passed by. I was once stopped by a plainclothes policeman who confiscated my camera and audio recorder. I was appointed to come to the police station the following day, where I was interrogated about my research, and it became clear that the police suspected that I might be organizing local university students in opposition to the ruling political party.

Partially in order to fill a socially acceptable role for a foreigner in Jimma and partially to facilitate my research, I began my study by teaching English to eleventh- and twelfth-grade students at the government vocational school. The recent introduction of vocational schools is a key aspect of shifts that have been made in educational policy to deal with the problem of youth unemployment. I was particularly interested in vocational education because many of the trades that are taught, such as woodworking and welding, are related to stigmatized occupations. In addition to teaching for one semester, I randomly selected students from each vocational field and met with them for individual interviews and group discussions.

Sampling was one of the greatest challenges that I faced in conducting research in an urban environment. I could move through the city and gradually develop relationships with the young men who passed their time in public space. These interactions were a valuable source of information, but I had learned though preliminary research that this method was also limited. It was almost impossible to meet young women in this manner. It was also difficult to meet young men who did not live in my neighborhood or who were not involved in a work or leisure activity that kept them in a public space. I solved this problem by relying on the assistance of neighborhood *iddirs* to select an initial sample of unemployed youth informants. An *iddir* is a burial association that is found primarily in urban areas. It is common for families to belong to multiple *iddirs* that have different criteria for membership (De Weerdt et al. 2007). Among their different memberships, most families belong to a neighborhood *iddir* that includes almost all residents, regardless of class, gender, ethnicity, and religion. I selected three neighborhoods with the intention of choosing places with differing levels of wealth and proximities to economic activity. These neighborhoods are described in more detail in Chapter 1. The leaders of each neighborhood *iddir* selected ten unemployed young people, and these thirty youth formed my initial sample of unemployed youth.

In the second half of my research, I decided to focus my attention primarily on young men. This was partially because of the difficulty of conducting participant observation with women and my reluctance to base my analysis on information gathered almost entirely through interviews. It is also significant that for many of the basic issues at play in my study—aspirations, opportunities, values concerning status, and class—the experiences of young men were very different from those of women. In the chapters that follow, I point out areas where the experience of young men was particularly gendered, but I do not attempt an in-depth analysis of the lives of young women.

The selection of working youth participants was opportunistic. I simply approached these young men as they worked and made casual conversation. After I felt that we had a comfortable relationship, I set up an appointment away from their workplace where I could conduct a formal interview.

During the second half of my research, I developed detailed case studies concerning twenty unemployed young men, eight working young men, five unemployed young women, and three working young women. I conducted a series of four weekly interviews with these young people in which I questioned them about their life histories, aspirations for the future, kin networks, and values concerning work and status. These youth also kept journals for me for a period of one month that documented all of their income from work and gifts, their expenses, and their daily activities. These journals provide the basis for my analysis of reciprocity in Chapter 5. This was the only portion of my research for which I directly compensated participants for their time. Generally I simply bought participants a drink at the cafés where we usually met, or I brought them unroasted coffee if we met at their home, but in this case I gave all participants two hundred birr (about twenty-five U.S. dollars) at the completion of the month of interviews and journaling.

During the course of my research, I conducted numerous other opportunistic interviews. Usually I became interested in a particular topic such as friendship, videos, or khat and then pulled together different groups of experts (for example, youth connoisseurs of video or khat) to discuss the issue. At times I also sought out government administrators to discuss policy regarding youth. Numerous nongovernmental development projects aimed at youth were also operating in Jimma, and I spoke with administrators and youth from many of these organizations. Through out my research, I sought out "elders," usually wealthy men, to interview regarding the history of Jimma city. Particularly in Chapter 1 I draw on these interviews to complement information that I gathered from secondary sources.

I use all of these different types of information in the analysis that follows. Life histories, casual conversations over a cup of coffee, my observations from an afternoon at a video house watching a Jackie Chan film, and data concerning a young man's total monthly income and expenditures are all combined to explore the complexities of life in urban Ethiopia. Each of these methods offers access to a particular type of knowledge. Some are useful for digging deep into the kangaroo's pouch, and others are better for stepping back and viewing the more abstract sunset.

Synopsis of Chapters

Chapter 1 discusses the historical and cultural background for this study, with particular attention to the manner in which urban class structure has shifted over time. I examine particular forms of stratification that accompanied the emergence of cities in Ethiopia. A major theme in most writing that concerns stratification in Ethiopia has been ethnicity. I do discuss historic ethnic relations in the Jimma region in Chapter 1, but these relations generally do not figure into my analysis of stratification that occurs in later chapters. Because of a number of interrelated economic and cultural shifts that took place around the turn of the twenty-first century, I argue that among urban youth in Jimma ethnicity is less salient for stratification than it was in the past. I make this argument in spite of the consensus among academics studying Ethiopia that under a policy of ethnic federalism, ethnicity is the most important source of differentiation between individuals and groups. Jimma's unusual history and high ethnic diversity means that other Ethiopian cities may have greater levels of ethnic-based stratification, but the argument I develop concerning aspirations, class, and status applies to urban Ethiopia more generally.

The remainder of this book is structured around an exploration of the construction of hope, barriers to attaining hopes, and strategies for maintaining the possibility of hope. Chapters 2 and 3 examine the construction of hope among young men. The everyday passage of time for young men is experienced as a source of stress, and activities such as consuming khat and watching international films are used to alleviate problems of time. In Chapter 2 I examine both the spaces in which khat and films are consumed and the discourses that surround these activities, in order to better understand the processes through which imaginative possibilities for the future are constructed. The chapter closes with a discussion of a government shutdown of video houses in relation to the imagination and the production of the social category of youth. In Chapter 3 I discuss narratives of progress. I argue that young men's notions of progress are based in part on their engagement with formal education. Progress is conceptualized in terms of experiencing improvement in one's position within social relationships. Young men's difficulties in actualizing their desires for progress represent an additional temporal problem. I analyze the temporal problems of young men in relation to discussions of time, progress, and boredom that have emerged out of a Western context.

For young men, the primary barrier to the attainment of hope is unemployment. As noted earlier, unemployment must be understood in terms of both the availability of work and young men's aspirations. In Chapter 4 I explore young men's decisions concerning work. I examine notions of stigma and prestige as they relate to occupational status. I argue that the stigma attached to some occupations is a result of locally specific values concerning hierarchy and social relationships. Case studies of working and unemployed youth are contrasted to demonstrate how values influence one's decisions concerning occupation. This chapter will be of interest to those who are doing applied work in relation to the problem of unemployment. It is often unclear how young people in urban Africa are able to economically sustain themselves in a context of extremely high unemployment. In this chapter I explore some of the strategies pursued by young men to meet their day-to-day economic needs and the implications of these strategies for long-term social reproduction.

Chapters 5 and 6 examine the strategies that young men employ to attain hope and connect the present to the future. In Chapter 5 I examine how contrasting patterns of reciprocity between working and unemployed young men produce multiple forms of inequality. I engage with literature on gift exchange to argue that differences in sharing behavior represent contrasting approaches to investing in social relationships and the accumulation of material wealth. The balance between investing in people and things has shifted over time, and I argue that historical changes associated with neoliberal capitalism have led to a decoupling of social relationships and material wealth.

Young men sought to solve their problems of time with the spatial solution of international migration, and I take up this issue in Chapter 6. In discourse and practice, migration represents a means of attaining hope. On one hand, international migration provides access to opportunities for earning higher wages. On the other hand, it also allows an escape from the social relationships that young men claim prevent them from taking on low-status work. I analyze space as an additional variable interrelated with time, production, and social relationships.

Together these chapters form an ethnography of young men in urban Ethiopia at the turn of the twenty-first century. Many of the dynamics faced by young men in Ethiopia are common to youth throughout the developing world. Youth face significant barriers to taking on the normative social responsibilities of adults partially because of global economic shifts associated with neoliberal capitalism. At the same time, the spread of formal education, increases in international migration, and greater availability of international media have elevated the aspirations of youth to unprecedented levels. The particular nature of the social category of youth as defined in terms of a process of movement toward an imagined future means that hope and hopelessness are common themes in the lives of young people. In this book I seek to explore the intersections of these global dynamics with cultural and historical processes that are specific to urban Ethiopia. Values surrounding occupational status, urban class hierarchies, and constructions of a good life all shape the aspirations and practices of Ethiopian young men. Examining the intersections between these local and global dynamics generates insights into theoretical questions concerning the nature of inequality, the experience of time, and conceptions of space. At the same time, I believe this book is important because it describes a particular population living in a particular time and place. The documentation of diverse cultural practices has historically been a goal of anthropology, and this is certainly one of my hopes in presenting this book.

1

The Historical and Cultural Roots of Unemployment and Stratification in Urban Ethiopia

Young men's struggles for hope emerge out of the particular class and status hierarchies of urban Ethiopia. This chapter examines the history of the city of Jimma and changing patterns of stratification in urban Ethiopia more broadly. I begin by examining shifts in class and status hierarchies during the mid-twentieth century and then trace these dynamics up to the present situation. The second half of this chapter is devoted to describing some of the qualitative dynamics of space within Jimma. Although I argue that *urban*, as a general term, is useful in grouping different types of space within a single category, differences in the qualitative nature of space within this category are still important. I describe neighborhoods and housing conditions in Jimma to give a sense of the different spaces that exist within the city and to provide a feel for the specific textures of life.

High unemployment rates in Ethiopia and in Africa more generally are a specifically urban phenomenon. Many of the issues that I explore in this book, such as the social category of youth, the experience of time, conceptions of modernity, and the nature of stratification, are also rooted in an urban context. *Urban*, therefore, as a term describing a particular type of place, is highly important for contextualizing my study. It is not, however, always completely clear what *urban* describes.

The ambiguity of *urban* is illustrated in the shifting definitions adopted by the Ethiopian government. According to the most recent national census, conducted in 2007, around 16 percent of Ethiopia's population is "urban" (Central Statistical Authority [CSA] 2008). For an area to qualify as urban it had to have at least one thousand residents who do not derive their livelihood primarily from agriculture. The qualitative difference between a town of one thousand

and Addis Ababa, a city of more than three million, is huge, and yet both are considered urban. Past government surveys of urban areas focused more on the qualitative nature of the urban experience. According to guidelines developed by the Ethiopian Central Statistical Office for carrying out surveys of urban areas between 1964 and 1968, an area could be classified as urban if the buildings and houses were contiguously aligned, meaning that they are side by side in rows (Bjeren 1985: 63–64). Other defining features of a town were the presence of a bar selling alcoholic beverages, a hotel offering lodging for strangers, a permanent shop, and a weekly market. This definition differs significantly from standards used in contemporary government assessments of urban areas, but in some ways it does capture many of the qualitative dimensions of urban life.

In everyday discourse, the term *city* (*ketema*) is used to mark the qualitative distinctions between rural and urban. A city has a density of economic opportunities and government services. A city should conform to particular patterns of spatial organization. Opportunities for leisure are also important. The hotel and bar that were markers of *urban* in earlier surveys are associated with modernity and European culture in that they first appeared primarily during Italy's brief occupation of Ethiopia (1936–1941). Contemporary urban residents, particularly men, seek out entertainment at bars and restaurants, but many also expect to have access to sports stadiums and cinemas. Opportunities for accessing health care, educational institutions, and other public services are also important components of a city. Not every "urban area" has these features, and a more qualitative notion of *urban* would necessitate the creation of much more specific analytical categories.

In 1998 and 1999 I served as a Peace Corps volunteer in Goha Tsion (known as Kare Gowa in Oromo), located about 185 kilometers north of Addis Ababa. With a population of four to five thousand, Goha Tsion is an urban area, but its status as a city depends on who is asked. Certainly for the farmers in the surrounding area, Goha Tsion is the city, but residents of Addis Ababa or Jimma would laugh at this designation. Goha Tsion is located on the main road leading north from Addis Ababa, just south of the Blue Nile Gorge that divides the Gojam region from Shoa. A single asphalt road bisected clusters of houses and dirt roads that I found unbearably muddy during the rainy season. If I walked at a brisk pace with my back to the asphalt, I was on the edge of town in five minutes, faced with a view of endless fields dotted by the occasional round house. The town had a weekly market that attracted a number of sellers from the surrounding area. There were schools up to the twelfth-grade level. There was no electricity, but a few businesses in town owned generators.[1] One of them, my neighbor, used his generator to power a TV and VCR that supported a small business in which customers, mostly children, paid a small fee to watch videos. Water came from a cluster of faucets that were shared by the entire town. A telecommunications office had a phone that rarely worked. A significant number of urban Ethiopians live in towns like Goha Tsion.

Addis Ababa, the political and economic capital of Ethiopia, is at the other end of the spectrum. In 2007, around 2.7 million of Ethiopia's nearly 11.9 million urban residents lived in Addis Ababa (CSA 2008). Addis has sprawling slums, neighborhoods of mansions occupied by expatriate embassy and development workers, shopping malls, and huge outdoor markets. Herds of sheep compete for space on the asphalt roads with the white Land Cruisers of the development workers. Small communities of Greeks, Arabs, Armenians, and Italians have lived in Addis for many years. Many residents of Addis go their whole lives without ever leaving the city, let alone going somewhere as provincial as Goha Tsion. For them, Goha Tsion is the *getter*, the countryside.

Jimma and Ethiopia's other regional centers are somewhere between Addis Ababa and Goha Tsion. With a population of more than 150,000, Jimma is one of the ten largest cities in the country (CSA 2006). It has a university, a cinema, a hospital, a small airport, and pleasant tree-lined boulevards. In some African nations, such as Nigeria, a place like Jimma would probably not be considered a major city, but in Ethiopia it is. Even Addis Ababa residents would acknowledge that Jimma is a *ketema* and not *getter*.

Although in a qualitative sense places like Jimma, Addis Ababa, and Goha Tsion are extremely different, from a quantitative perspective they are all grouped together within the single category of *urban*. This raises the question of which *urban* am I talking about—Goha Tsion, Addis Ababa, or Jimma? In this chapter, I argue that this broad category of the urban that includes all three areas draws attention to social dynamics that are important for understanding issues related to aspirations and unemployment.

The Development of Jimma City, Urban Occupational Status, and Class Structure (Late 1800s–1974)

Although the history of Jimma varies significantly from that of other urban areas in Ethiopia, its transition into an urban residential center during the twentieth century is associated with many of the same dynamics that are key to understanding issues of unemployment, aspiration, and stratification elsewhere in the country. Urban areas in southern and western Ethiopia have been associated with the expansion of primarily Amhara settlers from the North into the South and the creation of military garrisons that took place in the latter part of the nineteenth century. As northern Christians conquered the culturally and linguistically diverse groups living in southern and western Ethiopia, they established military outposts that later became cities. In contrast to other urban areas in Ethiopia, Jimma's long-term status as a center for long-distance trade was the result of the presence of an Oromo Muslim[2] kingdom, rather than an Amhara military garrison (Gemeda 1984, 1987; Hassen 1990; Lewis 2001). Jimma has been a center for trade for hundreds of years. The size and importance of the main Hirmata market in Jimma continued to grow during Abba

Jifar II's reign (1878–1932), and around the turn of the century the number of visitors to the weekly Thursday[3] market was estimated to be between twenty and thirty thousand (R. Pankhurst 1985).

The expropriation of land that accompanied the movement of northern settlers into southern Ethiopia during the late nineteenth and early twentieth centuries (Donham 1986; Zewde 2002a) also occurred in Jimma. However, in Jimma the process was delayed by the peace treaty that King Abba Jifar II made with Menelik II. In return for the payment of a yearly tribute to Menelik II, Jimma's relative autonomy from the central Abyssinian state was maintained up until Abba Jifar II's death in 1932. The heavy taxation and loss of land experienced in the rest of southern Ethiopia did not occur in Jimma until the reign of Haile Selassie, after the Italian occupation ended in 1941. Despite its unusual history, the emergence of Jimma as a residential city coincides with Amhara cultural and political domination and the development of a local government bureaucracy. Therefore, normative Amhara values concerning occupational status are particularly important for the study at hand.

Among the traditional rural highland Amhara, whose culture provides a reference point for much of contemporary urban Ethiopia, the range of occupational choice was limited. During the era of modern Ethiopian history that Bahru Zewde (2002a) defines as beginning in 1855 with the reign of Tewodros and extending until the expansion of modern education, the privatization of land, and increased growth of cities that took place under Haile Selassie, the most common occupation was farming. Some men became soldiers or priests, and it was also common for farmers to occasionally take part in military expeditions (Levine 1965). All of these occupations brought varying amounts of prestige depending on one's success in his field. Because most men opted for one of these three professions, occupation was generally not a primary variable in determining status. More important was one's position within hierarchical relations with others. The local lord, who held the right (*gwilt*) to collect taxes from farmers, as well as judicial and administrative authority over farmers on his estate, was able to foster patron/client relations with peasants who needed their lord's assistance in order to access land. In this sense, status was based on one's position within the relationships associated with the process of production. Status was gained by holding political office and using that office to distribute favors to others (Hoben 1970, 1973).

Although less has been written about occupation, status, and power relations among Oromo in the Jimma area, similar opportunities appear to have existed. Farming was the most common occupation, and this was valorized as being good work. No study with the ethnographic detail of Hoben's work concerning the Amhara exists, but Hassen (1990: 92–93) describes a class structure that developed in the Oromo states of the Gibe region. Nobility owned most of the land, free peasants had some rights to land, and landless tenants worked on the land of the nobility. Below them were slaves and stigmatized craft workers. It is not clear whether religious study and soldiering were options as full-time professions, but certainly men engaged in these activities, and particularly within the Oromo kingdoms of the nineteenth century, leadership in military battles was a proven means of accessing power. In contrast to the Amhara region, where merchants were generally viewed with suspicion, if not contempt, in Jimma trade had long been established as a viable means of making a living. Oromo traders, known as *afkala*, had a clear role in shaping the history of the region during the nineteenth century, but the significance of their continued influence is unknown (Hassen 1990). Little has been written about their presence during Haile Selassie's reign, and longtime Jimma residents claimed that if any wealthy Jimma Oromo merchants remained after the 1974 revolution, they fled to Saudi Arabia.

Among most Ethiopian ethnic groups and in East Africa generally, craft worker professions such as carpentry, blacksmithing, weaving, and pottery have been stigmatized. Although important ideological differences exist, the treatment of craft workers was similar to that of lower castes within the Hindu caste system (Levine 1974; A. Pankhurst 2001: 10–15). Alula Pankhurst (2001) explains that craft workers were marginalized in terms of space, economics, politics, and social life. Marriage with non–craft workers was prohibited, and craft workers frequently lacked locally defined rights to land. In most cases they worked as tenant farmers on the land of others, were required to give the products of their work to their patrons, and received only token amounts of grain in return. Craft workers did not observe the same food taboos as Muslims and Orthodox Christians. For example, craft workers are said to have eaten animals like the pig that do not have a cloven hoof and certain forbidden wild game such as monkey or hippopotamus. Sharing food and eating from the same dish is an important social activity for most Ethiopians, but craft workers were not permitted to share the same utensils or dishes with others. If craft workers were guests in the home of a non–craft worker, they ate from banana leaves or some other item that could be disposed of following the meal. Craft workers frequently were thought to possess an evil eye (*buda*), which also contributed to the general discrimination they faced in their day-to-day lives. Although discrimination against craft workers was officially banned during the Marxist Derg regime, it continues to influence notions of occupational status in rural and urban areas.

The traditional stigma against craft workers combined with the prestige of administrative authority formed a relationship between occupation and status that was further complicated by the process of urbanization. Mitchell and Epstein's (1959) foundational model for African urban occupation status is based on the colonialism experienced by other African countries. In this model, association with a European or "civilized" lifestyle motivates many urban residents to seek out white-collar professions instead of higher-paid positions that involve manual labor. In the Ethiopian case, the brief Italian presence does not appear to have impacted values surrounding occupation, and examining local history is much more useful for understanding status.

With the growth of permanent cities, notions of occupational status began to develop beyond the traditional stigmas applied to craft workers. Although it lasted only five years, Italy's occupation of Ethiopia was important for the transformation of Jimma from a trading center to a residential city. The Italians made Jimma the capital of the "Sidamo/Galla" region, and together with Dire Dawa and Addis Ababa it was one of the three capitals in the nation. During this period, the administrative center was moved from Jiren to the area surrounding the Hirmata market. Many of the major buildings and neighborhoods constructed during the Italian era still exist in Jimma. The Italians constructed a hospital, large hotels, a cinema, and numerous other government buildings and private residences. The city was segregated according to race and the Italians lived in what is now called Ferenj Arada and Mahel Ketema.[4] Although many of the buildings constructed by Italians have fallen into disrepair, Ferenj Arada and Mahel Ketema have an entirely different feel than other neighborhoods. Wide roads are lined by buildings with large verandas supported by pillars that today provide shaded spaces for street-side commerce. In Mahel Ketema, city blocks are organized so that storefronts line the street; behind the stores, in the center of the block, residential spaces open onto a shared courtyard.

Abdul Karim, grandson of Abba Jifar II, described to me the reign of Haile Selassie after the fall of the Italians as a "golden era" for Jimma. The coffee business was booming, and this brought numerous investors to town. A number of factories were constructed and work was said to be plentiful, attracting high numbers of immigrants from the countryside. The availability of disposable income led to numerous thriving businesses, particularly hotels, bars, restaurants, and nightclubs. Jimma had 27 hotels in 1953 (National Urban Planning Institute 1997). Trade in the city center came to be increasingly dominated by Arabs; 1,188 foreigners were living in Jimma in 1953, and 846 were Arabs who primarily worked as merchants (National Urban Planning Institute 1997). Three new schools and an agricultural college were also constructed under the reign of Haile Selassie.

Under Haile Selassie, government seizure of land and the introduction of high taxes meant that some Oromo peasants lost their land, but compared to other regions in the South, farmers generally were wealthy enough to pay these taxes (Gemeda 1987: 114). Haile Selassie gave Amhara and Shoa Oromo land grants in the Jimma area based on their role in resisting the Italians, and these individuals were able to expand their wealth primarily through growing coffee and trade. Although many Oromo Muslim farmers may have retained enough land for subsistence farming, most regional and city administrators who also owned large coffee plantations were Amhara or Oromo Orthodox Christians. The pattern was to grow coffee in the countryside, which would fund the construction of a house in the city and support involvement in trade.

With the creation of a wealthy land-owning class in Jimma, others were also attracted to the city. In particular, high numbers of people of Dawro, Kambata, Yem, and Kaffa ethnicity, who lived in the area surrounding Jimma, moved to the city in search of wage labor. Some came only to earn money during the coffee harvest, but others stayed and found work as servants or manual laborers for landowners. With little education or knowledge of Amharic, the national language of governance, it was difficult for these new migrants to find anything but the most menial of jobs. During this period, beginning after 1941, the prestige and desirability of government employment as an urban occupation appears to have developed in Jimma. The prestige of government work was partially based on the traditional hierarchical relationship between nobility and farmers. As Hoben (1970: 222) notes in describing Addis Ababa under the reign of Haile Selassie, the authority of the *"gwilt*-holding lord" (nobility with the right to demand tribute) had been replaced by the government administrator, and education had taken the place of military activity as a means for accessing social mobility. Markakis (1974: 183) claims that higher education almost "automatically" implied state service, which in turn guaranteed status and economic privilege. Owning land and a longer presence in the city increased one's chances of obtaining an education, and these qualities were concentrated mostly among Orthodox Christian Oromo and Amhara settlers, recently arrived from Shoa.

An occupational and ethnic hierarchy between those with or without government work began to develop. Government workers had both political and economic power; others generally performed the service work and manual labor necessary to maintain life in the city. To some extent a patron/client relationship existed between these two strata. In much the same manner that a lord could provide access to land, government administrators and landowners could give their clients urban employment, better housing, and other opportunities. The rise of a particularly urban form of stratification is based on the presence of a government bureaucracy and expanded opportunity for education. Government employment created class differentiation, and education was the means by which one accessed government work. To the extent that opportunities for government employment and education were present, this dynamic has been present in urban areas ranging from small towns to large cities.

Particularly in southern Ethiopia, the ethnic diversity of cities provided an additional variable that has influenced stratification. Gunilla Bjeren (1985) offers the most detailed description of urban stratification in Ethiopia before the 1974 revolution. On the basis of research conducted in Shashamene in 1973, Bjeren explains that ethnicity mapped onto economic and status hierarchies. The ethnicity-occupation hierarchy described by Bjeren appears to be applicable to prerevolution Jimma. Amhara and some (primarily Orthodox Christian) Oromo performed government administrative work and/or owned factories and coffee plantations while other ethnicities did service work or manual labor. It was not clear whether this was by choice or their urban land was forcibly removed, but local Muslim Oromo predominantly lived outside the city and worked as farmers. The low number of Muslim Oromo involved in the urban government may explain the predominance of values associated with Amhara Christians in what was largely an Oromo Muslim region. The Gurage people gradually took over most of the trade activities in the city, especially after the 1974 revolution, when many Arabs were expelled from the country. More menial jobs were performed by ethnic groups from the surrounding area, such as the Yem, Dawro, and Kaffa. In this manner ethnicity, wealth, and status overlapped to form relatively clear class groups. A lack of marriages between ethnic groups and unequal access to education allowed class hierarchies to be reproduced from one generation to the next. Dominant ethnic groups were better represented in education, and because education was necessary to access government work, social and economic power were inherited.[5]

Revolutionary Urban Ethiopia (1974–1991)

Beginning in the early 1970s, the Ethiopian economy began a long period of contraction (Arrighi 2002). With the Marxist revolution of 1974, all land was nationalized. Private ownership of coffee plantations and factories ended, facilitating the transition to associating local power predominantly with government work. A fall in the international price of coffee also led to a decline in the coffee industry and an increased reliance on public sector employment. This had already begun to occur in urban centers like Jimma, where owning land for agriculture was becoming less common and urban residents were relying primarily on income derived from trade and government employment. Before 1974 the children of most landowners were already established within the government. While some of these individuals were arrested or killed following the revolution, on the basis of life histories gathered from elder Jimma men, it appears that many of them made the transition successfully and found high-ranking positions within the new Marxist regime. During the Derg regime, nightclubs and factories shut down and opportunities for private employment disappeared, leading to a decline in the number of migrants moving to the city. While the Derg regime officially promoted equality among ethnic groups, institutionalized power differences meant that at least initially the cultural and economic dominance of Amhara and Oromo Orthodox Christians continued. In general the upper class from the prerevolutionary era maintained their power in the form of government employment.

The youth I studied were generally born during the final ten years of the Derg regime. Although the economic shifts associated with liberalization were just beginning, in terms of class these young men appeared to be in a very different situation than their parents. In Jimma and most likely in other cities as well, the emergence of a generation born in the city during the 1970s and 1980s has gone hand in hand with changes that have destabilized the close relationship between ethnicity, class, and status. Public education is free, and regardless of ethnic and class background children living in Jimma have been able to attend school. Many of these youth completed secondary school and became eligible for government employment. During the Derg regime, post-secondary education guaranteed government employment (Krishnan 1998). The urban environment also facilitated assimilation to the Amhara norm. At the time of my research, many individuals born in Jimma did not speak their parents' native language and were fluent in only Amharic, meaning that ethnicity was not always a social marker. Also important was that youth of all ethnicities were able to integrate into the Orthodox Christian Church, and predominantly for Oromo youth Islam provided access to powerful social networks as well.

Educated youth born into the city were no longer willing to accept the low-status work performed by many of their parents. These educated young people had a sense of entitlement to socially and economically desirable employment. In this sense the class situation of oppressed ethnic groups was not smoothly transmitted to the next generation. The expectations of youth for the future prevented them from willingly entering into the economic and social relations associated with the occupations of their parents. In urban areas, differing expectations and long-term unemployment disrupted the reproduction of class relationships.

An additional factor in changing class relationships is the emergence of urban households headed by single women. In her study of Shashamene, Bjeren (1985) claimed that women did not remain single for long, but this was not the case at the time of my work in Jimma. Many of the young men involved in my research came from families headed by women who had been single for at least five years and did not have plans to remarry. The economic opportunities for these women were limited primarily to petty trade and domestic work. The significant economic implications of women as household heads is one more factor reducing the salience of ethnicity in relation to class.

Postrevolutionary Urban Ethiopia and Youth Unemployment

Political and economic changes associated with the post-1991 EPRDF (Ethiopian People's Revolutionary Democratic Front) government have been important for disrupting patterns of stratification. These shifts must be contextualized within the global rise of ideologies and policies associated with neoliberal capitalism. Although the EPRDF initially espoused a Marxist doctrine, soon after taking power the government began to open national markets and privatize public holdings. This shift was at least partially motivated by a need to access funds through the International Monetary Fund (IMF). As with elsewhere in Africa, these policies have created patterns of uneven international investment and spiraling debt that have resulted in economic decline. At the beginning of the twenty-first century, Ethiopia has experienced economic growth, but also greater disparities in standards of living.

The implications of the EPRDF's policies directed toward liberalization were just beginning to become apparent in Jimma at the time of my research. The expansive Jimma Hotel was returned to its prerevolution owner, Qeñazmach Teka Genu. Two- and three-story hotels, one of which was the first in town to have a swimming pool, were being constructed near the bus station. Jimma College became Jimma University, meaning that the number of students, faculty, and staff was mushrooming and shifting the economic center of the city toward the university. Jimma University is the largest employer in Jimma. Certainly a few businessmen in Jimma have become extremely rich within a neoliberal context. At the national level no one has benefited more from these policies than Mohammed Al-Moudi, a billionaire of Ethiopian and Saudi descent. He is active in virtually all sectors of the Ethiopian economy, including gold, petroleum, and coffee, and he was a vocal supporter of the EPRDF government during the 2005 election.

Despite the success of a few individuals, most Ethiopians, like most Africans, have experienced the last twenty years as a period of economic stagnation or decline. With the 1989 failure of the International Coffee Organization to set a minimum international price for coffee, prices have steadily dropped. More than fifteen million Ethiopians earn a living from coffee, the nation's largest export. Jimma is located in a coffee-growing region, and although none of the young men who participated in my research were directly involved in the coffee trade, its decline certainly had negative implications for economic opportunity in the private sector. For most urban youth, job opportunities in Jimma consisted of finding work at the university or another public institution or trying to make money through entrepreneurial activities in the informal economy.

In terms of youth unemployment, the problem of economic dependence on the export of a single unstable commodity has been compounded by IMF-mandated reforms. In order to receive loans necessary for infrastructural development, Ethiopia was forced to drastically downsize its public sector. This was particularly devastating in urban environments, where education has conditioned young people to expect government employment after graduation. The fact that secondary school graduates are no longer virtually guaranteed government work is one of the causes of the massive urban youth unemployment that began in the mid-1990s. Unemployment among youth (ages fifteen to twenty-nine) increased by 60 percent between 1990 and 1994 and then decreased only slightly in 1997 (Krishnan 1998).[6] The number of young men and women employed in the public sector decreased by half between 1990 and 1997, and unemployment is highest among young people with a secondary education (Krishnan 1998). The fact that having a relatively high level of education increases one's likelihood of being unemployed is an indication of the relationship between expectations for one's future and choosing to avoid available forms of work.

In contrast, the situation faced by rural youth is much different. The rural areas surrounding Jimma tend to be ethnically homogenous, with Oromo people living primarily to the north and east, Kaffa to the southeast, Dawro to the southwest, and Yem to the west. On average, rural youth have far lower levels of education and lower rates of unemployment. In the rural areas surrounding Jimma, most young people progress slowly through school, as much of their time is devoted to farm work and domestic chores. For example, in 1999, 35 percent of rural youth (ages fifteen to nineteen) were attending school, compared with 75 percent of urban youth (Lloyd 2005). Although these youth certainly face struggles of their own, unemployment has less importance because most young people will become farmers.

In a context in which desirable forms of employment are eliminated, there is no means of maintaining stratification between ethnic groups, thus partially breaking down the relationship between ethnicity and employment. Analyses of census and survey data from urban Ethiopia also indicate that ethnicity does not have a major impact on employment (Bizuneh et al. 2001; Serneels 2007). Gurage men are less likely to be unemployed and young Amhara men are more likely to be unemployed, but the impact of ethnicity is small relative to education (Bizuneh et al. 2001). Slightly higher rates of unemployment among Amhara young men may be due to the fact that the Amhara have historically dominated public sector employment. As opportunity for government employment has decreased, these young men may experience the greatest disjuncture between their aspirations and economic opportunity, thus leading to extended periods of unemployment.

Other important shifts that occurred under the EPRDF were the advent of ethnic federalism and multiparty elections. Ethnic federalism divided Ethiopia into different regions on the basis of the ethnicity of the people historically thought to occupy the region. Jimma is located in the Oromo region, meaning that fluency in the Oromo language is necessary for accessing government employment. Non-Oromo speakers often claimed that this is a significant barrier to employment, but as the preceding numbers indicate, there is not a strong correlation between ethnicity and unemployment. Ethiopia held its first truly multiparty election in 2005. With close to 40 percent of the population between ages eighteen and thirty, the youth vote was very important. In Jimma, the ruling EPRDF and the opposition made various attempts to bring young people into the party and control their vote. Youth reacted to these attempts with contrasting narratives of cynicism and hope (Mains, forthcoming, "Cynicism and Hope"). Partially because of the high unemployment and economic decline, urban youth gradually came together in support of the opposition parties. After the opposition contested the results of the 2005 election, urban youth, particularly unemployed young men, took to the streets of Addis Ababa in support of the opposition. The Ethiopian government reacted by arresting tens of thousands of young men and holding them in detention camps outside the city. The state gave opposition parties much less freedom in the 2010 election, and similar youth uprisings did not occur.

Despite occasional outbreaks of resistance to the ruling party, most youth still aspire to public employment. In a recent study, half of the young unemployed were looking for government work, while a quarter claimed that they would accept any type of work. Aspiring to government work had a positive correlation with unemployment, and aspiring to self-employment had a significant negative effect on the likelihood that one would be unemployed (Serneels 2007). Serneels argues that public sector work is more desirable than self-employment because it is associated with higher wages.[7] He interprets the gap between public sector and self-employment wages as the primary factor leading young men to wait for government work. From this perspective the phenomenon of queuing for government work, which is associated with youth unemployment in many developing countries, is a rational decision based on a desire to maximize economic gain. Serneels, however, does not take into account the type of government work that most young people can expect to access. As I detail in later chapters, the lower-level government work typically aspired to by youth with secondary education did not generally provide wages greater than could be earned through self-employment. Furthermore, on the basis of a 1997 survey, Krishnan (1998) claims that differences in wages between the public and private sector were decreasing during the 1990s but that this did not appear to have impacted the behavior of job seekers who still desired government work. In other words, in waiting for work young men were not behaving like rational economic maximizers, and other explanations must be sought.

Homes, Class, and Status in Jimma

To concretize the patterns of stratification that I have described, it is necessary to examine specific urban spaces. I turn first to the home, where economic differences were often displayed. In terms of clothing and other forms of outward appearance, it was often difficult to identify class distinctions among the young men who participated in my research. A quick visit to their homes, however, nearly always provided a clear picture of their access to resources and social networks.

Like much of urban Ethiopia, in Jimma the home is a private place that is often hidden from the view of the passerby with walls of stone, tin, or bushes depending on one's finances. Although young men pass little time at home except to return for meals and to sleep, young women are generally always around the house working and visiting with friends and family. Most families in Jimma live in one- or two-room houses with walls made from a mixture of mud and straw. State surveys classify 37 percent of Jimma houses as overcrowded in that they are occupied by an average of three or more people per room. Most houses have tin roofs, and around half have concrete floors while others have simple dirt floors. Less than half of the housing units in Jimma have access to piped water, a number that is relatively low compared to other Ethiopian cities. Twenty-seven percent of housing units in Jimma have no access to a toilet of any kind, and for the most part the others rely on private or shared pit toilets. Four out of five houses have access to electricity (Abelti, Brazzoduro, and Gebremedhin 2001).

My neighbors during the first year of my research provide a good example of the standard of living for a middle-class family. They lived in a two-room apartment within a compound occupied by four other couples. The mother and father were both schoolteachers, and they had three children, all of school age. The house had walls made from mud and straw that were covered with plaster. The walls were adorned with different posters and calendars, although advertisements for Pepsi were particularly prominent, as the mother's brother was a distributor for Pepsi-Cola. A single glassless window, covered by a wooden shutter, was present in each room. The tin roof was separated from the living space by a thin manufactured ceiling. One bare lightbulb hung from the ceiling in each of the two rooms. The family shared a faucet and cement-floored pit toilet with ten of the other residents of the compound. Although the compound did have a cold shower, the family did not have access to it because the landlords felt they did not pay enough rent (access to the shower was limited by removing the handle on the faucet). The dwelling had cement floors that were covered with a thin patterned vinyl floor covering that was meant to simulate the appearance of tile. While wealthier families had this floor covering neatly stretching from wall to wall, my neighbors had purchased theirs many years ago, and it had sizable holes. Relative to other Ethiopian cities, wood was cheap in Jimma, and carpenters were highly skilled, meaning that most families had a large amount of high-quality wood furniture. The walls of my neighbors' home were lined with bureaus and shelves full of books, plates, clothes, papers, and other small items. A single bed sat in one corner of the room. A large wooden table with four wooden chairs sat next to the bed, but these were generally used only for guests. Like most Muslims, my neighbors preferred to spend most of their time on the floor mats and pillows that filled a large portion of the room. This was where meals were eaten, coffee drunk, and khat chewed, and where the children slept. The family owned a small television and a CD/DVD player. Much of the furniture and appliances in the main room were covered with handmade doilies. The other room in the dwelling was used primarily for storage and occasionally for food preparation, although this usually took place outdoors. Near the end of my research, my neighbors had a phone line installed in their home. Until that time they could receive calls only on their landlord's phone, and outgoing calls had to be made at a public phone. Like most families, they kept the phone's dialing apparatus locked to prevent the children from making outgoing calls. Mobile phones were introduced in Jimma in 2004. Initially they were confined to elites, but when I returned again in 2008 cell phones were everywhere and were owned by many middle-class families and most of the working young men who had participated in my study.

The presence of the television, the telephone, the manufactured ceiling, cement floors, and access to running water were all strong indicators of my neighbors' economic standing. Many of the young men involved in my research lived in houses that were not located in a locked compound and instead opened directly onto the street. In most houses the tin roof was exposed and floors were made of well-packed dirt. Furniture generally was limited to a few wooden stools, a large bed, and perhaps a wooden bureau. Toilets were pits dug directly into the earth, and water was accessed at neighborhood spigots. A radio was the primary source of news and nighttime entertainment, but it was common for young men without a television to watch programs at their neighbors' homes in the evenings. Whereas my neighbors had high-quality posters, other families might rely on photos from newspapers or magazines to adorn their walls. Most Orthodox Christian families had at least one glossy poster of a saint on their wall. Handmade doilies were common regardless of class.

Neighborhoods, Street Life, and Economic Opportunity

As soon as one leaves the home, whether through a metal compound gate or house door that opens directly onto the street, one is immediately immersed in social activity. For me, walking in urban Ethiopia, it is very difficult to see anything past the waves of people moving through the city on foot. If the pedestrians are the first layer of experience, then the vendors and beggars are the second. While the informal economy of urban Ethiopia is not as well developed as in other parts of Africa, the streets are dotted with women selling mangoes, boys with portable scales who weigh customers for a small fee, shoeshines, and children selling lottery tickets. Especially near churches and mosques, the beggars have a strong presence, each one exhibiting his or her particular physical ailment. Jimma is not a city that one experiences through expansive views and majestic urban architecture. Jimma is the people.

If the home is the inner sanctum where class is often made apparent, the neighborhood is the space where young men from various backgrounds mix and interact. Around neighborhood street corners, storefronts, and shady trees, young men gather to exchange stories, pass the time, and sometimes learn about opportunities to make a bit of money. The particular dynamics of neighborhoods mediated young men's class backgrounds and influenced opportunities to engage in relations of reciprocity.

The density of life and the sounds and smells all change from neighborhood to neighborhood. Occasionally a trip to the market or a walk through Ferenj Arada (described earlier) led young men to leave their home neighborhoods, but in general they preferred to stay where they were comfortable. In order to examine the importance of space in day-to-day life I focused my research on three types of neighborhoods: those with low incomes and low market activity, mixed incomes and high market activity, and mixed incomes and low market activity. By describing these neighborhoods I hope to provide a sense of what it feels like to live in Jimma and how these sensations change in different spaces.

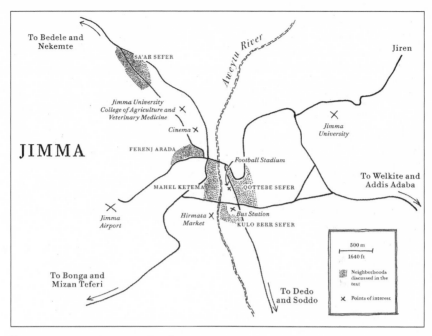

Jimma city map. (Courtesy of Walter Baumann.)

The importance of the qualitative dynamics of neighborhood for relations of reciprocity is analyzed more closely in Chapter 5.

Sa'ar Sefer: A Lower-Income Neighborhood with Low Market Activity

Sa'ar Sefer literally means "grass neighborhood." One explanation for this name is that "there is nothing there but grass," but a more accepted explanation is that it was the last neighborhood in Jimma to have a house built with a tin roof. This second explanation seems more likely because neighborhood residents could remember the owner of the first tin-roofed house and the date it was built. Sa'ar Sefer blended into an adjoining neighborhood called Matric Sefer. Matric Sefer takes its name from the matriculation exam that students take on completion of tenth grade (previously twelfth grade) in order to advance to postsecondary education. It was said that the young men in Matric Sefer fear this exam so much that they drink large quantities of *tella*, the local beer, before the exam and then fail miserably. The reputation for poor academic performance was also applied to youth in Sa'ar Sefer.

Jimma residents often claimed that Sa'ar Sefer had the highest rates of poverty and HIV/AIDS in the city. This was partially because of the presence of a large military camp in the neighborhood that eliminated space for economic growth and provided a source of disease transmission. The population of Sa'ar

Sefer was predominantly Orthodox Christian, most of whom were very pious. Most of the parents of youth with whom I worked had emigrated to Jimma from the surrounding countryside at a young age, and this was typical for the neighborhood. They were generally of Dawro or Kaffa ethnic descent, and they worked as domestic servants, day laborers, or low-level government employees. All of the young men involved in my research in this neighborhood belonged to households headed by single women.

Sa'ar Sefer had a distinctly different feel from other neighborhoods. The paved road turned to dirt upon reaching the neighborhood and then soon became impassable for motorized vehicles. There were more trees, and the air always felt a little cleaner and cooler. Instead of straight roads and large compounds, twisting trails meandered among clusters of houses, many still with grass-thatched roofs and no exterior fence. This meant less privacy for residents, as passersby could easily see into their houses. Whereas young men in other neighborhoods gravitated toward the city center, in Sa'ar Sefer, recreation was found by moving in the opposite direction. Young men sometimes took me for walks in the fields that began where the neighborhood and the city ended. They pointed out favorite trees for sitting and watching for wildlife and the best places for picking wild guavas. The young men I worked with in this neighborhood did not chew khat and had little gift income from their families or friends. They generally passed their time by attending Orthodox Christian Church and taking long walks outside the city.

Kulo Berr: A Mixed-Income Neighborhood with High Market Activity

The name *Kulo Berr* translates literally as "Kulo [a somewhat pejorative term for the Dawro ethnic group] gate [or door]." This neighborhood was clustered around the road that led to the Dawro region. Kulo Berr was also near the bus station and was one of the major trading centers in the city. Particularly for khat and other agricultural products, this was one of the first stop-off points where merchants sold their goods. The main market for sheep was also located in Kulo Berr. The streets were lined with small restaurants, drinking houses, barbershops, and other locations where any money earned could be quickly spent. The dynamics of Kulo Berr were similar to those of another neighborhood where I focused my research, Mahel Ketema (literally "city center"). Mahel Ketema contained businesses that necessitated a higher level of capital investment, such as shops selling clothing, gold, or shoes, and therefore was perhaps a slightly wealthier neighborhood, but the density of economic activity was similar.

In terms of ethnicity and religion, the neighborhood was very mixed, but there were particularly high numbers of Dawro Orthodox Christians and Oromo Muslims. Most of the money in the neighborhood was generated through trade, and many people were small-scale merchants. The wealthier members of the community were often owners of hotels or shops. Working youth felt that there was always money to be made in Kulo Berr, and they sometimes contrasted it with Sa'ar Sefer. Walking through Kulo Berr was a sensory overload that I found exhilarating, and I never ceased to be impressed by the density. Children, men carrying loads, donkeys, and the occasional vehicle crowded the main street. It reminded me of smaller Ethiopian towns like Goha Tsion with businesses lining a single asphalt road, separated from the houses by small bridges stretching across a mud-filled ditch. Businesses often sold locally brewed liquor and beer or simple meals. Crowds of children played everywhere; donkeys stood tied up outside various drinking houses while their owners enjoyed the profits earned selling goods at the market; khat was sold at all times of the day.

Many of the working and unemployed young men involved in my research passed time, resided, or worked in Kulo Berr. With few exceptions the unemployed youth were regular khat chewers, and this dominated their free time. They tended to have high levels of gift income and they always had enough money to attend a video, buy a bundle of khat, or have coffee at a café. It was not common for them to leave their neighborhood, and if I needed to track someone down, I could always find him simply by making a few queries.

Qottebe Sefer: A Mixed-Income Neighborhood with Low Market Activity

This was the neighborhood where I resided throughout my research. *Qottebe* means "savings." The name was given to the neighborhood because of the presence of a high number of government workers who were thought to be saving large amounts of money because of their regular salary and inexpensive government housing. The neighborhood was actually constructed specifically for government employees by the Marxist Derg regime. The heart of the neighborhood consisted of a neat grid of well-maintained dirt roads and large single-family compounds. Although renting out these houses for profit was illegal, it did sometimes occur. The name *Qottebe* was originally associated with the grid of government housing, but in practice it referred to the surrounding area as well. Although these residents were not necessarily government workers, they were still highly influenced by an ethos of public employment.

The neighborhood was dominated by government administrators and teachers, but it also contained private employees, domestic servants, and day laborers. Most of the government workers were Christian Oromo and not from the Jimma area. It was explained to me that because they were Muslim, Jimma Oromo had initially been resistant to public schooling and therefore did not occupy many government positions. It was not clear whether this was the case or local Oromo Muslims did not have access to education in the past, but Oromo from Shoa and Illubabor held most of the government administrative positions in the city. Other neighborhood residents represented a range of ethnicities and religions.

There was little economic activity within Qottebe Sefer. During the day a few shops were open and a couple of women sold vegetables on the side of the street, but compared to Kulo Berr the streets were empty. After around 7:00 P.M., when the sun disappeared, the gates to compounds closed and everyone remained indoors. The lack of street life made the constant presence of unemployed men even more conspicuous. There was always a crowd standing on what I called Qottebe Corner, hands in their pockets, eager for a new topic of conversation or some distraction from their day-to-day life. Khat was popular among Qottebe youth, but not as universally consumed as in Kulo Berr. Although many youth came from relatively wealthy families, money did not flow so easily and it was common for some youth to have little to do except wait out the day under the shade of a tree.

Conclusion

Although Jimma is distinctive in terms of cultural, historical, and spatial dynamics, I have argued that it is representative of urban Ethiopia in general. The history of Jimma extends back well before the northern conquest and therefore stands in contradiction to many assumptions about the development of cities in southern and western Ethiopia. That said, the values and norms associated with Abyssinian culture still took hold in Jimma and are particularly apparent around issues of occupational status. As in urban areas of varying size throughout the country, in Jimma government employment has been the basis for dominant class and status positions. In southern Ethiopia these positions were dominated by northerners, especially Orthodox Christian Amhara, Tigrayans, and to a lesser extent Oromo. Limited access to education was the means by which this hierarchy was preserved from one generation to the next. This dynamic has changed as the urban population and opportunities for education have grown. The gradual democratization of access to education caused ethnic differences to be diminished. Possibly more importantly, under the post-1991 political regime, the size of the public sector has decreased. The government employment that has been the basis of stratification is no longer available. In this context, youth unemployment has increased dramatically and is particularly high among those with a secondary education. This process has caused youth unemployment to be a particularly urban phenomenon. Although Addis Ababa is in many ways worlds apart from a small town like Goha Tsion, in relation to issues of unemployment and stratification the shared classification of urban still makes sense. In both cases the opportunities and aspirations of young people have been structured by the relationship between education and government employment.

Despite the shared economic and cultural context, Jimma is still a distinctive place, and within Jimma each neighborhood represents a particular place with particular ways of living. Neighborhoods are an example of the spaces within a space that I discussed in the introductory chapter. Although the lives of young men in these neighborhoods were certainly influenced by a fluctuating global coffee market, the downsizing of the public sector, and values concerning occupational status, differences between neighborhoods often led to contrasting patterns of reciprocity that had significant implications for local stratification.

2

Imagining Hopeful Futures
through Khat and Film

A key dynamic of life for youth in Africa and much of the global south
at the beginning of the twenty-first century has been the growing gap
between aspirations for the future and economic realities. As young
people fail to attain aspirations, they become frustrated with an inability to
place their own lives within a hopeful narrative (Hansen 2005; Jeffrey, Jeffery,
and Jeffery 2008; Ralph 2008; Schielke 2008; Weiss 2004a). Worries about
one's future are compounded by the excessive amounts of free time that are
associated with unemployment. In this context the imagination takes on great
importance. For youth, the ability to continually imagine desirable futures
enables hope to persist. In the moment that imagination fails, hope is cut.
Young men in Jimma relied on the day-to-day consumption of khat and international films to continually generate imaginative possibilities for the future.
Through these consumer practices, young men constructed narratives in which
movement toward a desirable future is possible.

Arjun Appadurai has argued that the imaginary is something "new in global
and cultural processes" (1996: 31). This claim is largely based on the emergence of new forms of technology of which Appadurai gives particular attention to cinema, television, and video. He also acknowledges the importance of
stories passed from person to person in creating a world in which "more persons in more parts of the world consider a wider set of possible lives than they
ever did before" (1996: 53). The increasing number of possible lives that individuals now have available to them creates a myriad of possibilities for social
change that did not previously exist.

Appadurai's argument should certainly be viewed critically. The description
of Jimma's history that I offer in Chapter 1 reveals that this region, like many

other places in the world, has been a center for the movement of people, ideas, commodities, and other potential stimulus for the imagination for hundreds of years. That said, massive exposure to international films, extensive conversations concerning global politics, and stories regarding family members residing abroad are certainly something new. Each of these developments generates new possibilities for living in a manner that is particular to the medium.

The same practices that allowed young men to imagine possible lives were social markers that contributed to the imagination of youth as a social category. Adults frequently made statements such as, "Youth are simply sitting and chewing. Today's generation is not interested in working; they are only interested in chewing." "Chewing" refers to the consumption of khat, and in Jimma it was often claimed that khat chewing had taken the place of work for the younger generation. For many adults, khat chewing among youth represented a lifestyle associated with unemployment, crime, and disrespectful behavior. Videos were the topic of a similar discourse. Videos and the houses in which they are shown were thought to expose young people to negative influences and encourage substance abuse, crime, and irresponsible sex.

In this chapter I explore the dual function of imagination in relation to the consumption of khat and films. Youth were imagined by others through these practices at the same time that they used khat and films to imagine possible futures for themselves. I begin with a description of a typical day in the life of an unemployed young man in Jimma, to illustrate young men's experiences of time. For unemployed young men, excessive amounts of unstructured time were sources of mental distress, which is specifically related to hopelessness. The inability to construct a narrative connecting the present to a hopeful future caused young men to experience time as an undesirable and overabundant quantity. Chewing khat and watching videos were activities that provided effective, if temporary, solutions to this problem. Both activities used excess time and allowed young men to reposition themselves in relation to the future, thus restoring a degree of hope. In contrast, among adults it was common to argue that khat and videos were at the root of youth unemployment and idleness. While the consumption of khat among young men was grudgingly tolerated (largely because most adult men also chewed regularly), video houses were sites where interventions were made into youth lives, and during the course of my research, a police sweep shut down all but one of the video houses in Jimma. I argue that the government shutdown of video houses demonstrates how the social category of youth is imagined through particular consumer activities. In this process, "youth" is constructed as a category that refers not only to age but also to gender, urban residence, and moral behavior.

The Dangers of Unstructured Time

Although the activities in which young men engaged varied widely, their day-to-day life conformed to certain patterns, which may be illustrated with a day in the life of Mulugeta, an unemployed young man described briefly in the introduction. Mulugeta was one of twenty young men involved in my research who completed a diary of their daily activities for four weeks. The following is a description of a typical day for Mulugeta. Although there was certainly variation in Mulugeta's activities, most of his days followed the pattern described here.

At 6:00 A.M. he wakes up and walks to the stadium, where he meets his best friend, Berhanu, and exercises. They run up and down the stairs at the stadium and then do upper-body exercises on a set of parallel bars. After exercising, Mulugeta returns to his parents' house, washes, and eats breakfast. By 9:00 A.M. he is standing on the corner in Qottebe Sefer where one of the main dirt roads meets the asphalt. Two other friends have also gathered there to take in the morning sun and watch the traffic of people going to school or work. They talk for a while about a European Premier League soccer match from the night before and crack jokes at the expense of different passersby. Around 10:00 A.M. one member of the group announces that he has a couple of birr and invites the others to go to a video house with him. They walk to the town center and watch an action movie starring Steven Seagal. After the film, Mulugeta returns home for lunch, takes a short nap, and then returns to the corner. At this time of the day the heat is oppressive, and with the sun straight overhead, there is little shade to be had. After standing around for twenty minutes, Mulugeta goes to Haile's house, the popular gathering place that I describe at the beginning of the introductory chapter. Although Mulugeta does not chew khat, he enjoys the conversation, and he spends two hours at Haile's, mostly listening to the others as they chew and tell stories. As the afternoon heat begins to dissipate, Mulugeta emerges and returns to the corner, where a crowd of young men gradually forms. Other youth come and go, and Mulugeta stays for more than an hour before his friend Berhanu arrives and suggests they take a walk. They walk to Ferenj Arada, a neighborhood that is particularly popular among young people for evening strolls. Ferenj Arada is lined with pleasant cafés, and many students from Jimma University can be found there in the evening. By chance they run into another friend, who invites them to a café for coffee. They accept the invitation and sit talking for an hour. When Mulugeta finally returns home, it is around 8:00 P.M. He eats his dinner and watches television with his family until 11:00 P.M., when he retires to sleep.

Although many of the events in Mulugeta's day were contingent on running into friends, certain patterns were present. He almost always exercised in the morning. Not all youth exercised, but most engaged in a regular activity such as attending church or chewing khat that provided some structure to their day. He generally ate his meals at home, meaning that three times a day he returned to eat and in most cases immediately emerged again. Unemployed youth with wealthier parents took more of their meals at restaurants, but returning home for lunch and dinner was still common. The heat of the afternoon provided another source of regularity, as there was always a need to be somewhere cool.

Despite these patterns, for young men, the most salient characteristic of time was its lack of structure. In describing their condition of extended unemployment, young men in Jimma frequently complained about an excess of time. Time was something to be "passed" (*yasallafal*) or "killed" (*yasgedal*).[1] Michael Ralph (2008) describes similar discussions among unemployed young men in Dakar in relation to tea consumption. In both cases, economic restructuring has led to unprecedented levels of youth unemployment, which in turn has created problems of excess time, particularly for young men. Tea in Dakar and khat and videos in urban Ethiopia are activities through which young men creatively imagine solutions to their problems of unemployment and time.

In Jimma, the burden of too much time was a privilege of gender and urban residence. In terms of family background, all of the young men in my study were born in the city and therefore at least had the minimal social networks necessary to meet their daily needs for food and shelter. Young men were expected to perform little household work, and in contrast young women spent nearly all of their time performing tedious household tasks such as collecting firewood, fetching water, and preparing food that were essential to the running of the household. While young men expressed an interest in working partially as an escape from unstructured time, young women explained that the best part of their day included activities such as drinking coffee with friends when they were free to relax and socialize.

Craig Jeffrey (2008: 745–746) notes that cultures of waiting are often linked to class. Young men with too much time on their hands are often relatively privileged and can choose to avoid low-status work. Passing time may also be a way of signaling one's class status to others. To some extent this argument works in the Ethiopian case. Rural young men and urban women were not worried about killing time, largely because of their marginal economic position. As indicated in the introductory chapter, however, unemployed urban young men came from a wide range of different economic backgrounds. Mulugeta, for example, was certainly part of the poor working class, and yet he struggled on a day-to-day basis with having too much time. Perhaps as a result of the wide range of urban young men who participated in this culture of waiting, an excessive amount of leisure time was not a source of distinction. As I discuss shortly, the attraction of khat and video houses was partially the ability to escape the public gaze, so that one's unemployment was not advertised for all to see.

Young men explained that unstructured time was problematic because it led to thinking about their prospects for the future. Young men evaluated activities in terms of their ability to focus one's mind away from his present condition. "Thought" (*assab*) was a key term in these narratives. It represents a broad range of concepts including stress and depression, and a state of "thoughtlessness" was often described as the desired goal. Brad Weiss (2005) explains that young men in urban Tanzania use the Swahili term for *thought* to describe worries associated with one's relationship to one's future.[2] In Jimma the problem of thought was also related to the future, but this was not because of a gap between the present and "limitless prospects of the future" discussed by Weiss (2005: 110). For young men in Jimma, the stress of thought and unstructured time was a result of the perceived lack of potential for achieving one's aspirations in the future. Young men explained that excessive amounts of time led to introspective contemplation of one's long-term unemployment. They did not want to think about their continued dependence on their family, their inability to marry, and the indefinite continuation of their joblessness. Time stretched in front of young men, and the future seemed relatively certain but definitely not desirable. It was not simply thinking that young men sought to avoid, but specifically introspective thought in which one contemplates the bleak future that he faced. Young men consumed khat and international films partially to facilitate the generation of imaginative possibilities for the future.

My intent is not to suggest that evaluations of time in relation to work existed on a continuum, with not working as the least desirable and full employment as the most desirable. While there was no culture of "waiting for the weekend" or desiring more free time, it was also clear that no one envied day laborers who generally performed physical labor with minimal breaks for eight hours a day. Young women who were expected to perform large amounts of housework never complained of excessive unstructured time. The ideal relationship between time and work was not fully conceptualized among unemployed young men, but they did speak about the value of work in terms of enabling them to be busy and avoid the stress of introspective thought. Libraries and gymnasiums were sometimes mentioned as potential solutions to the problem of unemployment because they would provide young people with a productive means of passing their time. In other words, unemployment was not simply an absence of work but a problem of time.

This is a theme that I explore in later chapters. Work was not necessarily, or even primarily, conceived of in relation to the process of production. If work was valued because of the structure it added to one's life, the process of working was also essential for establishing one's social position. Working in different occupations placed one in particular relationships to others, and evaluations of these relationships often affected occupational choice. I return to issues of occupational choice in the following chapter.

Spaces of Escape: The Video House and the Khat House

Both the spaces and practices associated with watching videos and chewing khat were ideal for dealing with the problem of excessive unstructured time. For me, the video house was always an overwhelming sensory experience that I could withstand for only short periods of time. Upon entering, one is met with a blast of heat generated by the tightly packed bodies and the sun radiating off the tin roof. The houses are medium-sized rooms, usually not more than 15 feet by 20 feet, and often hold as many as a hundred customers, mostly young men. The customers sit on low wooden benches facing a television, which provides the only source of light in the room. After adjusting one's eyes to the sudden darkness, it is more or less possible to find a place on a bench, depending on the popularity of the film. Many video house customers were younger than the young men involved in my research, and they ranged in age from around twelve to their early thirties. The older customers usually chewed khat as they watched the film. Khat is said to produce a "heat" within one's body, and this, combined with the temperature of the room, created an intense experience that heightened the customers' enjoyment of the film. Talking between customers was rare. Audiences were fully engaged with the films, cheering for the heroes and occasionally shouting words of warning when the villain prepared an ambush. The video house provided a feeling of total escape. After entering, customers forgot the outside world, and presumably that world forgot about them as well. Although a customer could be sitting with a hundred people, the darkness and intensive focus of attention on the film provided a sense of anonymity in which he could forget himself.

While the interior may be a space in which the individual interacted directly with the film, outside the video house was a site for socializing. Small groups of young men sat on stools talking, chewing khat, and drinking tea and coffee. Table tennis and other games that could be played for a small price were usually found nearby, making the video house a center of activity for young men. Films were a common topic of conversation among the small groups of youth who gathered outside video houses. These discussions frequently took the form of comparing and contrasting what one had seen in a film with day-to-day life in Ethiopia. The physical space of the video house enabled distinctive experiences of inside and outside. Within the house, heat, darkness, and consumption of khat all provided an intense connection between the viewer and the film. Outside in the bright afternoon sunshine, that connection quickly dissipated as young men discussed and debated the relative merits of different films.

Khat was consumed in a variety of locations, but it is worth briefly exploring the khat house in order to understand the relationship between space, imagination, and an escape from time. Khat houses were generally smaller than video houses, often no more than 10 feet by 10 feet. In Jimma, customers at khat houses were almost exclusively young men who did not have access to a space of their own where they could chew with friends. The houses were run by women who earned money selling tea and coffee. Although the crowd was smaller, the charcoal burner for boiling coffee meant that the heat of the khat house was often even more intense than the video house. Smoke from charcoal, cigarettes, and incense created a haze in the room that enhanced the experience for chewers. In contrast to the video house, the khat house was usually not a center for other youth activities. Small groups of chewers converged on the house from different directions. They entered, chewed (sometimes for hours), and left. Socializing was confined to the house and not the space surrounding it.

The social dynamics of khat houses varied considerably in terms of the space present for interaction. At one house where I spent time, young men lounged on mattresses chain-smoking. Some young women were present, and they were chewing as well. Ja Rule and Eminem (popular American rap musicians in the early 2000s) blasted from a small boom box, making conversation nearly impossible. Youth on the mattresses leaned on each other, sometimes joking with the person sitting next to them, but mostly staring off into space or singing along with the music. At another house that I frequented with one of the participants in my research, Alemu, the atmosphere was entirely different. This house was known as the Hoolaa Café. It was explained to me that *hoolaa* is the Oromo term for "sheep," and the name was given to the house because of its close proximity to the daily sheep market. The house was made from sheets of corrugated tin and had wooden benches instead of mattresses. At the Hoolaa Café the main attraction was conversation. This house attracted a crowd that was interested in talking about current events, and chewers sometimes brought a newspaper with them in order to initiate conversation. I observed only young men chewing at the Hoolaa Café. The customers were usually in their twenties and although they were mostly unemployed, they frequently had a year or two of postsecondary education. Whereas the clothing of the youth at the first house tended toward baggy jeans and sports jerseys, the young men at Hoolaa Café preferred the more conservative style of button-down shirts tucked into pants. Although the customers appeared to be segregated roughly in terms of class, both houses were in the same neighborhood and the price of coffee was the same.

Like videos, khat provided an escape from time, but the spatial dynamics were very different. The video house created an isolated interaction between viewer and film. The area outside the video house supported conversations among peers, but these did not have the same intensive focus as those at the khat house. The khat house constricted interactions to clusters of people. At the first house, interactions might be with one other person, while at the Hoolaa Café they involved a small isolated group. Both the khat house and video house manipulated the relationship between the individual and the social group. The inside-outside dynamic of the video house created sites for individual experience and social interaction. The khat house facilitated interaction, but within a highly controlled setting. By constricting interactions with others, the khat house provided the chewer with more control over his experience.

The escape from stress that khat provided was often explicitly described in terms of the problem of excess time. One young man who occasionally worked as an assistant at a video house explained:

> Mondays are the worst day of the week. On Monday everyone is going to work or school and running errands. No one comes to the video house because they are too busy. If I had a real job or I was a student, I would love Mondays. On Mondays I have to chew khat. There is

nothing else to do. On other days I can take it or leave it, but on Mondays I have to have it. How else can I pass the time?

In alleviating the feelings of depression that accompanied a person's inability to live his life as he desired, khat served the dual function of passing time while also making it more enjoyable.

Videos also served the function of using time. Youth often commented that one of the factors behind the popularity of Indian films is that they are up to twice as long as American films and therefore are a better value for one's money, and more importantly they use up the excessive quantities of time that young men experienced as a source of stress. The value of films was sometimes described in similar terms to khat—"films kill time" or "films pass time." Some youth claimed that they had an "addiction" (sus) to videos, and they often watched two or three films a day. Video houses generally screened the first film at 10:00 A.M., followed by a showing at 1:00 P.M.; the most popular time slot was at 4:00 P.M., and then there was an evening showing at 7:00 P.M. One young man who regularly watched two videos per day commented, "In America no one would watch a film at ten in the morning, but here in Ethiopia we have nothing else to do." There was a sense among young men that the experience of time was specific to their location and economic condition. From their perspective, in contrast to much of the rest of the world, in Ethiopia there is no work, and in this absence activities such as khat chewing or video watching use time while providing a mental escape.

Spatial dynamics are also related to conflicting imaginations. Contrary to Appadurai's conception of cultural flows, my discussion of video and khat houses draws attention to the importance of particular spaces in relation to understandings of imagination. If video houses provide a space in which youth can interact with film and imagine possible futures, this is clearly not a process in which all are free to participate. Occasionally young women did attend videos, but for the most part, they were occupied with household work and had restrictions placed on their movement outside the home. It would have been shameful for a young woman and her family if she were to be seen at a video house. It was rare for families to own VCRs or DVD players, and therefore young women had little exposure to films. It would seem that their ability to imagine possible futures through film was constrained.

It was also considered shameful for adult men to visit a video house, and in this sense they were similarly constrained in their engagement with international media. The video house and the khat house were places for young men. However, while adults may have been limited in their exposure to film, this did not prevent them from directing their own imaginations toward video houses, khat, and youth. As I describe shortly, particularly in the case of the video house, the actual space provided a site of contestation. The isolation of international culture within a specific space was key to the conflicting imaginations of adults and young men. Rather than Appadurai's notion of flows, James

Ferguson's (2006) discussion of point-to-point global connections appears to more accurately describe the spatial dynamics of international culture in this case. Cultural goods may be accessed only within particular spaces, and that isolation often creates struggles over the right to imagine possible futures and to reclaim hope.

Videos and the Possibility of Hope

Intuitively it seems that films that expose young men to lifestyles, technologies, and commodities that are vastly beyond what they are capable of attaining would generate a sense of anguish and unfulfilled desire. However, in discussions concerning videos, young men generally did not speak about films as a source of desire but rather as a means of negotiating problems that they already faced. Like youth elsewhere in Africa (P. Richards 1996; Masquelier 2009), young men in Jimma frequently spoke about the value of videos in terms of "learning." Videos were seen as an educational tool. In contrast to the "lessons" learned from popular theater in Nigeria (Barber 1997), learning was often indirect and did not generally involve taking a message or moral directly from a particular story. Youth listed topics as varied as English words and models for dating as information that could be obtained from videos. Action films were thought to be particularly educational. Like Paul Richards's (1996) study of youth in Sierra Leone, young men spoke of learning how to solve difficult problems from watching heroes in action movies extract themselves from seemingly impossible situations. James Bond and Jackie Chan were mentioned as great teachers in this regard. Loyalty was also noted as a trait that could be learned from action movies in which soldiers "left no man behind." In the process of learning, young men felt that they were accessing a window into the realities of life abroad. Glimpses of technology and cultural behavior were remembered for future use. Young men did not simply aspire to become part of the worlds observed through film. As Lila Abu-Lughod (2005) notes, consumers of visual media are often ethnographers in their own right, critically evaluating other places and cultures. In some cases young men positively evaluated aspects of foreign cultures such as the traits associated with action films or the prevalence of personal automobiles. In other cases foreign cultures were perceived negatively, and different young men drew conclusions about racism in the United States based on the common portrayal of African Americans as criminals in Hollywood films. Brian Larkin explains that among Muslim youth in Nigeria, Indian films provided "a way of imaginatively engaging with the changing social basis of contemporary life that is an alternative to the pervasive influence of the secular West" (1997: 434). Although the spatial and religious dynamics were different in Ethiopia,[3] as in Larkin's study films were tools that youth could use in examining their own identity in a context in which desires for the future often did not match economic realities. Similar to Larkin's (2008) description of an "aesthetic of outrage" in contemporary Nigerian cinema that reflects an environment of economic instability and corruption, Ethiopian film also offers an exaggerated depiction of issues concerning love and money that young men may discuss and reflect on.

Youth entered the video house with some notion of what they needed to learn, and the lessons that they took from the films conformed to those desires. While learning English and dating skills may seem distinct, in fact they were both related to the anxieties of young men regarding becoming an adult in an environment of limited economic opportunity. Developing intimate relationships with women was seen as especially difficult because of a lack of employment. In the video house, young men sought and found solutions to this problem. Lack of comprehension of English was regarded by many youth as preventing them from advancing to postsecondary education. Although many consumers of films were no longer students, learning English while watching films provided them with the sense of moving in a direction associated with advanced education and desirable employment. English was also associated with travel abroad, a key element in youth narratives for future success. In consuming films, youth developed elaborate plans for the future that often involved international travel.

The manner in which youth used films to explore problems associated with massive unemployment is particularly apparent in relation to Ethiopian films. While American and Indian films were discussed abstractly, particular plots and themes were less likely to be analyzed. The language barrier and the contextual differences prevented many youth from fully engaging with foreign films. The handful of Ethiopian films that were released in theaters and on video were quickly seen multiple times by nearly all young men and became common points of reference for discussions regarding issues of love and money. Youth noted that watching Ethiopian films filled them with a sense of pride and excitement. There was a sense that these films were part of a movement away from "backwardness" (*hwalakerinet*) because local realities were being represented through cinematic stories. During my research Tewodros Teshome, a director born and raised in the Mahel Ketema neighborhood of Jimma, released two films. While these films were well received throughout Ethiopia, they were especially popular in Jimma, where the young director had many friends among the local youth population.

The first and more popular of these films was titled *Kezkaza Welafen* ("Cold Flame"). It tells the story of a beautiful college student, Selamawit, who loses her boyfriend in a car accident in the first scene of the movie. Her older godfather pressures her into accepting a marriage proposal by refusing to give her mother money for medicine and evicting Selamawit's family from their home. Selamawit is saved from marriage at the last moment in a scene in which her mother intervenes during the wedding. Just as the suitor lifts her veil to kiss Selamawit, her mother announces that there can be no marriage without an HIV-negative certificate (it is not clear how it is known that the suitor was HIV positive). Selamawit's mother is confident in intervening because another suitor has given her a large sum of money. The second suitor is a nice but somewhat homely man who repeatedly has sought Selamawit's affection, and during the first half of the film his lack of success brings much in the way of comic relief. After Selamawit learns about the gift to her mother, she becomes close friends with the second suitor. He supports Selamawit through college and immediately gives her a job in his office after she graduates.

After the first marriage proposal is resolved, the second relationship is largely based on economic need. Selamawit's opinion about this young man, Biruk, changes drastically after he helps her financially. He drives a high-priced SUV, talks on a cell phone, and has a decent-sized belly—all signs of wealth. They discuss the issue of love and her indebtedness to him in a scene shot at Lake Langano (a popular vacation site among the international community in Addis). In the end, Selamawit does fall in love and agrees to marry Biruk.

The second film, *Fiker Siferd* ("*Love Verdict*") is more of a thriller with a plot that contains many twists and turns, but it also features a love story that crosses boundaries of class and religion. In this case the beautiful young woman is from an extremely wealthy family and she is pursuing a poor policeman.[4] She is Christian and he is Muslim, but their class and religious differences do not stand in the way of their love.

For young men, these films contained models of Ethiopian modernity and success. Values such as religious piety and honesty are combined with symbols of success such as university education, personal vehicles, and international vacations (in the second film, the lovers travel to Kenya on their honeymoon). After expressing his appreciation for the references to HIV running through the plot of *Kezkaza Welafen*, one unemployed young man commented that the male protagonist in the film could have never succeeded in winning the love of Selamawit without money. He felt this was true to life. In young men's narratives, sex was continually linked with money and employment status. Young men argued that in Ethiopia there is no love; there is only money. Without work or access to money, it was difficult for young men to marry or have girlfriends. According to one unemployed young man, women want *bizness* (material support) for the simple reason that "there is no work" (*sira yellem*). He did not appear bitter about this situation; it was simply a fact of life. A film like *Kezkaza Welafen* exaggerates conditions—the difficulty of love in an environment of extreme poverty—that youth are already quite aware of, thus providing an excellent medium for discussion. In general young men were empathetic with the conditions Selamawit faced and her dependency on different men for economic support. In the end she found a benefactor whom she was able to love, but most young men saw this as a happy coincidence and not a condition that should be expected.

The film *Fiker Siferd* provides a contrasting message, in that the poor policeman was able to marry a beautiful and wealthy woman. Their class differences are highlighted in a scene that cuts from the policeman taking a bucket bath in his squalid apartment to the young woman luxuriating in a huge tub full of bubbles. In this film love is not bound by economic necessity. At one point the young woman's father refuses to support her love for the policeman, and she leaves her father's mansion to move in with her lover. The film provides another shared story that young men could insert into their preexisting discourse on love and money. While youth may not have found the possibility of a wealthy woman pursuing a man of limited economic means to be realistic, the story was happily consumed and discussed.

As in Masquelier's (2009) study of youth television consumption in Niger, young men in Jimma were also evaluating the meaning of love through the consumption of film. The contrast between love and money assumes a possibility for true love that is independent of exchange. Although I do not have adequate evidence to substantiate a comparison with the past, this conception of love may have been new and closely intertwined with the stories told in both national and international films. Economic conditions that created a greater need to receive material goods in exchange for intimate relations were thought to be a relatively new phenomenon, and perhaps so was the notion that relationships between men and women could exist without some level of financial dependence.[5]

In contrast to Abu-Lughod's (2005) discussion of melodrama and the creation of modern subjectivities in relation to Egyptian television serials, young men's narratives did not conform to the melodramatic love story that was common both in Ethiopian films and televised dramas. Telling stories about themselves or others was not common among young men. Instead ideas were conveyed with more generalized statements, logical arguments, and often proverbs or riddles. Love was a topic of interest, but at least among young men there was no marked tendency to insert themselves into the format of the love story.

In a context in which ideals of wealth and marriage were clearly unattainable for most young men, Ethiopian films provided stories in which different possibilities could be explored. These stories were particularly compelling, partially because they were told in Amharic and partially because they dealt with locally relevant issues such as HIV and religion. The escape from time associated with film was important, but so was the construction of narratives that enabled youth to think through an uncertain future. Youth interacted with films to imagine other possibilities and worlds. It was not that films created a false belief among young men that bridged the gap between their aspirations and economic realities. The process of imagination allowed young men to contemplate this gap in a way that did not necessarily imply success or failure.

To the extent that film provided young men with a means of reconstructing narratives connecting the present to the future,[6] they facilitated a reengagement with hope. When hope is cut, the attainment of desires in the future is no longer possible. Through interactions with film, young men can rethink their relationship to their future and avoid many of the anxieties associated with unstructured time, introspective thought, and hopelessness. Videos and khat alleviated this problem by using time and allowing young men to imagine positive futures.

Chewing Khat and Dreaming of the Future

Jimma is widely believed to be one of the centers in Ethiopia for khat consumption, and many residents claim that after Harrar and Dire Dawa, Jimma has the highest per capita rate of consumption. In the absence of official statistics on khat consumption, I simply asked youth to estimate how many young men chew khat regularly. Nearly all estimated that 70 to 85 percent chew at least weekly, and at least half of these chew daily. They stressed that khat use in Jimma varies significantly with neighborhood and religion. For example, in a predominantly Christian neighborhood, approximately 50 percent of youth may chew khat, while up to 90 percent of Muslim youth may do so. Although these figures do not necessarily correspond with the actual number of young chewers, they certainly reveal a perception that khat consumption is widespread.

Beginning in the late nineteenth century, khat began to play an important role for Ethiopian Muslims in prayer, celebrations, and community discussions (Gebissa 2004). In areas of Ethiopia with high concentrations of Muslims, khat has been popular for day-to-day use for some time, particularly among adult men. Heavy khat use among Christians is a new phenomenon in Ethiopia and largely confined to young men in urban areas. In the popular press and adult discourse, khat is associated with unemployment and is said to make the chewer lazy.

For habitual chewers, especially among the unemployed, the first half of the day is usually spent trying to scrape together a few birr for khat. The price of khat is relatively low in Jimma, and two or three birr (0.25 U.S. dollars) is usually enough for one person, although five birr is the preferred amount if finances are available. Among the unemployed, money for khat sometimes came from odd jobs such as running errands or occasionally serving as a broker, but gifts from friends or family were more common. Most young consumers of khat had a few friends with whom they regularly chewed, and if one could buy khat he shared it with his close circle of friends. The process of sharing and chewing together was important for creating bonds between young men, and I discuss sharing relationships in more detail in Chapter 6. In general, despite being unemployed, one way or another most habitual chewers seemed to manage to obtain khat on a daily basis.

For the unemployed, khat chewing usually began in the early afternoon after lunch. Khat chewing was nearly always a social activity involving at least two or three friends. If one of the young men had access to a house where they could chew without being disturbed, this was the ideal location. However, in many cases parents did not permit their children to chew at home, and youth used the khat houses described earlier.

Approximately one hour after beginning to chew, a high is reached that is known as *mirqana*. For most youth the purpose of chewing khat is to reach mirqana. During mirqana the heartbeat is noticeably faster, one begins to sweat, and there is a general sense of happiness and satisfaction with life. Thoughts and conversations turn to hopes for the future, youth begin to dream (*hilm*), and the particular social interactions associated with khat emerge. Chewers described the "opening of the mind" (*amro yikefetal*) and a sense of unlimited possibility. The following discussion of mirqana comes from a group discussion I conducted with Habtamu and two of his friends as they chewed khat. At the time of my research, Habtamu was in his midtwenties and unemployed. Together with his friends he chewed khat almost daily.

> HABTAMU: During mirqana you *arrange*[7] your mind. Now, for example you might be thinking about doing some kind of work or some kind of study. That thing becomes very broad. Your mind thinks about it. Anything that you want to do, your mind is able to grasp it very quickly.
>
> DANIEL MAINS: For example, if one person has a problem and he chews khat, he will find a solution very quickly?
>
> HABTAMU: Yes. *Around the table* a good *diplomat* will be created. This is the main thing about khat. When there is an argument about something—for example, if there is a problem between husband and wife—among Muslims they will give the elders one sheep and a lot of khat. The elders will chew the khat and solve the problem.
>
> FRIEND 1: Yes. There is another thing. When you chew khat, you think, "Tomorrow I will buy a car. Tomorrow I will get money from the bank and buy a house."
>
> FRIEND 2: When you're chewing.
>
> FRIEND 1: But in the morning if you ask me, I have nothing.
>
> HABTAMU: Usually it is like this.
>
> FRIEND 1: It is mirqana.

If possible, youth preferred to chew with the same two or three friends. These were friends with whom they were comfortable and who had similar interests and conversational styles. Individuals usually came in and out of the conversation, sometimes giving passionate monologues that lasted five to ten minutes, and at other times staring off into space, lost in their own thoughts. For youth who watched videos while chewing, conversation was limited. In their case the video appeared to act as a stimulus that allowed their thoughts to travel outside the boundaries of normal life.

At the time of my research, Alemu was twenty-nine and had been without regular work during most of the nine years since he finished grade twelve. He lived with his mother, who owned a small shop, and he had been chewing khat daily since finishing secondary school. Some of his friends called him *mulu qen,* or "full day," because he chewed during the entire day. He explained that during mirqana his future seemed "very bright" and all of his dreams were within reach. "When I chew khat I get happiness; if I think about New York City it is like I am actually living there." This process of "dreaming" appears to bond khat chewers together as a social group. Alemu classified others in terms of chewers and non-chewers. Especially during mirqana he preferred to be around chewers. He described chewers as dreamers who are able to go places in their mind, while non-chewers are continually caught up in day-to-day affairs. During mirqana, everyday reality seemed very dull. Chewers did not want to talk about anything "normal." They preferred an atmosphere that allowed them to escape into explorations of hopes and desires for the future.

In terms of identity, young chewers also considered themselves more knowledgeable and experienced than non-chewers. While non-chewers some-times insulted chewers by calling them *duriye* (defined later in this chapter), chewers referred to non-chewers as *farra* ("rural" or "backward"; the opposite of "cosmopolitan"). Many of the non-chewers with whom I spoke were students at the Jimma Technical School. For the students, dreaming and discussions about seemingly unrealistic hopes for the future were cited as key reasons for avoiding khat. They gave examples of the sort of wild fantasies that chew-ers entertain during mirqana. Chewers talk about owning seven airplanes or building a four-story hotel. Non-chewers argued that this type of conversation is meaningless. The students were still in the process of pursuing their goals through the traditional means of education. For them it was better to focus on more realistic aims that were close at hand and could be attained by passing through clearly defined levels of education and work. Critiques of chewing and dreaming also pointed out that all of the planning and discussing of the future that takes place during mirqana is lost the following morning. While khat stimulates the mind to form detailed plans for achieving even the most impossible desires, chewers cannot seem to remember these ideas once the mirqana has passed.

Khat chewers also acknowledged this problem. In the group discussion quoted previously, Habtamu described how he feels the morning after chewing khat.

> In the morning I don't want to talk with anyone. I won't even greet my friends. You try to remember what you were thinking about the day before, but it just won't come. Nothing helps; you can drink coffee or try anything, but you just feel bad. In the afternoon, after khat, you can deal with people again, and all of the plans from yesterday come back.

Most of the unemployed chewers spoke of an intense depression that occurred on the days when they did not obtain khat. Chewing with a group of friends in the backyard of his mother's house, an unemployed man in his midtwenties explained that without khat in the afternoon, the only way to pass the time is to wander around. The sun burns into a person's head and he begins to think about all of his problems—the lack of a job, friends who have died of AIDS, and the hopelessness of the future. He claimed that if he did not get khat, he inevitably ended up spending a night or two in jail. I found this surprising because this young man had an extremely calm and polite demeanor. However, without khat he wandered around in a cloud of depression. He explained that he would eventually run into an acquaintance and begin exchanging insults, which then escalated into a fight that attracted the attention of the police.[8] Only partially in jest, some of the technical school students argued that this is why the Ethiopian government does not ban khat. It prevents people from thinking too much about the problems in life, and as long as they obtain their daily khat, they are unlikely to disturb the government.

For unemployed youth, consuming khat played a key role in the construction and fulfillment of desire. Although it was not always openly discussed, sex was often the most immediate desire experienced by young men. Young men claimed that during mirqana, once a person begins thinking about sex it is nearly impossible to think about anything else.[9] One unemployed young man described a process in which the chewer's desire is so intense that a woman may absorb his "heat" and increase her sexual appetite. For some young men, having sex after chewing khat was described as a physical necessity.[10]

The narcotic effect of khat combined with intense conversation in order to escalate sexual desire to potentially uncontrollable levels. The need for sex was intertwined with the condition of unemployment. As one young chewer put it, "Without money I must sit with my desire." At least temporarily, khat allowed this problem to be overcome. The notion that the heat of desire that is produced during mirqana may be transferred to a woman illustrates how something that is made difficult by economic constraints not only seems possible during mirqana but is believed to be facilitated by the act of chewing khat.

Other youth conceived of khat very differently in terms of its relationship to sexual desire. In a group discussion among unemployed young men regarding khat, the conversation took a tangent toward women and relationships. These young men argued that relationships with women could lead to a number of problems, including illegitimate children and HIV/AIDS. One member of the group argued that the solution to this problem was to chew khat. He explained:

> Usually if you don't chew, you get these problems. If you don't chew and you are on the street, some women will come, you greet them, invite them for coffee, *communication* is created, and a relationship begins. After that you will enter into bad problems. Therefore, if you chew, you enjoy mirqana, you go home, you watch TV, you read, that's enough—you sleep. *Morning*, you get up at ten, you eat breakfast, you eat lunch, and then you chew khat.

Chewing khat removed one from the public space that enabled interactions with women that could lead to potentially serious consequences. As the conversation progressed, these young men soon adopted the exact opposite point, arguing that in fact khat leads to irresponsible sex.

As in my discussion of film, my intent is not to establish a causal relationship between khat and sexual behavior. Young men experienced intense desires that were interrelated with issues such as unemployment and HIV/AIDS. In addition to passing time, khat facilitated an exploration of these desires and the barriers to their fulfillment. Contrary to claims of adults and some youth, khat did not cause the spread of HIV/AIDS or unemployment as much as it provided space for constructing one's own position in relation to these issues. An idea was presented (for example, khat leads to irresponsible sex) and then evaluated and critiqued. The conclusions that were reached in discussions fueled by khat were often forgotten, but the process itself was important. The simple act of discussion allowed young men to momentarily come to terms with the gap between their desires and economic realities.

Conversations that took place while chewing were often repetitive, and as many young men chewed daily, what began as fantasy could eventually be perceived as a realistic possibility. Possibly even more common than discussions of women and sex were conversations about migration, especially to the United States. Through these fantasies, aspirations were developed in a manner that was intertwined with economic behavior. The following comes from the conversation between Habtamu and his friends quoted earlier. They are describing the types of conversations that they have during mirqana. They are also experiencing mirqana as they are describing it, and this most likely influences the flow of the discussion.

FRIEND 2: If you are thinking about the *future* or another thing . . .

HABTAMU: *Future?!* In the name of God! Stop! [*implying that he could talk about this all day*]

FRIEND 2: If you buy khat today, you will become bright. You will plan ten years ahead. [*He names off one thing after another—work, marriage, children—snapping his fingers after each one.*] Now if I am experiencing mirqana and you ask me, I will tell you about America. After arriving in America, I will go to Atlanta.

HABTAMU: Is it Atlanta today?

DANIEL MAINS: My town.

FRIEND 2: Yes, yours. There, good work. A private car. A good house.

FRIEND 1: *Palace.*

FRIEND 2: After I win the DV [Diversity Visa lottery], I will do all of this. But sometimes it gives me a headache. Thinking, "Why can't I do this?"

FRIEND 1: Why is it this way? *America life* and *Ethiopia life*—there is one hundred years' *difference.* An American will never think about finding something to drink or something to eat. For us we eat breakfast at home; after that we don't know where we will find lunch. This is a problem.

In this manner the relationship of young men to their future is shifted. During mirqana, time is no longer a source of anxiety because introspective thought about one's future brings pleasure rather than stress. The shift is not complete. As the comment about the headache indicates, the ability to achieve this fantasy is continually questioned. However, these doubts appear to be overcome by the patterned nature of the conversation. It is not only electronic media that facilitate the imagination of possible lives in the manner envisioned by Appadurai (1996). In this case, khat-fueled conversations generate imaginative futures. When Habtamu's friend mentions that he plans to go to Atlanta, Habtamu's response indicates that they have had this conversation before and the only difference is the name of the city.[11] These young men are engaging in *chewata*, which literally translates as "play," but is used to refer to conversation more generally. As Cindi Katz (2004) explains in her ethnography of childhood and development in Sudan, play is a process through which alternate realities are explored and new possibilities are constructed. Young men's conversations are creative but within boundaries, and these boundaries shape the construction of the possible.

In Brad Weiss's discussion of imagination among urban young men in Tanzania, he notes that it may be useful to theorize the interconnections between imagination and habitus (2002: 98). Aspirations are one of the key areas through which habitus is expressed. While I discuss aspirations in more detail in later chapters, it is worth noting that activities like chewing khat and watching videos were processes through which both limits and new possibilities for one's own life were constructed. In building detailed fantasies around the Diversity Visa lottery and migration to the United States, khat chewers were both opening and closing certain possibilities. As I detail in subsequent chapters, the option of working locally was avoided because of both a lack of opportunity and stigmas that were associated with available occupations. Through conversation while chewing khat, migration appears to be a real possibility for one's future. As this possibility is imagined, the economic behavior that links habitus to class is potentially changed. Newly imagined aspirations cause shifts in economic behavior. The creative construction of fantasy is one factor leading young men to accept long-term unemployment as they anticipate an eventual opportunity to travel abroad. This in turn has implications for the reproduction and subversion of class hierarchies, as fantasies of migration constructed through chewing khat lead young men to avoid working locally.

The consumption of film functioned in a similar, yet distinct manner. In the case of khat, ideas were continually interrogated with the assistance of active partners. Young men did not simply adopt the values that were conveyed through films, but there is something necessarily passive about interacting individually with a form of technology that cannot respond to questioning. Although the creative role of young men was reduced in consuming film, it was still possible to appropriate received messages in a manner that had new and unusual implications for their lives. Young men grappled with issues of love, money, HIV, and gender relationships with the help of film. A singular synthesis of these issues did not emerge in youth discourse, but in general the experience of viewing and discussing films enabled young men to come to terms with a new and challenging situation. New possibilities for living were not generated specifically by film. Regardless of their exposure to film, young men in Jimma were forced to engage with new economic and social conditions. However, film did influence the manner in which youth experienced these new conditions by enabling them to compare and contrast individual experiences with fantastic stories that were well known among their peers.

In the remainder of this chapter I shift perspectives and move beyond young men's experiences of film and khat. Rather I examine the primarily adult discourse that surrounded these activities and the way that youth was imagined through this discourse. I begin with a brief discussion of the term *duriye*, because it was in some ways synonymous with "youth," and demonstrates how young, male consumers of khat and films were perceived.

Duriye

In discussions of the problem of youth unemployment it was common for adults to claim that today's youth are *duriye*. When I asked for the English equivalent of *duriye*, the most common response was "vagabond" or "hooligan," but neither of these terms really works in contemporary American English. Perhaps "punk" or "thug" may be a better equivalent, depending on the Western subculture that one wishes to reference, but the terms are still not quite right. Brad Weiss's (2002) discussion of "thug realism" in Arusha, Tanzania, does resonate with the use of *duriye* in an Ethiopian context, but there is one key difference. In my experience it was rare to find someone who referred to himself as a duriye. Whereas a "thug life" has been valorized in popular American rap music, and young men in Arusha referred to themselves as *wahuni*, which appears to be the Swahili equivalent of *duriye* (Weiss 2002: 108), there was no sense that a duriye life (*duriyenet*) was desirable among young men in Ethiopia.[12] The category of *bikhet* in Papua New Guinea also appears to be similar to *duriye*, but again, in contrast to Jimma, a degree of pride is associated with being a *bikhet* in some areas of Papua New Guinea (Demerath 2003).

I was never able to find a satisfactory English translation for *duriye*, and my sense of what a duriye is was often contradicted. Initially, I thought that all of the young men who spent most of their time standing on the street corner near my house were duriye. These men were generally unemployed, lived with their families, and devoted much of their leisure time to videos or khat. Similar groups could be found on corners in every residential neighborhood in Jimma. Coming and going from my house I often joined these fellows for a bit of conversation, and on one occasion it came out that I considered them duriye. They were shocked and very defensive. These young men explained that a duriye sleeps on the streets and lives from crime. They lived with their parents and were well behaved. Although they may not have had work, this was common and they certainly were not duriye.

In other situations, I encountered much looser definitions of *duriye* that would have certainly encompassed these young men. Sometimes it seemed that the term *duriye* was associated with unemployment, ample free time, and hanging about in public. Particularly during the first half of my research, I had people shout insults at me to the effect that I was a duriye because I was perceived to be wandering around aimlessly. I eventually concluded that almost every young man who was not a student or gainfully employed was in a losing struggle to avoid being defined as a duriye. The occupation (unemployed or working in low-status jobs), recreational habits, and social position of young men made it difficult to avoid this identity. Although it was not likely that one would self-identify in this manner, the discourse surrounding youth made the *duriye* label an ever-present reference point.

Video House Raids and Conflicting Imaginations

Around six months into my long-term research, I ran into Yonas, the dreadlocked owner of a video house in Ferenj Arada. After exchanging greetings, I asked him about business, and he told me that the police had shut down all fifteen video houses in Jimma. All of the owners were arrested and then released with dates to reappear in court for sentencing, and their equipment (DVD and videocassette players) had been confiscated.[13] Most video houses were back in business within a few weeks, but the loss of their equipment was a significant setback. At various times after the shutdown, video houses closed on their own because they feared a police sweep, and this resulted in a loss of income. By this point in my research I had made contacts with a number of youth involved in the video industry. Compared to other youth businesses, video houses created high profits and jobs for multiple young men. Given the high rate of youth unemployment, I was curious why the government would suddenly close these houses down.

I heard a variety of explanations as to why the shutdown had been ordered. Like many businesses, video houses operated without a license, and this was one possible reason behind the shutdown. Others argued that it was a copyright issue. In Addis Ababa, local musicians had recently staged a march in protest of the money they were losing because of pirated audiotapes, and many youth and adults assumed that the government was reacting to this in preventing unauthorized showing of films. Another possibility concerned the environment within the video houses. Video houses were thought to be places where duriye passed their time, and there was a fear that younger children were being exposed to bad habits such as smoking cigarettes and chewing khat. Others argued that violent or pornographic films exposed youth to negative influences, and this was the reason for the shutdown.

Clearly there was no shortage of reasons why the government might seek to regulate video houses. In order to investigate the matter further, I sought out the government office that had ordered the shutdown. After a week of phone calls I was able to get a meeting with the head of the Jimma Office of Youth and Sport, who then referred me to Ato Seifu, the head of the Culture and Tourism Office. I knew Ato Seifu when he was employed as a teacher at the preparatory school, and he was willing to speak with me. Unfortunately he had been at the office for only a few weeks and was not present when the order to shut down the video houses was given. However, he was able to explain that the police generally raid video houses every year. Their policy seemed to be one of organized harassment, confiscating the equipment of video house owners but not actually holding them in prison. Ato Seifu explained that the logic behind this was that films were considered a negative cultural influence. A culture that was explicitly defined as "foreign" (*wich hager bahil* or *ferenj bahil*) was responsible for encouraging young people to engage in irresponsible sex, crime, violence, and disrespectful behavior.

Many adults repeated this idea and argued that there is a distinction between foreign and local culture. Adults explained that young people lack the knowledge to understand foreign practices they observe in films and simply imitate what they see. They claimed that without maturity, young Ethiopians were not ready for foreign culture. In other words, this culture was not inherently negative, it was just not right for young people. Near the end of my research I presented some suggestions for reducing the problem of youth unemployment at a community meeting. Many adult members of the audience responded that "the problem of youth" could not be solved without addressing underlying factors such as the negative cultural messages conveyed through videos. Although youth saw videos as being a temporary solution to the problem of time associated with unemployment, adults argued that unemployment was caused in part by viewing videos.

A similar discourse was common among adults regarding khat, and this was occasionally expressed in the popular press as well. A quote from Dr. Nigussie, a professor at Alemaya University, in an article in the Addis Ababa–based English paper *Fortune* on the closure of khat houses in Addis Ababa is typical. Dr. Nigussie states, "No question about it khat is a stimulant, it kills work enthusiasm, wastes time, deflects the working force from productivity, shortens one's life span, and thus it hurts the economy as a result" (Negatu 2004: 3). Within this discourse, khat is the force behind unemployment and the idleness of youth. Although both adults and youth used phrases like "killing time" in discussing khat, the implied meanings were different because of contrasting conceptions of time. Adults did not express any awareness of the difficulties associated with the experience of time for urban young men and how khat or videos might be useful in dealing with these problems. For adults, killing time meant wasting time that could be devoted to other activities. Among young men there was no assumption about how time could or should be used. As noted previously, time's lack of structure was its most salient quality, and to kill time was to negotiate this lack of structure.

The reactions of young men to the closing of video houses were mixed and reveal that a simple dichotomy between the views of adults and youth cannot be made. A few weeks after the shut down I caught up with Yonas hanging out at the Titanic Barber Shop, across the street from his video house. In a voice dripping with sarcasm, he told me that the government radio had described the raids on video houses in Jimma and claimed that fifty-one *adegeñña bozeni* (dangerous/criminal unemployed youth)[14] had been arrested. Yonas argued that most of the youth who were arrested at his video house were around age twelve and posed no threat to anyone. He clearly felt the shutdown was a waste of everyone's time and looked forward to being able to reopen his business.

More surprising were some of the opinions expressed by video house customers. Many of the same young men who expressed an interest in action and pornographic films also claimed that these were a bad influence and could lead to irresponsible behavior. Two unemployed young men in their late twenties explained:

> At video houses anyone can watch these films. It doesn't matter how old you are or what the film is. Children go to the videos and learn very bad behavior. They watch films and imitate crime and the sex from the erotic films. The films are all right for some people but not these children. Kids skip school to watch films. Parents do not enforce the idea that some time is for films and some is for studying. There are also a lot of duriye at video houses. These people chew a lot of khat, smoke cigarettes, and do not live with their family or attend school. Young kids will learn bad behavior from these duriye.

Other young men commented that although they missed watching films, they believed the video house closure was for their own good. Consumers of khat often adopted a similar perspective, arguing that although they enjoyed chewing khat, in the long term they believed it would have negative consequences.

The contrasting perspectives surrounding khat and videos as sources of negative youth behavior are based on a differing understanding of the process of imagination. On one hand, for many youth khat and videos act as a stimulus that allows them to reconstruct hope for desirable futures. From this perspective, imagination is an essentially creative act that facilitates one's ability to move beyond economic constraints. In the case of sex and gender relationships, films allowed young men to think through problems they were facing concerning issues of love and money. From the other perspective, the economic behavior and values associated with unemployment or delinquent behavior are directly generated by khat and videos, and there is no interaction between the individual and the stimulus. Young men were simply acting out behavior they had observed in video houses. Watching a pornographic film (referred to as "love films" or *erotix* by young men) would lead young men to engage in irresponsible sex, and action films would cause violence.

The second perspective conceives of khat and video houses as sources of beliefs and behavior that young people are unable to control and therefore legitimizes the intervention of the government into youth lives. This contrast cannot simply be defined in terms of generation. Young men also expressed the notion that videos may produce negative behavior in youth, but as the preceding quote indicates, this logic was generally applied to those who were younger than the speaker. In other words, the ability to consume videos appropriately was thought to come with experience and maturity. Educated adults often used the English words *use* and *abuse* to differentiate between ways of consuming khat. Adult chewers felt that they were able to chew responsibly and enjoy valuable discussions during mirqana, while khat fueled heavy drinking and delinquent behavior among youth.

In discussing khat and video consumption, adults and to some extent young people were constructing what it meant to be a youth. Youth were passive receivers of information and not creators. Videos and khat acted on youth, and youth were not capable of using them for their own purposes. Related to this notion of youth was a lack of understanding regarding the problems faced by young people. The difficulties of negotiating time and one's relationship to the future were generally not understood by adults. The same is true of students who did not yet face vast amounts of unstructured time and an unknown future. As a result it was difficult for adults to comprehend how youth were using khat and videos to solve a particular problem.

The discourse surrounding khat, videos, and the problem of youth also indirectly constructs youth as a narrow social category. In this discourse, *youth* refers to a young underemployed urban male and is almost synonymous with *duriye*. In Chapter 1, I described the economic factors associated with the emergence of an extended period of one's life referred to as *youth*. Controversies that surrounded khat and films created an opportunity to talk about youth, and through that discourse the category has been further defined. In describing youth culture in Nepal, Mark Liechty writes, "In Katmandu young men are more likely to be implicated in the cultural construction of 'youth' than are women. . . . To say that 'youth culture' in Katmandu is largely a male experience is to underline again the fact that 'youth' is a culturally constructed category: 'youth' is a specific cultural construction not only of age but also class and gender" (2003: 233–234). Jennifer Cole argues that in Madagascar, youthful femininity is constructed as one of the primary qualities of "youth" (2004: 576). As in Katmandu and Madagascar, in urban Ethiopia *youth* refers to more than age. In speaking of the "problem of youth" in relation to khat and video houses, specifically male activities defined the category of *youth*. With few exceptions, young women did not chew khat or watch films.[15] The problems of crime or disrespectful behavior that were thought to be generated by exposure to films were not associated with women. Furthermore, the experience of time that conditioned the consumption of khat and films was particular to men, as unemployed young women did not experience unstructured time as an overly abundant quantity.

Discursive practices that addressed youth in relation to specific leisure activities also excluded rural young people. The privilege of too much time that contributed to the interest of young men in khat and films was also a product of a relative class position associated with urban residence. Most young men born in Jimma had families who were capable of providing them with at least minimal economic support. Especially compared with young people living in rural areas, they were better educated and possessed a social network that allowed them to exist without work for long periods of time.

Finally, there is a clear moral dynamic to discourse surrounding khat and video houses. These activities were associated with duriye—an intrinsically negative identity. In this sense, youth was not simply an age group but a problem. Interventions such as police raids of video houses were necessitated because consuming khat and watching videos were perceived as threatening the well-being of the community. Young men did not always dispute this perception and often accepted the notion that their behavior was problematic. Consuming films and khat were effective tools in dealing with their temporal problems, but many young men still felt that these activities were somehow morally reprehensible, and it was in their own interests for the government to exert control over their use of leisure time. Employment did not necessarily provide exemption from this moral discourse and the label of *duriye*. Working young men engaged in many of the same consumer activities as unemployed youth, if not more. Even worse, because of the nature of their work, working young men in the informal economy often had ample idle time, meaning that they were frequently in public view, sitting alongside the road, chewing khat. Being a young urban male in Ethiopia brought many privileges, but it also meant that one's existence was defined as a social problem. In seeking to overcome their problems of time, young men inevitably engaged in activities associated with duriye, and this dynamic was at play in many of the struggles over status that I examine in later chapters.

Conclusion

Young men's consumption of khat and videos represent day-to-day processes through which hope is constructed. In the absence of employment, time presented itself as a potentially dangerous quantity. Chewing khat and watching videos were effective means of both using time and rethinking one's relationship to one's future. Just as youth used khat and videos as tools to imagine different futures, these commodities were signs that influenced adult imaginations of youth. In the following chapter I continue my exploration of time and youth aspirations through an investigation of education. As with khat and videos, through formal education youth construct desires for the future that are inseparable from their day-to-day experiences of time and their conceptions of the future.

3

"We Live Like Chickens; We Are Just Eating and Sleeping"

Progress, Education, and the Temporal Struggles of Young Men

"We live like chickens; we are just eating and sleeping" was often repeated to me by young men who were frustrated with their inability to achieve their aspirations. They contrasted a life of "eating and sleeping" or "simply sitting" with one that involves "progress." Living like chickens implies that life lacked meaning, simply moving here and there without any purpose besides filling one's stomach. Ideally most young men aspired to a life course consisting of a series of linear and incremental improvements. For the most part, however, young men were uncertain whether they would ever move out of their parents' home and start their own families. Even working youth often did not see their employment as a potential means of escaping their current situation, and many young men did not work because they believed available employment opportunities would not allow them to experience progress.

In Chapter 2 I argue that through the consumption of khat and international films, young men constructed hopes for the future. Chewing khat and watching films allowed young men to negotiate an overabundance of unstructured time and reconstruct hopeful narratives in which they could move toward a desirable future. In this chapter I continue my exploration of the relationship between time and hope through an examination of young men's specific values and aspirations. Young men's conceptions of progress shape the economic processes and forms of stratification that I describe in later chapters.

Education is often held to be the cornerstone of economic development and the reduction of poverty in the global South. Ethnographic studies from a variety of regions have shown that although the implications of education for economic development are ambiguous, education certainly has a major impact on young people's aspirations and desires for the future (Demerath 2003; Jeffrey, Jeffery, and Jeffery 2008; Knauft 2002b; Liechty 2003; Stambach 2000; Willis 1977). In the global South, education is often associated with economic success and experiencing progress at an individual level. The model for economic success that emerges through education has a close relationship with modernist visions of development in the sense that it involves linear progression through time. This chapter begins with a general description of young men's hopes for the future. The young men I spoke to sought to experience long-term progressive changes with the passage of time rather than what they considered temporary and fleeting pleasures in the present. I argue that the progressive nature of young men's hopes is related to the expansion of formal education that began in Ethiopia during the mid-twentieth century. The importance of education in securing employment and the intrinsically progressive nature of the education process led many young men to expect linear improvement in their lives.

This is not simply the case of a modern institution associated with the West (secular education) producing values associated with Western notions of modernity (a desire for progress) in a non-Western context. Ethnographic research demonstrates that what at first glance appear to be modern desires are better understood as local engagements with global discourses and institutions (Cole 2004; Demerath 2003; Hansen 2000; Liechty 2003; Stambach 2000). In the Ethiopian case, although new values and worldviews certainly emerge among young men through their engagement with education, both the process in which these values are produced and the manner in which they are expressed are locally specific. Progress and modernization are conceived of specifically in terms of social relationships, and the social nature of progress supports a novel conceptualization of time as relationships.

Young men in Ethiopia seek to reposition themselves within relationships with the passage of time. The social category of youth is conceptually linked with processes of modernization in the sense that ideally it is a stage within a linear and progressive transformation from child to adult. Young men struggle to transition beyond the social category of youth, as unemployment prevents them from establishing their own households. I argue that the movement from child to adult may be conceptualized in terms of a shift in one's position within relations of reciprocity.

The Ethiopian case supports critical engagement with the anthropology of time and modernity. James Ferguson (2006) has usefully critiqued the recent proliferation of analyses of alternative modernities within anthropology. I agree with Ferguson that celebrations of alternative ways of being modern should not prevent an examination of existing and new inequalities. In the case at hand, however, examining the particular manner in which Ethiopian young men conceive of progress provides valuable insights into issues of time, space, and stratification. Young men's experience of time may be usefully contrasted with Elizabeth Goodstein's (2005) discussion of boredom and Jane Guyer's (2007) investigation of contemporary shifts in conceptions of "the future." The phrase "hope is cut" highlights the importance of the relationship between the present and the future for urban young men. The temporal struggles of young men are in part a result of the absence of a progressive series of events that connect the present to the future. Ultimately, the complex interconnections between work and social relationships support a rethinking of Marxian theories of time and production.

Young Men's Narratives of Progress

When I first met Solomon, he was twenty-nine and had been unemployed for most of the seven years since he had graduated from secondary school. In response to a question about the meaning of a good life, Solomon explained, "A good life means that if I have a friend with a problem, I can do something to help him. A good life is working and seeing improvement in my life. To not be dependent on my family and to have a mind free from thoughts is a good life. It is not important to be rich, but I do want to help others." A few key ideas are expressed in this brief explanation of the good life. A good life involves improving one's life, being free from thoughts, and helping others. Each of these themes was common in young men's discussions of their hopes for the future, and I address each of them in more detail in this chapter, beginning with the desire for improvement or progress.

The aspirations of young men followed a general narrative that placed individual success secondary to one's relationship to family and community. Each step in this narrative contributes to the attainment of the next step. Young men often explained that after finding quality employment, they wanted to first help their parents and siblings before starting a family of their own. Younger brothers and sisters should be supported through education so that they could progress in the same manner. Once this was accomplished, young men expected to leave their parents' home, usually for the purpose of marriage. After marriage, children were thought to be a natural consequence. In keeping with the principles of good family planning, most youth expressed a desire to have only two or three children. A small number of children would be easier to educate so that they could live a better life than their parents. For most young men, after first helping their parents and siblings and then starting their own families, the ultimate goal was to help their community. This was often conceived of as starting a nongovernmental organization (NGO) or business that would help youth and create jobs.

More short-term consumer-based aspirations were certainly present as well. Youth often spoke of the good life in terms of wealth and "getting the things that you want," which was defined largely in material terms, with clothes being commonly mentioned as an example. However, it was also explained that this type of consumption was particular to youth. Young people claimed that they had especially high levels of desire for consumer goods, but they assumed that as they aged and took on more financial responsibilities this money would be directed away from personal expenses and toward their family.

Unemployed young men often criticized other youth who earned regular incomes but devoted much of their money to consuming clothes, food, alcohol, and khat. I questioned a group of unemployed young men about the success of young owners of video houses who were able to dress in the latest fashions and easily visit cafés and bars. They were not impressed and argued that this type of consumption was meaningless. Although it provided certain benefits in the present, in the long term it would not allow a person to significantly change his life. After five years of hanging out and chewing khat, these youth would not have advanced to a "better place." A similar criticism was often directed by unemployed youth toward Afwerk, a bicycle repairman discussed in more detail in the following chapter. Jokes to the effect that if khat chewing and *tej* (honey wine) drinking were Olympic sports, Afwerk would easily earn two gold medals highlighted the lack of success that other youth predicted for him in life. Although it was debatable whether Afwerk earned enough money to significantly change his life, most youth were critical of his lifestyle and argued that spending time and money on excessive chewing and drinking was simply wasting one's life. In this sense, abstract notions of progress were generally prioritized over day-to-day consumption.

In contrast to a life that was not marked by significant improvements, progress was perceived as good in itself. Siraj and Mohammed both sold watches on the side of the street. They had migrated to Jimma from the Wollo region within the last five years, but while Siraj was from Kombulcha (a city similar in size to Jimma), Mohammed was from a rural area. Siraj often criticized Mohammed as someone who could be happy "just eating." Mohammed was married and had two children. He earned enough money from his work to support his family in a simple manner, and he claimed to be satisfied with this. He worked, chewed khat, attended the mosque in the evenings, and then ate with his wife and children. Mohammed argued that if a person was happy with life, he should not always be striving for change. Always dreaming of progress just brought stress when a person had no hope of achieving his goals. Siraj countered that this was fine for someone like Mohammed who was from a rural background and was satisfied with electricity and a full stomach, but someone like himself who had been raised in the city needed to see progress in his life.

Although Siraj's comments about Mohammed were laced with humor, in some ways his stereotype accurately described the experience of a previous generation of rural-urban migrants. Ato Bashu was the father of an unemployed daughter. He lived in the Kulo Berr neighborhood and worked as a self-employed tailor in Mahel Ketema (see Chapter 1 for a description of neighborhoods). At age ten he moved to Jimma from the Dawro region to live with his older brother and attend school. He studied until grade five and then quit for economic reasons. He gradually learned his trade by working as an assistant in a tailor's shop and eventually opened his own business. Life in the countryside had been difficult for him. He lived a day's walk from the nearest school. Although his family was never without food, day-to-day sustenance was a constant struggle. In this sense, movement to the city provided a significant and positive change in his ability to access education, work, and a more comfortable lifestyle. After establishing his business, he married a woman from his birthplace and brought her to the city, where they had four children together. At the time of my research, Ato Bashu had been the head of the Mahel Ketema *iddir* (a burial association) for a number of years. Despite the fact that he was employed as a tailor, a traditionally stigmatized profession, he occupied a respected and powerful position within his community.

The contrast between Siraj and Ato Bashu illustrates two key points about the condition of young men in Jimma at the time of my research. The first is that they had extremely elevated desires. Like Ato Bashu, Siraj had migrated to Jimma and worked in a low-status occupation. However, Siraj was not satisfied with his position and frequently complained of a lack of progress in his life and spoke of a need for change and improvement. Mohammed was essentially living a similar life to Ato Bashu, but Siraj was representative of most of the young men in my study in that he evaluated this lifestyle negatively. Young men like Siraj were born in the city and therefore took things such as access to education, electricity, and health care for granted. These amenities were the status quo and did not constitute improvement. Like Ato Bashu and Mohammed, Siraj could marry, but this type of marriage would not fit with his progressive ideals concerning a family. The second point is that the opportunity structure in urban Ethiopia was different for previous generations. Although children and marriage were a possibility, it was very difficult to imagine someone from Siraj's generation advancing to a respected position such as that of an *iddir* head if he was employed as a tailor with only a fifth-grade education. Educational inflation and reduced opportunity had left an entire generation with little chance for experiencing the progress they desired.

The contrast between generations is even more dramatic for women. Most of the mothers of youth in my study did not have more than an elementary education, and if they were employed at all it was in extremely low-status and low-paid occupations such as baking *injera* or brewing beer in their homes. Life histories revealed that although urban life and divorce had forced many of them to work for money, employment had not formed a significant part of their childhood aspirations. Their daughters had completed secondary school and aspired to professional employment. Although some daughters did help their mothers in *injera* baking or brewing *tella* (beer), they never voiced the idea that this might be a potential career. Young men and women desired a different life from their parents', one filled with progress and change.

Education and Expectations of Progress

I began my research in Jimma by spending a semester teaching English to eleventh- and twelfth-grade students at Jimma's vocational school. However, like Jeffrey and colleagues' (2008) study of unemployed young men in northern

India, my focus in this section is on discourses concerning education rather than what actually takes place in an Ethiopian classroom.[1] In contrast to Jeffrey and colleagues' study, for the most part, unemployed young men did not speak about education as transformative in the sense that it creates a qualitatively different type of person. This is in part because of my focus on young men who had not advanced beyond secondary school. At the tertiary level, young men spoke of a sense of difference between themselves and other young men of a similar age in their neighborhood, but these university students were in a definite minority. Among the young men in my study, education was conceived of primarily as a means to ends. Although these young men associated a sense of progressive achievement with the movement from one grade to the next, for the most part they valued education for its power to open up opportunities for employment.[2]

At the base of young men's narratives of progress was the notion that education should enable a person to achieve his goals. Both adults and youth often repeated the Amharic proverb "The one who eats and learns will never fail" (*Yebelana yetemare wodeko ayewodikim*), which expressed a widespread belief in the value of education. Being well fed and well educated are similar in that both provide resources to withstand difficult times. In Chapter 1, I explain that long-standing norms concerning relations of power caused access to education to be a virtual guarantee of government employment during much of the twentieth century, and that with the expansion of education and changes in the urban opportunity structure the value of education has declined. Despite the apparent decrease in the utility of education in creating access to employment, most young people in Jimma were still convinced that education was the key to their success.

I often asked young men and women to differentiate between the value of education as a means to knowledge versus accessing more material goals. For the most part, they argued that it is difficult to differentiate between knowledge (*uket*) and wealth (*habt*), and that for practical purposes the two are inseparable. For example, youth explained that an engineer is someone who is thought to have a high level of knowledge, and because this knowledge is valued by society, the engineer will be able to earn a large amount of money as well. Even a person who inherits wealth still must be educated, or this money will be quickly squandered. As the proverb indicates, education is valued for utilitarian reasons, but it is also assumed that knowledge is always useful. Levine (1965: 109) describes similar ideas among students in Addis Ababa during the early 1960s. He explains that students "have become obsessively aware of the 'value' (*tiqem*) of further schooling, namely, as the surest way to a job that pays well." It appears that education as a means of obtaining work and achieving aspirations has been an established narrative in urban Ethiopia for at least the past fifty years.

From my perspective, the continued belief in the value of education in improving one's life often appeared to be irrational. Early in my research I con-

ducted a series of interviews with a group of young men who worked as waiters at a medium-sized restaurant/hotel. The highest level of education among
them was grade seven, and all came from other regions of Ethiopia. Their salary
at the restaurant was low, and they all hoped to move on to something better
in the near future. When I asked them how they expected to improve their
life, the answer was always the same: education. After an interview one of the
young men continued to sit with me, repeatedly explaining that his only hope in
life was to return to school. The hopes of these young men were unrealistic on
a number of different levels. All of them were at least eighteen years old, and
returning to elementary school at that age would have been difficult, especially
given the fact that they had to work to support themselves. Aside from practical difficulties if they were to return to school and graduate from grade ten,
the types of employment available to them would not be significantly different
from their present situation. I pushed them on this issue and asked about the
large number of unemployed secondary school graduates. They explained that
these young men were unemployed because they failed their examination to
advance to postsecondary education, but there was no sense that they might
also find themselves in this situation. The notion that education is the primary
solution to achieving one's goals was voiced time and again by young men and
women from a variety of different backgrounds.

My line of questioning placed these young men in a difficult position. In
their conversation with me, it was probably emotionally difficult for them to
directly acknowledge the hopelessness of their situation. Education provided
them with a possibility for future success. However, education was by no means
the only option available to them. Although it may have also been unrealistic
in practice, the possibility of saving money from work in order to open a small
business was no less likely than advancing through education. Achieving goals
through education was a conceivable option. It was an established narrative for
success, and in this sense it existed while other options did not. This was interrelated with the stigmatization of available forms of work, as conceiving of success through education did not bring the stigma associated with working in a
low-status occupation. For young men like the service workers who were already
performing low-status work, it would seem that their evaluation of education
was not based so much on a fear of stigmatized occupations as a general cultural
milieu in which education is constructed as the primary path to success.

The powerful faith in the value of education that I encountered in Jimma
may be contrasted with other studies that describe increasing cynicism toward
schooling as education fails to produce tangible economic benefits. For example, in a study among the Manu people of Papua New Guinea, Demerath
(2003) found that most students were highly critical of education, rebelled
against teachers and authority, and valued school primarily for its role in creating social relationships with peers. Despite the struggles that secondary school
graduates faced in finding work, in urban Ethiopia the belief in the value of
education was still quite strong at the time of my research.

The rapid growth of private schools and colleges is good evidence of this. Despite the poverty that most Ethiopian families faced, they could often scrape money together to send a son or daughter to school. During an interview with Ato Uta, the father of an unemployed son and daughter, he tightened his belt as he spoke to demonstrate the sacrifices he was making to pay for his son to attend an evening engineering program at Jimma University. At the time of the interview, Ato Uta was working irregularly as a day laborer and his wife sold traditional bread (*ambesha*) at the market. The cost of his son's education was literally taking food away from his family, but Ato Uta saw it as an investment in the future.

In Jimma one private elementary school had been established in 2002,[3] but for the most part private schools focused on either kindergarten or postsecondary education. Computer schools were especially successful, but schools also existed for English, typing, hairstyling, cooking, and various other trades. One particularly successful school trained students to become teachers at private kindergartens. The owner of the school also owned a private kindergarten in Jimma, and she was able to hire many of her first round of graduates. The apparent success of students in finding work attracted many more student-customers in subsequent years.

The utility of private education in securing employment is debatable. While I knew many young people who remained unemployed after obtaining a "certificate" from a private institution, there were also some who had found work. Parental investment in private education reveals it as not just a primary option for achieving success but such a highly valued opportunity that parents were willing to endure great personal sacrifice in order to support it. Education was conceived as the first step toward government employment and a good life, while other options were generally not acknowledged.

The long-standing obsession of students with the Ethiopian School Leaving Certificate Examination (ESLCE) demonstrates that education leads to work not because it provides skills but because it provides a certificate and official credentials. A standardized exam was given to twelfth-grade students beginning in the 1950s. The highest-scoring students were able to advance to postsecondary education. Levine describes protests occurring in Addis Ababa when the proportion of students failing the exam was increased to 60 percent in the early 1960s (1965: 110). Although the ESLCE was abolished in the early 2000s, in practice it was simply replaced with another exam that is administered two years earlier, after grade ten. Essentially, the ESLCE was the test that determined whether one's twelve years of schooling were wasted time or the first step toward government employment. During my experience teaching English in an Ethiopian secondary school as a Peace Corps volunteer, students with little speaking ability could easily conjugate English verbs in the present perfect tense. This was a reflection of students' prioritization of preparing for the grammar portion of the ESLCE over learning English communication skills. For most students the process of education was about preparing for a test that would eventually provide them with access to government employment.

Results from the ESLCE also determined the field that a student would enter after graduation. In describing students in the early 1960s, Levine (1965) explains that many of them were uncertain about the work they would like to engage in because they were not familiar with modern urban occupations. Although young people in Jimma were quite aware of the different occupations available, they also had few aspirations regarding specific forms of work. They wanted "good work" or "government work." Those who had failed to pass the ESLCE wished to return to school in order to pass their exam, advance to higher education, and obtain "good work." Even with knowledge of the options available to them, young people did not conceptualize their future as something that they could control. The path to a good life was clearly defined as participating in education, passing a test, and then receiving employment.

The decrease in the value of education described in Chapter 1 created a gap between one's probable life trajectory and aspirations and the development of a situation similar to what has been described as a "diploma disease" (Dore 1976; Gould 1993) or "diploma inflation" (Bourdieu 1984: 142–143). In the absence of jobs that young people believe are fitting with their educational status, many youth accept extended periods of unemployment. This dynamic is common in African countries, but although a decrease in the value of education and access to government work has led youth to create opportunities in the informal sector elsewhere (Cole 2004), in Ethiopia this is not common. While dissent was occasionally expressed, for the most part, values surrounding occupational status and education appeared to be quite rigid. In the absence of jobs that young people believed fit with their educational status, urban Ethiopian youth of all class backgrounds frequently accepted extended periods of unemployment. I discuss the relationship between expectations, values concerning progress and prestige, and employment further in Chapter 4.

The expansion of education also provides a point of generational contrast that contributes to differing perceptions of time and progress. Reinhart Koselleck ([1979] 1985) explains that notions of "progress" appear at a certain point in history when the relationship between experience and expectations shifts. Expectations for the future are generally based on what one has experienced in the past, but with the development of a belief in the inevitability of progress, this changes. In discussing the advent of progress in Europe, Koselleck explains, "What was new was that the expectations that reached out for the future became detached from all that previous experience had to offer" ([1979] 1985: 279). In other words, progress is the expectation that the future will not be like what one has experienced in the past, and instead it will be qualitatively better. Education has not only created expectations among urban youth that they will be able to attain high-status government employment; it has also conditioned them to expect continual progress in their lives.

Contrasts between unemployment and life as a student are revealing. At the time of my research, many young men had completed secondary school within the past five years and remained unemployed after graduation. For these young men, school was the last time they were involved in a structured activity. One difference from unemployment is simply that school makes a person busy and therefore eliminates the problem of passing excessive amounts of time discussed in the previous chapter. Possibly more significant is a person's relationship to his future. As one young man who had been unemployed for two years after completing grade twelve put it, "When I was a student I had no thoughts. I learned, I studied, and I didn't worry about the future. Now I always think about the future. I don't know how long this condition will last. Maybe it will be the same year after year." When one is a student, time is divided into neat units, and change is experienced as linear improvement. When one advances from grade to grade, it is assumed that this movement has created a change within oneself as well. The educated individual expects to be transformed so that his future will be better than the present. Unemployment is the absence of change. Days pass, but one's material and social positions remain the same. Long-term unemployment prevents youth from imagining a desirable future and placing their day-to-day lives within a narrative of progress.

Writing in the mid-1980s, John Boli and colleagues (1985) argued that mass education has homogenizing characteristics. They claimed that "mass education is institutionally chartered to conduct the socialization of the individual as the central social unit" (1985: 149). It is not clear that education has necessarily produced such an individuation in the Ethiopian case. However, the standard process of schooling that is characteristic of formal education throughout much of the world appears to have contributed to the development of a distinctive relationship to the future and the passage of time.

Because of the expansion of education and urbanization, the young men I studied were far more embedded in an ideology of progress through education than previous generations. Most urban youth were the sons and daughters of parents who were raised in rural environments and did not advance beyond primary education. Despite living through a Marxist revolution that was associated with particular notions of modernity (Donham 1999b), their lack of education meant that the parents of youth in my study often did not internalize an ideology of progress as it pertained to their own lives. It was common for parents of unemployed youth to explain generation differences in terms of education and desire. Adults claimed that their children had much greater levels of both. A similar perspective was voiced by a young man who explained, "Today's generation is different. In the past everyone expected to do the same work as his parents. Today everyone wants to learn and to have a better life. If someone's father is a farmer, then he wants to be a modern farmer, or else to do a different job altogether." For both young people and their parents, education is linked with elevated aspirations for the future. In describing their life histories, most parents spoke of the movement from a rural area to Jimma as a major shift in their life. Upon arriving in Jimma, they generally accepted whatever work was available and were not as concerned with issues of status as their children. Parents often argued that their children's lives should be different from their own specifically because of their higher level of education, and they were disappointed when this was not the case.

Progress, Relationships, and Becoming an Adult

The relationship between formal education and the production of progressive aspirations is complex. It is not simply the case of a modern institution producing a modern worldview. As I explain in Chapter 1, the value of education in accessing desirable employment was largely due to the particular nature of traditional Ethiopian power relations, especially as they existed in the northern highlands. Education provided a means by which those power relations could be mapped onto an urban context in the form of a government bureaucracy. The ideological implications of formal secular education are perhaps less dependent on context. Education is generally a progressive process in that it involves linear change in which each step in the process is assumed to be more desirable than the last. The evidence that I have offered indicates that education had a significant role in producing an ideology of progress among young men. Local values concerning social relationships shape the manner in which progress is conceived.

The challenges faced by Solomon, the unemployed young man quoted earlier in the chapter, demonstrate the social nature of young men's notions of progress and the manner in which their aspirations have been ruptured. Like many of the unemployed young men in my study, Solomon had graduated from secondary school and therefore completed the first stage in the narrative of progress espoused by most young men. After completing twelfth grade, he spent an additional year studying mechanics at a vocational school. He was able to find work in a garage, but he quit in order to pursue a government position. He did not get the government position, and he did not return to the garage because the pay was too low.

When we met, Solomon still lived with his parents and generally passed his days in a similar manner to what I describe for young men in Chapter 2. He spent as little time at home as possible. In the mornings he left and spent his day talking with friends and chewing khat at tea houses. At night he returned after drinking honey wine and sat quietly watching television, trying not to disturb his family. His continued dependence on his parents was a particular burden. Although young men commonly lived with their parents until marriage, Solomon constantly had to deal with the stress of knowing that at his age he should be helping his family instead of the reverse. Young men in their early twenties pointed out those like Solomon, approaching thirty and still living at home, relying on daily handouts from their parents, as models to be avoided. This was a critique of both marital status and economic dependence.

I have argued that young men's desires for progress emerge as a result of engagement with urbanization and education and therefore are specific to the current generation of youth. However, this does not imply that youth possessed a completely new set of values in relation to aspirations. As described in Chapter 1, educated urban young men sought an established lifestyle that was associated with government employment and high status. Within this model, success is defined in terms of relationships. Progress may be conceived of as a movement from dependence on one's parents to offering assistance to one's family and community. Young men's inability to experience progress was directly linked with their struggles to attain economic independence, marriage, and fatherhood.

Although young men aspired to be a source of material support for others, in practice they depended on their families for unprecedented lengths of time. Unemployed young men had a strong sense of ambiguity regarding their dependence on their parents. They insisted that their parents appreciated having them in the house. This was true even for older men who were working but living with their parents. Although a man in his forties who had not married was sometimes the subject of derisive gossip, it was generally agreed that he was doing a good thing by living with his parents. Working young men who elected to live on their own sometimes felt great stress regarding leaving their parents' home. One friend of mine in his late twenties rented an apartment of his own, but told his parents he was staying with friends in order to study and continued to spend at least one night a week at his parents' home. It was a great relief for him when his parents found out about his apartment through another source and he did not have to confront them directly.

Despite the culturally accepted model of living with one's parents until marriage, young men still expressed significant stress regarding their situation. Although direct conflict with their parents was rare, young men explained that "you feel something." The experience of long-term dependence on their parents was described as "difficult" and "stressful." In some cases, youth reached a point where their relationship with their parents began to become strained. This was particularly true for young men who stayed with their parents until their late twenties and spent most of their time and resources on chewing khat. Alemu, an unemployed young man discussed in Chapter 2, received two or three birr almost daily from his mother. He also occasionally received money from his sister, who worked at Jimma University. Despite receiving consistent economic support, Alemu felt that in recent years his relationship with his family had changed. "They don't need me," he explained. His family was willing to provide enough support for him to get by, but they appeared to be unwilling to invest emotionally in his future.

Occasional tension with their parents did not prevent young men from continuing to rely on them for daily handouts in order to avoid working. Alemu made an interesting comment during an afternoon I spent with him at the Hoolaa Café. Outside we could hear the sound of day laborers at a construction site breaking rocks for eight birr a day. Alemu pointed to each of the young men who sat chewing khat on benches lining the walls and claimed that they could all afford to be there chewing instead of working because of their parents. Even if they did not receive money, they always knew that they could go home to eat. They would never resort to working as day laborers unless all other sources of support were exhausted.

In describing their ideal life course, young men claimed that marriage should follow economic independence. Studies from across Africa argue that marriage is one of the most important markers of becoming an adult and experiencing change within one's life (Hutchinson 1996; Johnson-Hanks 2006; Stambach 2000). Older men who were not married were often the objects of disdain even if they were otherwise successful. Marriage meant participating in the local *iddir*, having children, and essentially becoming a full adult. Regardless of all other indicators of status, marriage generally brought a certain level of respect that was otherwise unavailable to young men.

Without quality work, marriage was thought to be impossible. Solomon explained to me that he wanted to marry, but a person must "first pack his bags before setting out on a trip." He cannot live with his parents and be married. He has to be able to provide money for food, rent, clothing, and all of the other expenses associated with living independently. Even before marriage, money was thought to be necessary in order to attract a potential wife. As noted in Chapter 2, in general young men believed that women were interested only in a romantic partner capable of supporting them financially. Young men were not bitter about this and often explained that in the current environment of poverty and unemployment, it was only natural that women should seek out wealthier men.

Women, on the other hand, provided a different perspective. Although they certainly did not object to the possibility of a wealthy spouse—as one young woman pointed out, "the poor marrying the poor is meaningless"—young women usually claimed that they would not marry until after they had found work. This would provide "equality" and make for a better, longer-lasting relationship. Few of the young women I spoke to complained about the lack of wealthy marriage prospects, and they did not assume that they would eventually be supported financially by their husbands. However, given that employment prospects for young women were even bleaker than for men, it is unclear how these women would ever have the means to move out of their parents' homes.

In addition to the difficulty of attracting a wife, hosting a formal wedding required a significant monetary investment. Weddings in urban Ethiopia had become sites for conspicuous consumption and the performance of class differences. It was not uncommon to rent out large hotels and hire musical groups, professional photographers, and numerous cars for transporting guests. On his own initiative, Solomon once wrote for me what was basically a rant concerning marriage and money. Money was necessary to attract a wife, and then a wedding was also expensive. The couple had to invite all the neighbors to a lavish feast in order to avoid gossip and "backbiting." In the end, unless a person was wealthy, marriage was impossible.

Young men generally believed that insurmountable financial barriers prevented them from dating, marrying, and having children. They often claimed that they would not marry before age thirty or thirty-five and then only if they had become wealthy. Children were seen as a natural and desirable result of marriage—the next step in youth narratives of progress—and the financial burden of raising children was an additional factor preventing young men from achieving their aspirations. Simply raising children did not involve any great costs, but most young men desired a future for their children that would be better than their own. Kebede, an unemployed young man, first explained to me that he would not accept available forms of work such as carpentry or waiting tables because they would not allow him to change his life. He then explained:

> Without something big [a source of money], I won't even think about marriage or children. Even if I am rich, I will never have more than two children. With two kids I can educate them properly so that they can reach the university. If they don't reach the university, I will send them to America. Of course, I could get a job and have children now. Even if I were making only a hundred birr a month, I could feed them *shuro*[4] [chickpea paste], but that kind of life is not good for children. They will not learn properly, and they will end up shining shoes or something like that. You want your children to have a better life than yourself. You want them to improve and have a good life.

A similar perspective comes from a young man who earned money by making and selling sandals made of tires but continued to live with his parents:

> I don't want to marry unless I have a different type of work. I need something different before I try to start a family, but once I arrange my own life, I definitely want a family. I want only two children. In the past people have just been having kids without saving money or thinking about the future. In my neighborhood, kids are everywhere. This is fine if you have a big compound, but in my neighborhood there are no compounds; all of the houses are packed in together. People sleep three or four to a bed. At my house we all sleep in one room. We all come home at night and watch TV, and then when the programming ends at 10:00 or 11:00 P.M., we turn off the TV and go to sleep. If you want to stay up and study, you can't because there is only one light for one room and you can't keep everyone else awake. Then in the morning we all wake up at the same time. Everyone in my neighborhood is like this.

In these statements education and small families[5] are contrasted with symbols of lower-class urban life such as *shuro* and sharing rooms, in order to construct different future trajectories. One possible future is based on repeating what were seen as the mistakes of one's parents, while in the other it is assumed that fewer children will allow a heavy investment in education and open up more opportunities for higher learning and desirable employment. The notion that education and smaller families should lead to modernization and progress resonates with a discourse of development (Escobar 1995; Karp 2002) to which youth were regularly exposed through school and government mass media. Smaller families and education as means to realizing this goal were development-based strategies, and the desire to progress was contrasted with previous generations who had been satisfied simply getting by and raising children ("living like chickens").

In a different conversation, I asked Kebede about the qualities of a good father. Like most young men, the first thing he mentioned in response was providing an education. He specifically explained that a free public education would not suffice. A good father must provide his children with a private education and help his children study in the evening until they have surpassed his own ability. He explained, "In order for my children to reach a good place they must have everything. Good school, good clothes, and good food. If my father had been a driver, I could have been a doctor."

The cases of Mohammed and other young, married workers with children demonstrate that starting a family was possible, but it was not simply a family that Kebede, Solomon, and other young men desired. They wanted a family in which their children would lead modern progressive lives that involved more than "eating and sleeping." Young men defined progress in terms of the types of relationships that could be developed with others. To lead a progressive life was to avoid the undesirable relationships associated with low-status occupations, move from a position of dependence to one of support in relation to others, and offer one's dependents the chance to lead similar progressive lives. Because achieving these relationships was felt to be impossible through available work, many young men elected to remain unemployed.

To the extent that young men were failing to shift their position within social relationships, they were failing to become adults. For young men, the movement from child to youth to adult may be conceptualized in terms of one's position within relations of reciprocity. As a child, one is completely dependent on others. Young men sought to first attain independence and then offer economic support to a gradually increasing number of dependents, beginning with their immediate family, expanding to extended kin, and eventually supporting neighbors and other community members. In this sense young men sought to attain a particularly masculine notion of adulthood that has been documented in other studies in Ethiopia and elsewhere in Africa (Cole 2004; Johnson-Hanks 2006; Poluha 2004). Unemployment prevented young men from experiencing progress in their relationships with others and moving out of the social category of youth toward adulthood. In the following section I delve more deeply into the relationship between young men's expectations of progress and their experience of time.

Progress, Boredom, and the Future

The problem of time for unemployed young men in Jimma is that they are unable to actualize their progressive aspirations. In this disjuncture, unstructured time in which young men experience their lack of progress most acutely is spoken of as a source of stress and unease in the manner detailed in Chapter 2. Brad Weiss (2004a: 10) has argued that something similar to the compression of time and space described by David Harvey (1990) has also been experienced by urban youth in Africa. He explains, "Time may seem to rush forward and temporal spans may seem to narrow precipitously, while in the same moment, the grounding of the future in the present—the ability of persons to comprehend and anticipate even their day-to-day routines—seems markedly insecure." The problem of time for young men in Jimma was quite different in that they could anticipate their day-to-day routine, and this routine was not expected to bring change or enjoyment. It was precisely the lack of change that young men often lamented.

A lack of progressive change causes hope, that tenuous thread connecting young men to their future, to be cut, leaving them stranded in the present. The experience of time among unemployed young men has interesting parallels to Elizabeth Goodstein's (2005) discussion of the emergence of a discourse of boredom in nineteenth-century Europe. Goodstein argues that progress, as described by Koselleck ([1979] 1985), "constitutes the condition of possibility for modern boredom" (2005: 122–123). In Goodstein's analysis, the production of boredom is based on the existence of a notion of progress similar to what I have described, in which the future is expected to be different and better than the past. This is combined with a sense that the reality of life is not equal to what one had imagined. Boredom is the feeling not only that one has too much time but that that time is not meaningful because it is not passed in the progressive manner that one has come to expect.

However, unlike Goodstein's discussion of Western discourse on boredom there is no sense that "the subject both registers and rebels against the regulation of lived, subjective time by the inhuman demands of technological progress" (2005: 124). Goodstein links the emergence of boredom with romanticism and an intense desire for meaning that often valorized the experience of the individual. The Ethiopian case is different in two important ways. First, rather than being overwhelmed by technology so that a sense of individual humanity is lost within waves of progress, in Ethiopia there is simply a lack of progress. It is not just that progress is not occurring in the utopian manner that one imagined, but that progress is not occurring at all. Second, a notion of romantic individualism is far from the experience of unemployed youth. As I detail in the following chapter in relation to occupational status, young men sought to conform to traditional norms for social relationships. Unease and frustration with an abundance of unstructured time were not based in romantic visions of the self, but in an inability to experience progress in the form of desirable social relations with others. Ethiopian boredom[6] is the combination of unstructured time and an unfulfilled desire for a self that is constructed through social relationships. Employment is the barrier to the construction of relationships that would alleviate the stress of unstructured time, and therefore the problems of time and youth unemployment are inseparable.

The emergence of boredom among young men in urban Ethiopia connects with Jane Guyer's (2007) suggestion that in the twenty-first century, experiences of the "long-term" and the "present" are increasingly prioritized over the "near future." Guyer explores the idea that economic and religious trends mark a shift in the way Americans conceptualize time. In contrast to developmentalist models of modernization, such as W. W. Rostow's (1971) "stages of growth," time is no longer broken into regular increments. For example, for American evangelicals the present consists of a period of waiting that is punctuated by significant events, the most important being the second coming of Christ.

In the Ethiopian case, urban young men struggle with time in the present, partially because the passage of time is not marked by benchmarks, changes, or progress in the near future. The lack of opportunity for progress causes young men to experience the present as an indefinite period of waiting. Young men are mired in the present in part because a downsizing of the public sector has greatly constricted local economic opportunities. They wait for the future and invest their hope in particular events such as the Diversity Visa lottery that have the potential to instantly transform their lives.

The case of Ethiopian young men reveals that this shift in the experience of time and the emergence of boredom cannot be attributed entirely to contemporary economic and cultural changes. The importance of the present is due in part to long-standing values concerning occupational status and social relationships. To work in a low-status occupation is to be placed in a subordinate position and to be subjected to gossip in a manner that is experienced immediately in the present. In this sense, hopes for the future and the experience of time in the present are mutually constitutive. The absence of an ascending ladder of attainable goals in the near future leads young men to experience something like boredom in the present as they wait for the sudden change that will reconnect them to their hopes. At the same time, the desire for a particular quality of social relationships in the present leads young men to forgo available employment and wait for instant transformation in the future.

Time as Relationships

The interrelationship between time, work, and social relationships may be explored further through a parable told to me by a young man. An Ethiopian was resting under a mango tree. A *ferenj*[7] (foreigner) approached the Ethiopian and suggested that he gather up all of the mangoes and sell them in the market. The Ethiopian did this and made a large amount of money. He found the *ferenj* and asked him what he should do with all of the money that he made. The *ferenj* advised him to take his money and go on a vacation and relax.

The obvious interpretation of this story is that it questions the need to work in order to access leisure when it is already possessed in abundance. However, if this story is placed in the context of local conceptions of occupational status, then the interpretation changes. From an Ethiopian perspective, the absurdity of the Western contrast between work and leisure is that it divides activities into the categories of *productive* and *nonproductive* without regard for their implications for constructing social relationships. Bourdieu ([1963] 1979) describes a similar dynamic in the context of the development of a market economy in Algeria. In that case, work was appreciated less as a means of reaching an economic goal than as a way to demonstrate one's conformity to the value of industriousness. In his discussion of young men and tea consumption in Dakar, a case that has remarkable parallels to Ethiopia, Ralph (2008) also notes the difficulty of analytically separating work and leisure. By defining value as "a meaningful consequence of human activity, transformed into social relationships that structure a system of production" (2008: 17), Ralph argues that activities typically classified as labor and leisure are both directed toward shifting social relationships. In a similar manner, for the young men in my study, decisions regarding employment were based primarily on how working or not working would shift the manner in which one relates to others.

The concept of surplus labor presumes that labor may be quantified in terms of time and categorized as necessary or surplus. In the Ethiopian case, work is not always conceived of in this manner. I explore conceptions of work in far more detail in Chapter 4, and for now it is enough to note that in urban Ethiopia, working positions one within relations of power and exchange in a manner that produces identity. This work may last two hours or eight, and the implications for identity are the same. One *is* a shoeshine or one *is* a teacher. In Ethiopia the government worker is the paragon of this dynamic. The government worker receives a salary that depends not on the number of days or hours worked, but on his position. He is thought not to produce, but to mediate between individuals. The model of the government worker, on which the aspirations and values of youth are largely based, produces no surplus value. He gives and receives as a result of his position in relation to others. Youth sought government work to transform themselves from one who gives rather than receives support. At the same time, available work was often declined because it did not offer the potential for one to experience progress in social relationships. In this sense, young men do not evaluate work simply on the basis of what they receive in exchange for a particular quantity of labor, but in terms of how the performance of that work allows them to reposition themselves within relationships, in both the present and the future.

If work is measured in terms of relationships, then relationships are measured in terms of an abstract notion of time. In his Marxian analysis of time and labor, Postone (1993: 200–216) explains that within capitalism, time becomes an independent rather than a dependent variable. In classic anthropological analyses of time in noncapitalist societies, such as Evans-Pritchard's *The Nuer*, time is measured on the basis of seasonal changes in nature or daily activities, and in this sense time does not exist independently. Postone argues that with the advent of capitalist production, time is increasingly abstracted and measured in terms (i.e., hours or minutes) that do not reference human activities. E. P. Thompson (1967) has described in vivid detail the process by which notions of time change with industrialization and the spread of wage labor. Time is no longer measured in terms of tasks; rather, the reverse is true and tasks are quantified on the basis of the abstract time they require to be completed and the monetary value of that time.

In the case at hand, time also functions as an independent variable. Unemployed young men conceive of the passing of time independently of human activity, and activities are assessed based on this abstract notion of time. However, even in the case of work, activities are generally not quantified in terms of production. Instead, activities are assessed on the basis of their ability to shift one's relationship with others. Among urban young men in Ethiopia, time is not money. Perhaps it is better to say that "time is relationships." Time is taken as a measure of human activity, but it is used to measure and quantify relationships rather than labor and its corresponding monetary value. For example, young men were often reluctant to disclose their age because they felt that their accomplishments in terms of marriage and having children were not what one would expect for people of their age. The attainment of particular social relationships was evaluated on the basis of an abstract measurement of age, rather than the reverse.

Temporal problems faced by young men are caused by the stress associated with unstructured time and the inability to experience progress in social relationships. Day-to-day activities are evaluated in terms of time, and this evaluation is relative to progressive changes in one's relationships. Ethiopian young men experience their unstructured time as a potentially dangerous quantity because it does not match their progressive expectations, in which they achieve linear improvement in their relative social position with the passage of time. Stress is generated for young men not because of a lack of productivity but because their social relations are not changing in accordance with an abstract notion of time.

Conclusion

In summary, through engagement with formal education, urban young men develop expectations of progress. Young men conceive of progress specifically in terms of changes in their relationships with others. Frustration with their inability to progress from a position of dependence to providing support for others causes young men to experience time as an overabundant quantity. This disconnection between the present and a desired future is related to the emergence of a sense of boredom, in which the day-to-day passage of time is no longer meaningful. Ultimately the close connection between employment, time, and social relationships supports a rethinking of Marxian analyses of time and production.

The analysis of time I present in this chapter emerges out of the particular contrast between hopes for the future and economic realities. Young men construct hopes that are nearly impossible to fulfill in a context of extremely limited economic opportunity. The contrast between hope and reality causes young men to feel as if they are trapped in the present, unable to become adults and to move through time in the manner they desire.

The manner in which time is conceived of in terms of social relationships supports a rethinking of development more broadly. Young men evaluate time and progress not so much in terms of production or accessing economic goals but rather as repositioning themselves within social relationships. The passage of time is evaluated positively if one can achieve a progressively better social position. Although young men's aspirations are structured around a progressive notion of time, the manner in which progress is conceived of is decidedly uneconomic. In this sense, economic development must be evaluated in terms of its implications for social relationships. The problems faced by urban young men are a result of not only joblessness but also an inability to engage in activities that situate them positively in relation to others. The Ethiopian case indicates that strategies of economic development aimed at creating employment, without giving attention to the meanings associated with different types of work, may be subject to failure.

Education policy as a component of economic development continues to be a major topic of debate in Ethiopia and elsewhere. Policies are often evaluated in terms of their effectiveness in preparing students to find work. Such economistic interpretations of formal schooling have long been critiqued by social scientists. My analysis adds an additional layer to these critiques. Schooling certainly plays a role in the production of aspirations, which in turn influence economic behavior and class. The particular nature of aspirations, however, is embedded in local cultural norms. Rather than interpreting this situation as a barrier to effective schooling, the purpose of education must also be reevaluated. Just as the goal of development cannot be only economic growth, the goal of schooling cannot simply be the acquisition of jobs. Education must support the locally relevant desires and hopes. In the Ethiopian case, this involves providing students with the tools necessary to reconstruct their social relationships with others.

At this point I have described the progressive nature of young men's hopes for the future and the manner in which their hopes are based on social relationships. In Chapter 4, I take this story one step further by examining unemployment, the primary barrier that young men face in attaining their aspirations. The particular decisions that young men make concerning employment are based on their hopes for the future.

4

Working toward Hope

Youth Unemployment, Occupational Status, and Values

There are so many unemployed young people here because
youth don't respect work. No one appreciates work. Everyone
wants to start at the top. No one wants to start in a small job
and work their way up.
  —A young woman working shining shoes

In Ethiopia there is work, but many people won't do it.
Ethiopians don't respect work. People are afraid to do lower
jobs because they think, "What will people say about me?"
  —A tenth-grade student

I could find work in a cafeteria or as a day laborer, but that
kind of work does not bring satisfaction. I can't do that kind
of work because of *yiluññta*. People will talk about me. My
friends will leave me. If I lived in the United States, I would
do anything. I would wash dishes. But I can't do that kind of
work here.
  —An unemployed young man

n his analysis of urban young men's unemployment in Ethiopia, Pieter Serneels (2007) argues that long-term unemployment is largely a result of rational decision making aimed at economic maximization. "The average young
unemployed man in urban Ethiopia has a strong incentive to wait in unemployment for a 'good job' in the public sector" (Serneels 2007: 182). His argument
is based on the wage differential between employment in the public sector and
other forms of available employment, the likelihood of eventually obtaining a
public sector job, and the average length of time spent waiting for work. From
the perspective of an individual seeking to maximize his income, the decision
to wait for public sector work is rational.[1]

The preceding quotations offer a different perspective on urban youth unemployment. Like Serneels, they indicate that young people choose not to pursue private sector employment, but they also demonstrate that this decision is not motivated by rational economic maximization. Cases of people not acting in their best economic interests are not unusual and have often been analyzed in terms of the reproduction of stratification. Working in very different contexts than urban Ethiopia, Paul Willis and Pierre Bourdieu investigated the relationship between values and occupational choice in order to understand the reproduction of class. In Willis's classic study, *Learning to Labour* (1977), he argues that the values of working-class young men ("the lads"), particularly surrounding issues of masculinity and camaraderie, lead them to devote little effort to education and instead enter into working-class jobs. The lads evaluate a working-class lifestyle positively, and therefore among their peers factory work is a high-status occupation. The lads actually seek out a subordinate class position in order to access status within their peer group.

The behavior of the lads in Willis's study may be conceptualized in terms of Bourdieu's habitus (1977: 81). Bourdieu explains, "In short, the habitus, the product of history, produces individuals and collective practices, and hence history, in accordance with the schemes engendered by history" (1977: 82). Put simply, a class situation generates a particular set of dispositions that in turn tends to reproduce that class situation. Aspirations are a key part of this process. Bourdieu (1984) explains that aspirations are conditioned not only by values but also by expectations for one's future. Expectations limit aspirations in the sense that the occupation to which one aspires is generally based on what one can typically expect given one's educational background and other relevant factors for obtaining employment. Willis's study demonstrates that youth do not simply recognize structural limits to class mobility and consciously lower their aspirations accordingly. Willis's "lads," for example, desire working-class jobs not because they see this as the only opportunity available to them but in order to fulfill local masculine ideals.

Much of Bourdieu's discussion in *Outline of a Theory of Practice* (1977) takes the approach of structure producing individual dispositions and practices in a manner that reproduces structure, and this logic has rightly been criticized for leaving little or no room for social change. However, in other writing, Bourdieu makes it clear that empirically reproduction of economic stratification rarely takes place in this manner (Bourdieu and Wacquant 1992: 129). Individual variation and historical change are always present and often subvert the reproduction of class hierarchies. Particularly after dramatic historical shifts, there may be changes in the opportunity structure for employment. In these cases aspirations do not match the level of opportunity, and individuals are unable to choose their occupation as they would like. The Ethiopian case exemplifies this situation. Young men aspire to jobs that are far beyond what may realistically be expected given their class background and level of education. As I explained in Chapter 1, in urban Ethiopia a rise in education combined with a dramatic reduction in available public sector employment has created a disjuncture between expectations and opportunity that disrupts any simple reproduction of class. In Ethiopia, as in much of the global South (Jeffrey 2008), at the historical moment when expectations of earning membership in an urban middle class through education were expanding, economic opportunity decreased dramatically. Although the urban unemployed come from different class backgrounds, they are united in a desire to be members of the middle class, primarily associated with public sector employment.

In this chapter I investigate the relationship between young men's values and their decisions about employment. Just as young men engaged in different economic strategies, they had different ideals and expectations concerning the meaning of a hopeful future. For unemployed young men, status was a key value in relation to their decisions regarding employment. In many ways, occupational choice for young men appeared to be based on exchanging one's labor in a manner that maximizes status rather than income. Therefore, I begin this chapter by defining the often vague, but highly important, concept of status, and then examine youth discourses and practices concerning low-status and high-status occupations. I argue that young men's avoidance of particular occupations is based on the manner in which these occupations position them within relations of power and exchange.

The contrast between economic maximization and social relationships has long been central to anthropological discussions of exchange. Anthropologists have argued that it is often impossible to understand decisions about exchange from the perspective of an individual actor seeking to maximize control of material goods. In urban Ethiopia, employment is a means of reaching a hopeful future, but young people's hopes are often based on access to social relationships rather than material goods. Each of the statements quoted earlier indicates that young people choose not to work and to remain unemployed because of social relationships. Youth often make the economically irrational decision to forgo an income from work because they are worried about what others will say about them.

The history of anthropology is rich with studies documenting similar apparently irrational economic behavior. In the African context, Paul Bohannan's classic study of spheres of exchange among the Tiv of Nigeria argued that exchange is motivated by a desire to access prestige rather than simply accumulate material goods. Maximization was certainly present in this case, but it was governed by a system of values quite different from that associated with industrial capitalism. On the basis of his analysis of cattle ownership in Lesotho, James Ferguson has explained that "it is clear that a structured social practice such as livestock keeping cannot be understood simply as the outcome of choices by 'rational individuals,' as the utilitarians would have it, for we have seen that what the 'choices' will be and what will count as 'rational' are themselves part of the system of rules which is at issue" (1985: 668–669). This does not imply an end to rational choice theory or the value of neoclassical economics, but rational choice is meaningful only in the context of a detailed examination of the system of values in relation to which decisions are made (Donham 1999a). It cannot simply be assumed that Ethiopian youth strive to maximize material accumulation.

In the second half of this chapter, I examine case studies of working young men. Their divergent strategies for actualizing hopes are partially a result of differing values concerning work and social relationships. For different reasons, the working young men in my study were positioned outside normative values concerning occupational status. They constructed identities that were somehow distinct from their community. This meant that their internal sense of status was not threatened by external social judgments in the same manner as unemployed young men. In this sense working young men were free to pursue hope through strategies directly related to material accumulation.

Implicit in my analysis is that contrary to many recent anthropological discussions, work is essential to the construction of youth identities. Focusing on stylistic practices related to consumer behavior, anthropologists have recently argued that youth identities are constructed primarily in terms of consumption. This argument is based partially on assumptions regarding cultural shifts associated with late capitalism. Within late capitalism, economic growth is driven by technological innovations that facilitate the production and marketing of commodities to increasingly narrow consumer groups (Baudrillard 1982; Harvey 1990).

Particularly for youth, anthropologists have argued that identities are constructed largely through the semiotic manipulation of commodities, rather than through one's position within the process of production. In the African context, examinations of youth consistently conceive of identity and future desires in terms of consumption (De Boeck 1999; Gondola 1999; Friedman 1994; Masquelier 2005; Newell 2005; Weiss 2002). In his study of Kathmandu, Mark Liechty (2003) argued that the social category of youth is inseparable from the construction of identity through consumption. Liechty's argument is based on the relationship between the emergence of a middle class and the heightened importance of consumption. In this sense, Liechty does claim that class continues to be highly important for youth identities, but class is increasingly defined in terms of what one consumes rather than one's position in the process of production.

As my discussion in Chapter 2 indicates, I certainly do not deny the importance of consumer practices. However, one of my goals in this chapter is to highlight the significance of work and production for youth identities and stratification. In the Ethiopian case, the significance of work is a result of not only one's position in relations of production and exploitation but also how it positions one within relations of exchange and power and creates hierarchies of status. To a great extent, a job is assessed in terms of its implications for social relationships rather than the material wealth it generates. A thorough investigation of occupational status is therefore necessary to understand the relationship between work, identity, and stratification for young men.

Defining Status

Status can often be a frustratingly vague concept. Max Weber contrasts *status* with *class*, explaining that "'classes' are formed in accordance with relations of production and acquisition of wealth, while 'status groups' are formed according to the principles governing their consumption of goods in the context of specific 'life-styles'" (1978: 54). Weber used the notion of occupational status as a means to differentiate between the implications of work for constructing identity and providing access to material goods. The association Weber establishes between status and lifestyle is certainly important, but it does not tell us how we may assess and evaluate differences in status. For this it is helpful to look toward more ethnographic analyses.

One of the clearest explications of status in an African context comes from Jennifer Johnson-Hanks's (2006) discussion of honor in relation to decisions surrounding childbirth among young women in Cameroon. Johnson-Hanks uses the term *honor*, but I prefer *status* because of I am primarily concerned with decisions surrounding occupation. In Johnson-Hanks's review of anthropological literature on honor, she notes that most discussions have emphasized either external or internal dimensions of honor. Notions of honor that emphasize external dimensions generally define *honor* as socially recognized rights (2006: 61). From this perspective, the extent to which one possesses honor is manifested in the qualitative nature of one's social interactions with others. Analyses that emphasize internal dimensions of honor prioritize self-perceptions and pride. Honor is therefore based on the skills or qualities of personality that generate positive self-perceptions (2006: 63). Johnson-Hanks seeks to develop a notion of honor based on a synthesis of these two perspectives. She explains that in her study of the Beti in Cameroon, honor "requires the re-formation of the subject from the ground up; the external becomes both a sculptor and an indicator of internal honor" (2006: 64). A positive self-identity is important, but it is meaningful only in the context of relevant local values and perceptions. Social norms regarding honor are not static. For example, among the Beti, an internal sense of honor has been transformed through interactions with the Catholic Church and schooling (2006: 75).

The value of Johnson-Hanks's synthesis between internal and external dimensions is that it demonstrates the importance of social relationships for the construction of the self. Status is a product of social relationships and may be assessed in terms of qualitative changes in one's relationships with others. On the other hand, the implications of these relationships are always mediated by individual self-perceptions. For example, as I detail in Chapter 6, young men who lived away from their family and friends were far more likely to work in stigmatized occupations because they were not exposed to negative judgments from others, thus demonstrating the importance of external dimensions of status. On the other hand, case studies of youth entrepreneurs in the informal economy that I discuss in this chapter demonstrate the importance of internal dimensions of status. For these young men, their self-perceptions were based on a fit between their unique values concerning work and their interactions with others. Working young men selectively internalized the judgments of others, meaning that their sense of status was partially based on personality and individual values. This is not to say that status is always relative to individual perceptions. The measurement of movements of gifts between people that I explore in Chapter 5 represents one possible means of quantifying status.

Low-Status Occupations

At the time of my research in Jimma, long-standing stigmas against craft workers were closely related to qualitative evaluations of work. After the 1974 revolution, discrimination against craft workers was formally banned. In large urban areas like Jimma, strict restrictions on the behavior of craft workers were not present, but young people claimed that a powerful stigma was still directed toward many types of work. Stigmatized occupations were often those that involved menial labor or were associated with traditional craft workers. Even professions that did not exist in the past, such as welding, had negative connotations because of the association between metalworking and the previously stigmatized occupation of blacksmithing.

The key contrast between occupational stigma in the past and present is that in recent years individuals have not been born with stigmatized identities. One is not a carpenter or a welder because one's parents worked in these occupations. Although craft workers are almost exclusively from relatively poor families, at least in theory, occupations are chosen. In this sense young men can exert a degree of control over their status position, with the choice to work or not to work in a low-status occupation. In discussing decisions concerning occupation, young men often claimed that status was a major deterrent from engaging in certain professions. For example, a twelfth-grade student in the woodworking program at the Jimma vocational school explained to me that although he enjoyed carpentry, if he were to pursue this career, he would prefer to do it away from Jimma in a place where he did not have family or close friends. He did not come from a family of woodworkers and would not have been thought to have an evil eye or face any traditional forms of discrimination described in Chapter 1. In fact, he was popular among his peers partially because of his reputation as an excellent soccer player. He feared that by working in a stigmatized occupation, he would expose himself and his family to insults and disrespect. How this would specifically affect his life was unclear, but in any case, the fear was powerful enough to discourage him from doing woodwork in his hometown of Jimma.

Stigmas against craft workers appeared to be particularly strong in certain neighborhoods. In discussing the desirability of different professions, a group of young people living in a poor outlying neighborhood, Sa'ar Sefer, ranked carpentry as very low, despite the fact that carpenters earn more money than many of the better-ranked occupations. They explained that carpentry is "dirty" (*qoshasha*) or "bad" (*metfo*) work. Even young men who explicitly rejected this perspective as ignorant or belonging to the past acknowledged that others might think this way and that working in particular occupations could make it difficult to form relationships with others and especially limit potential girl-friends.

Youth discourse surrounding traditionally stigmatized occupations was not significantly different from that regarding other forms of work that are generally considered "lower" or "inferior" (*ziqqiteñña sira*). In regard to carrying loads at the bus station for money, one unemployed young man claimed, "In this country no one wants to do that sort of work; it disturbs your mind." Similar to the quotes at the beginning of this chapter, he explained that in Ethiopia work is not appreciated or respected (*sira yinakal*).[2] The phrase *sira yinakal* was repeated again and again by youth in regard to local attitudes about work. Youth were intent on conveying the idea that work was not a valued activity and many types of employment would not bring prestige, regardless of one's effort.

Although youth occasionally commented on the social slights that they would suffer from performing certain types of work, fear of what others might think or say about them appeared to be the greatest threat. I often questioned youth about specifically what would be said if they worked in a lower occupation, and they claimed that they would not necessarily be directly insulted. Instead youth described working and having acquaintances pass by and look at them and make comments like, "Did you see him? He is working as a shoe-shine now." In youth discourse it was the act of being recognized, evaluated negatively, and spoken about in relation to a particular occupation that was at the root of their fears. As I noted in the introductory chapter, this almost obsessive fear of what others are saying and thinking about one's self and family is described with the Amharic term *yiluñña*. To be recognized and spoken about as a shoeshine would have been emotionally devastating. The simple statement that "in Ethiopia there is *yiluñña*" was offered by many young men to explain the difficulty of working. The thought of what others might say about them and how this would affect their family caused such a great degree of mental distress that many youth preferred not to work at all.

Government Employment and Occupational Prestige

If certain occupations were avoided because of status concerns, others were desired because of their ability to bring prestige. The role of government work in shaping urban class structure that I have described in Chapter 1 also meant that it had significant implications for perceptions of occupation and status.

Although "government work" (*mengist sira*) encompassed different types of employment ranging from administrator to clerk to janitor, in everyday discussion the single term was often used to refer to all types of public employment. When asked what type of work he or she wanted, it was very common for a young person to respond with the answer "government work." The specific type of position desired was usually based on what could be expected given one's education level, but in most cases the classification of government work was more important than the particular job.

In assessing values concerning occupational status, I asked youth to individually rank different professions in terms of prestige and income, and then we discussed these lists as a group. While "government worker" was not generally placed first on the occupational hierarchy lists, it was always near the top, especially in terms of prestige. There was some debate over whether the government worker was actually feared instead of respected for doing good work, but all agreed that a government administrator wielded a large amount of power. The power of the government administrator was visible on various trips I made to government offices to deal with different bureaucratic issues. Waiting was always part of a visit to a government office. The government official was usually at least fifteen minutes late to a meeting, and in some cases, he (in my experience, it was always a male) did not show up at all. At large meetings the highest-ranking government officials are always the last to arrive— indicating that they have the power to make others wait and that their time is of particular value. On one occasion, I visited with a friend of mine who was an older man, the head of his *iddir*, and quite respected in the city. Normally walking down the street with my friend meant that everyone stopped to greet us, always addressing us in the most respectful form possible. In the government office, this suddenly changed, and it was my friend's turn to show deference, standing to greet officials who were far younger than he was and patiently waiting for our appointment with a man who never arrived.

Youth pointed out that the government worker did not receive a particularly high salary but did have access to a number of perks and benefits. For all workers these included basic benefits such as a pension after retirement, working only forty to fifty hours a week (most workers in the private sector worked at least seventy hours a week), and having time off for holidays. Depending on the level of the worker, other fringe benefits might include the ability to place one's family in other jobs, access to education opportunities, better housing, and bribes. These benefits were important not only for oneself but also for one's family, and a government worker had a heightened degree of ability to redistribute wealth. Even low-level workers who could not directly provide these benefits had day-to-day access to administrators who were capable of delivering help. The definite knowledge that a paycheck was coming at the end of the month also allowed workers to budget money for a child's education or to support extended family. To some extent, the ability to redistribute wealth allowed government workers of all levels to participate in the patron/client relationships that Hoben (1970) describes as being crucial for the development of prestige among Amhara in the mid-twentieth century. I describe this dynamic in relation to the construction of status in the following section.

More intangible benefits to being a government worker could also be observed in day-to-day life. Regardless of one's specific position, the government worker was part of a larger community composed of all other public employees. It provided an identity in a way that many other forms of employment did not. In describing Sa'ar Sefer, an older man noted that it was a neighborhood full of government workers. This was a poor neighborhood, and the workers were mostly cleaners or guards. While the authority of the high-level administrator was certainly desired, for those who could not hope to reach that level, simply identifying oneself as a government worker was still a source of pride. It was a mark of quality that revealed something about the people and the neighborhood where they lived.

That tight community and sense of camaraderie that existed among government workers was clear during the semester I spent teaching and conducting research at the vocational school. The predominantly male staff formed an informal men's club providing support for each other in times of joy and sadness. The staff had a soccer team that competed with other city teams. Postgame celebrations usually involved consuming large amounts of meat and beer, at least partially at the school's expense. Twice during the course of my research the staff used the school's bus to take tours of the country, visiting tourist destinations and other schools. On both occasions they returned bleary eyed and tired with stories of late nights carousing in different cities.

Being a government worker also gave individuals some ability to transcend boundaries of class and power. This was especially apparent at weddings and funerals. If a government administrator sponsored a wedding, all employees of his office, including cleaners, guards, gardeners, and others, were invited and expected to attend. For those who lacked funds to host a lavish wedding, coworkers contributed so that a celebration could still be enjoyed. When a government employee died, all of his or her coworkers were expected to attend the funeral. Government vehicles were often made available for transportation, and contributions were made at the office in order to help pay for the costs associated with feeding all of the mourners. Both weddings and funerals were extremely important events in establishing and revealing social status in Ethiopia. Young men sometimes commented that no one would attend the funeral of a wealthy person who was not generous with his money. He might have been given deferential treatment in life, but in the end the funeral was far more important.

This must be contrasted with the lower occupations described earlier, where workers were often left out of these important social events. Even high-level private employees were often unable to attend funerals because they were not given permission to leave their work. In day-to-day life the lower worker was spoken to only to give orders, while the government worker was generally treated as an equal regardless of the nature of his or her work. The government worker was greeted on the street while the lower worker was ignored. Status hierarchies were often expressed as qualitative differences in one's interactions with others.

The positive discourse surrounding government employment was by no means universal. A critique of government work was especially strong among students from the vocational school who were learning skills such as metal-working that were often stigmatized. Neighborhood was another important factor in shaping the opinions of youth concerning government employment. Generally youth from neighborhoods where a relatively high percentage of adults were government employees evaluated government work favorably. In Sa'ar Sefer, the same neighborhood where young people were especially critical of traditionally stigmatized professions, youth were very positive in regards to government employment. In Mahel Ketema (literally "city center") where most of the city's successful merchants were located, youth were less interested in government work. In contrast to youth who desired the stability of a monthly paycheck, Mahel Ketema youth appreciated that a shop owner received income daily and could invest his or her money without any restrictions.

Occupational Status, Power, and Exchange

The varying levels of prestige and stigma associated with different occupations sheds light on young men's contrasting values and decisions concerning employment. I argue that stigma results from the manner in which occupations place one within relations of exchange and power. While lower forms of work did not have the established culturally prescribed restrictions on social interactions found in the past with craft workers, performing these types of work still placed one in a different social category—a type of person who is treated differently from others. My analysis demonstrates that work is not simply a means of accessing income, but of situating oneself in relation to others, in both the present and the future.

Working in lower occupations meant placing oneself at the bottom of relations of authority. Hierarchical relations have historically been common in Ethiopia. In their early ethnographies of the highland Amhara, Allan Hoben (1970, 1973) and Donald Levine (1965) claimed that hierarchies are a key aspect of Amhara culture and that they are partially rooted in Orthodox Christianity. Hoben states, "It is a fundamental postulate of Amhara culture . . . that social order, which is good, can be created and maintained only through hierarchical, legitimate control deriving ultimately from God" (1970: 194). In her ethnography of school children in Addis Ababa, Eva Poluha (2004) claimed that hierarchy and social order that roughly correspond with a patron/client model continue to be highly valued, and as I explain in Chapter 1, Amhara culture acts as a point of reference for much of the social interaction that takes place within urban Ethiopia. However, there is a significant difference between the hierarchical relations associated with the patron/client model and in subordinating oneself within the process of exchange. Subordinating oneself within a patron/client relationship is thought to be a sign of good character. The individual to whom others defer is expected to provide some level of protection or guidance for his or her subordinates. As Poluha (2004) explains, the parent/child and teacher/student relationships are good examples of this dynamic. In contrast, showing deference in the context of work does not involve a personal relationship. The worker is simply following orders to access money, and there is no expectation of a deeper relationship. The worker exists at the bottom of a power hierarchy without a corresponding personal relationship of protection and obedience.

Analyses of stigma among craft workers in rural areas are helpful for understanding how urban occupational status is inseparable from one's position within social relationships. Alula Pankhurst and Dena Freeman (2001: 341–344) note that notions of personhood are important for maintaining the marginalization of craft workers in rural areas. In their study, farmers asserted that craft workers are not fully human. Despite a discourse centered on factors such as cleanliness and eating habits, Pankhurst and Freeman argue that the continued low status of craft workers is based on their lack of access to land and the social relations that are involved with land rights. Even when craft workers become wealthy, this does not translate into status and full personhood unless they are able to obtain land rights. The inability to own land constricts one's interactions, and this in turn leads to negative status evaluations, which are manifested in social relationships. As with marginalized rural craft workers, in Jimma the particular dynamics of subordination and exchange were responsible for the low status of many occupations. Money alone was not enough to transform a status position that was determined largely by the person's position within social relationships.[3] In the Ethiopian case, work is evaluated primarily in terms of social relationships rather than income.

In some cases, a form of relationship does exist between the worker and his customers. In Amharic, both the vendor and customer are referred to as *demibeña* if a relationship exists between them. To have a *demibeña* relationship implies a degree of loyalty. The customer should not buy elsewhere, and the vendor should give a favorable price. While the *demibeña* relationship is important, it exists only at the moment of the transaction. The vendor and seller are on equal terms for a moment, each helping the other to obtain his or her needs, and then that relationship ends until another purchase is made. It does not generally encompass other aspects of social life. One's *demibeña* would not be expected to attend the funeral or wedding of a family member. It is a means of establishing civility in an otherwise tense interaction, but it does not imply the existence of a relationship that extends beyond the moment of exchange.

The *demibeña* relationship may be contrasted with the prestigious position of the government worker described previously. The contrasting status evaluations that urban Ethiopians gave to different occupations resonate with Marcel Mauss's notion of "total prestation." Many of the material benefits controlled by government workers are connected to access to powerful individuals and the chance to distribute better housing, education, and employment. Giving and receiving in this context take place because a relationship exists, not just at the moment of the transaction but in all aspects of life. The prestige of the government worker derives from the fact that work-related subordination and exchange take place on the basis of relationships that extend into all aspects of life and are not limited to the moment of the transaction, as they are for the low-status worker. A government administrator, for example, will attend the funeral of a janitor working in his office, indicating that their relationship extends well beyond the workplace.

Charles Piot's (1999: 62–66) distinction between the qualitative nature of gift exchange and the quantitative nature of commodity exchange is also helpful for understanding the difference between prestigious government employment and stigmatized work in the informal sector. Piot distinguishes between using people to access things and using things to access people. In the case of gift exchange, a thing is used to form a relationship between people. Because the desired result is the relationship, an equivalency between things is unimportant. For government workers, giving, receiving, and subordination are present, but there is little sense that one is directly exchanging one's labor for what one receives. For workers in the informal economy, the sale of commodities or one's labor time is quantified so that particular services or things are equated with specific amounts of money. In contrast, the salary of government employees does not directly correspond to production. Government workers often spend long periods of time away from work attending funerals and other social events, which implies that they are not directly compensated for time spent at work. Qualitative exchanges associated with government employment build relationships in a way that is not possible for young men working in the informal economy. As I explain in Chapter 5, this contrast is also relevant for understanding distinctive patterns of reciprocity between working and unemployed young men.

This contrast should not be conceived of as exchange for profit versus relationship-based forms of exchange, in which exchange for profit represents the intrusion of a market economy (Taussig 1980). As Parry (1989) has argued, the notion that social relations and accumulation of wealth should be separate spheres of activity often leads anthropologists to assume that an antipathy toward commerce is present. In the Ethiopian case, accumulation through exchange was not necessarily evaluated negatively. James Ferguson (2006: 72–73) differentiates between prosocial and antisocial forms of accumulation. For government workers, material accumulation is prosocial in the sense that it is inseparable from the maintenance of social relationships. Workers access material goods through relationships and must invest materially in these relationships to ensure their maintenance. For workers in the informal economy, there is a greater degree of separation between relationships and accumulation. This does not imply that working young men earn their living at the expense of others or that they are involved in exploitative forms of accumulation. The day-to-day exchanges they rely on to accumulate wealth are not, however, dependent on the maintenance of long-term relationships to the same degree as government employees. I complicate this basic dichotomy between working and unemployed youth in the following chapter, but at this point it should be clear that occupational prestige and stigma are associated with contrasting models of exchange.

In this sense, youth evaluated an occupation not only on the basis of its utility in accumulating wealth but also in terms of its association with a particular quality of social relations. The government employment that most youth desired provided a secure form of income, and it placed one within a vertical hierarchy of power that was accompanied by close personal relationships. Because of local and international economic shifts, government work was not available and most youth chose unemployment. Nevertheless, it is perhaps not quite accurate to conceive of youth as choosing between unemployment and employment. Youth were faced with a choice between contrasting ways of positioning themselves socially, and the shame of *yiluññta* often prevented them from engaging in socially undesirable work. This was true of not only relatively well-off young men but also those who came from families with few economic resources. To work or not to work was a social decision.

This is important for two reasons: First, it indicates that the problem of unemployment is not simply an economic issue. The absence of work represents an inability to control the manner in which one is positioned within social relationships. The problem of unemployment is perhaps best conceived of not simply as an absence of work, but as an inability to construct a desirable identity through social relationships. Second, it reveals that an investigation of stratification in relation to unemployment must not be confined to economic difference. Youth decisions regarding employment are not simply driven by a desire to maximize income but are shaped by cultural norms concerning work and relationships. This conclusion demands a new perspective from which to approach the issues of inequality and stratification. I return to this discussion in the following chapter and explore how inequality may be understood in terms of one's control over social relationships.

Before moving on, it is necessary to emphasize that compared to traditionally stigmatized craft workers, the marginalization of different occupations was relatively flexible in urban settings like Jimma. Unlike traditional stigmas, the negative status associated with lower occupations was not permanent and showed a high degree of variability in its influence over one's social interactions. Ellison (2006) cautions against constructing occupational status groups as overly rigid, and my research indicates that flexibility in identity and status has increased in a contemporary urban setting. For example, one of the wealthiest and most powerful men in Jimma, Qeñazmach Teka

Genu, was said to have begun his working life as a shoeshine. He became very wealthy under Haile Selassie's reign, lost much of this wealth during the Derg, and then regained many of his previous properties with the coming of the Ethiopian People's Revolutionary Democratic Front (EPRDF). The fact that he came from such a low background was seen as a sign of strength on his part and not anything inherent about him as a person. Another example is Afwerk, the bicycle repairman described in more detail shortly. On one occasion I observed Afwerk greeting a small girl, and her mother quickly pulled her away, scolding her for touching someone who was dirty from working on bicycles. Similar greetings between strangers and small children were common and accepted in Jimma. Despite this woman's avoidance, Afwerk did have close relationships with other small children from the neighborhood where he worked and sometimes served as a temporary caretaker for one child whose parents owned a nearby shop. In this sense the discrimination faced in one situation might not be present in another, and one's status at the moment was not permanent.

Choosing to Work

The lives of working young men reveal the variation that exists in young men's values and economic behavior. In the Ethiopia case, class is clearly relevant, but it is not the determining factor in relation to aspirations and occupational choice. None of the working young men in my sample came from middle-class families, indicating that if one had substantial social support, then taking on low-status work was generally not an option that one could conceivably choose. Most urban young men, however, were from poor families. Some of them worked, and many of them did not. The diversity of practices among young men with similar class backgrounds implies that occupational choice was based on more than class. Individual case studies of working young men reveal great variation in the reasons why some individuals are willing to take on lower forms of work. In the cases of working young men that I describe shortly, each was in some way distanced from social judgments and norms, so that the power of *yiluññta* in relation to occupational status was reduced.

Young men with a secondary education could potentially access a variety of different jobs, including low-level government work, working in bars and restaurants, manual labor, petty trade and manufacturing, and various other informal entrepreneurial activities. With the exception of government work, youth felt that all of these occupations carried a negative stigma. I focused the bulk of my research on working young men whose occupations were not particularly physically demanding but provided substantial incomes, approximately as much as a low-level government employee (at least two hundred birr per month). This excluded day laborers who perform grueling labor for a daily wage and restaurant workers who earn very low wages (approximately fifty to eighty birr per month).

Over the course of my research, I developed detailed case studies for ten working young men. They include a bicycle repairman, two owners of small shops (both of whom also rented bicycles), an assistant in a video house, two barbers, a Hindi-to-Amharic translator who was employed at a video house, a watch salesman/repairman, an assistant on a minibus taxi, and a young man who made and sold tire sandals. The four case studies described in this section demonstrate the variation and commonalities among working young men.

Afwerk: Bicycle Mechanic

I begin with Afwerk because he was one of my favorite people in Jimma. He fixed bicycles on the side of the road near a hotel where I stayed during my first extended visit to Jimma in 2002. I walked past him every day, and we quickly developed a friendly relationship. He was a sort of philosopher, always ready to put his tools aside and talk to me about various topics such as religion or local gossip. For this reason he was one of the people to whom I always turned when I needed a bit of information about something, related to my research or otherwise.

Afwerk worked on a busy street approximately one block from the bus station. Both sides of the street were lined with teahouses, barbershops, and various small shops selling locally produced butter (*qibay*), coffee, and household goods. The street received a fair amount of foot traffic and was also one of the two main lines that minibus taxis traveled down. Afwerk's workstation was positioned on a side alley so that he was able to take advantage of the shade from a high, corrugated metal fence and stay out of the way of pedestrians.

Afwerk worked seven days a week. His days usually began around 8:00 A.M., when he left the small house he shared with his mother and sisters and bicycled to a tea house for coffee and a bite to eat. From there he set up his workstation. This consisted of dragging a heavy wooden box of tools from where it was stored at a nearby shop to the corner where he worked. It was common for self-employed young men to rely on local businesses for help with things like storing their tools. The rest of Afwerk's day was more or less unstructured. If someone came by needing a bicycle repaired or a tire filled, he would do it, but if this did not happen he simply sat on his box of tools, chatting with whoever happened to stop by. Chewing khat and eating lunch were the only activities that broke up the day. After breakfast Afwerk bought a small bunch of khat. Khat that is chewed in the morning is called an *ehjebena*, which is an Oromo word that translates roughly as "eye-opener." For Afwerk, lunch was usually a hearty meal, and he was especially fond of a dish called *cha-cha* that is made from a sheep's stomach. After lunch he purchased a larger bundle of khat to chew during the afternoon. Afwerk also smoked cigarettes whenever he was chewing khat. Around 5:00 or 6:00 P.M. Afwerk usually had a plastic bottle of *tej* (honey wine) concealed by paper wrapping that he sipped from. He stayed at his workstation until around 6:30 P.M. and then packed up his tools and cycled to a *tej* house. After drinking until around 9:00 P.M., he returned home and fell asleep.

Afwerk had been working as a bicycle repairman in the same place for around four years. He originally learned the trade from a friend, working as an apprentice until he was able to operate on his own. He enjoyed his work and took a great deal of pride in developing innovative solutions to fix bicycles without the proper tools or technology. Everything was repaired and reused. I once pointed out that the inner tube that he was patching appeared to be more patch than tube, and he responded that this was far better than spending four times as much money on a new tube. Occasionally Afwerk had a younger assistant working for him in hopes of learning the trade, but these helpers never lasted more than a week or two.

For Afwerk business had its up and downs, but he always seemed to have money in his pocket. On a bad day he might not have any business, and on a good day he could earn up to twenty birr. Occasionally someone in the neighborhood offered him a day's work doing light construction or unloading goods, and he was always happy to do so. During the month when I tracked Afwerk's income, he earned 266 birr (approximately 30 U.S. dollars). Sometimes Afwerk supplemented his income by renting out his bike. This brought the risk of theft, and on more than one occasion he had to spend a few days at the police station trying to recover a stolen bicycle. The large amount of money that Afwerk spent on alcohol, khat, and restaurant meals meant that he had little or no savings. He owned a high-quality bicycle, which was rare among young men in Jimma, but other than that all of his money went toward his recreational habits.

As I have noted, Afwerk was very sociable and he did have several friends who would stop off for a cigarette or a bit of khat and some conversation. However, these friends were not well respected, even among youth. Many of them lived on the streets and made money by carrying loads at the bus station. In terms of social status, among working young men Afwerk was at the low end of the spectrum. This was partially due to the nature of his employment. Like all of my primary informants he was not a government employee, but his work was also literally dirty and it did not require an education. Also important was the fact that he worked on the street. This meant that he was constantly exposed to the gaze and the judgment of anyone who passed by. Afwerk's lifestyle was also a source of his low status. While working he usually wore a ragged T-shirt and a couple of layers of grease-covered pants, and his after-work outfits generally involved removing one layer of pants. He chewed khat and smoked cigarettes in public, and even drank *tej* on the street. I know of no other person in Jimma who would drink in public. In general urban Ethiopians look down on such public consumption of intoxicants.

Getanet: Barber

Getanet had the air of a cosmopolitan young man. He had been raised in Jimma's commercial center and therefore was accustomed to being around all types of business, music, and nightlife. He generally dressed in youth fashions and his name was well known among other working young people. Getanet was unique among the young men closely involved in my research in that he was married. During the course of my research, he experienced the birth and the death of a child.

Both of his parents died at a young age, and this pushed him to leave school and begin working. He began by shining shoes and selling lottery tickets. Lottery ticket sellers rove the streets looking for customers, and in doing this he began to spend a large amount of time hanging out at barbershops and gradually learned the trade. Getanet had worked as a barber in many of the different small towns around Jimma. Between 2003 and 2005, he worked at three different barbershops in Jimma. In each case, he left because of a falling out with the owner.

Especially for young men, barbershops are sites where people gather to listen to music, talk, chew khat, and generally hang out. This may have been part of the reason that Getanet was so well known. Different levels of barbershops are available, and they vary in terms of cleanliness, the skill of the employees, and price. Getanet always worked at the highest standard of barbershops. These shops charged five birr (0.60 U.S. dollars) for a haircut. The barber kept half of the fee for himself and gave the other half to the owner. The barber also kept any tips that he was given. The owner was responsible for all expenses. The barber did not receive any additional salary from the owner. The high level of social and economic activity that surrounded barbershops sometimes brought additional opportunities, and Getanet occasionally made money on the side by acting as a broker between buyers and sellers. During the month that I monitored his income, he earned 432 birr (around 50 U.S. dollars). Getanet's wife did not work outside the home, and he was responsible for all of their household expenses. Although rent was low because he had a government-owned house, other expenses prevented him from saving much money from month to month.

Getanet generally worked seven days a week. He began each day around 9:00 A.M. and worked until 10:00 P.M., but he was able to take numerous breaks through out the day. Especially when business was slow in the afternoon, he often left for a few hours to hang out with friends or run errands. Usually two or three barbers worked at any shop and served the customers on a rotating basis. This meant that even at the shop, Getanet had plenty of time to socialize with friends, read, or listen to music. It was common for barbers to chew khat as they worked, and Getanet usually chewed small amounts throughout the day.

Unlike many of the other lower occupations that I examined, cutting hair had the advantage of being indoor work. It was possible to maintain some privacy and conceal oneself from the public's gaze. However, some barbers commented that others consider their work "dirty" because it involves touching another person's hair. Like other forms of lower work, cutting hair was thought to require very little education and was not seen as an important profession. Despite these negative associations for some youth, working at a barbershop had the advantage of immersing the barber in youth culture. Getanet always wore a unique but generally admired haircut. He sometimes gave free haircuts to friends, meaning that he had the power to dispense style and fashion. He used his time at the barbershop to familiarize himself with local and international music, and he occasionally worked as a disc jockey at a bar that was popular with young people. In general, Getanet and other youth workers involved in the culture industry were often seen as cool (*arrif*) by their peers.

Siraj: Watch Repair and Sales

Like Afwerk, Siraj was someone with whom I developed a relationship during my first extended visit to Jimma in 2002. The nature of his work meant that he often had time to talk, and I was always welcome to pull up a stool and sit with him as he worked discussing news, politics, the United States, religion, and whatever else was on our minds. Siraj worked side by side with his good friend Mohammed. Mohammed was only a couple of years older than Siraj, but he was married and had two children and was therefore on a very different trajectory in life. The contrast between Siraj and Mohammed is discussed in Chapter 3 and reveals how two young men with the same occupation may have very different goals and expectations in life.

Siraj worked at a shady spot on the side of a busy road that led to Jimma's main market. In terms of foot traffic the road was one of the busiest in the city. He was positioned next to a small shop that sold bread and in front of an unmarked café that sold various nonalcoholic grain-based drinks that were made on site. Around five other watch vendors were spread out in front of this café, and Siraj shared one particular corner with Mohammed. There was no difference in the services that any of these young men provided, but there appeared to be adequate business for all of them. Working in close proximity allowed them to watch another person's goods if he needed to leave, and each man occasionally referred customers to another vendor if he did not have the desired part or watch.

All of these watch vendors were Muslim, and most of them were from the Wollo region—two to three days' travel from Jimma. Siraj moved to Jimma in search of work in 2001. When he arrived, he quickly found acquaintances from his birthplace. They were all working with watches, and they invited him to join them. He was able to learn the trade within a month. He did not particularly enjoy his work, but it was a way to pay the bills. The watches sold in Ethiopia were generally poorly made, meaning that there was no shortage of customers, and he was able to earn a decent income. During the month that I monitored his income, he made a profit of 554 birr (around 65 U.S. dollars). Watch sales involved a large amount of negotiation. Customers looked at a watch, a price was stated, counteroffers were made, haggling ensued, and in many cases the customer elected not to buy. The price was usually relative to the perceived wealth of the customer. Although bargaining is a part of many transactions in Ethiopia, the price of watches seemed to be especially flexible, and this may explain the lack of a friendly relationship between Siraj and most of his customers.

Siraj lived alone and was responsible for all of his daily expenses, but he was still able to save money. He estimated that he saved two thousand birr in his first three years of work. All of this money was spent on gifts for his family when he made his first trip home in 2004.

Siraj's day-to-day life followed a consistent pattern. He worked seven days a week, sometimes working only a half day on Fridays. He arrived for work around 9:00 A.M. and stayed until 6:00 P.M. Although he sometimes chewed a morning *ehjebena*, he usually chewed khat only in the afternoon. He took a break for lunch and to go to the mosque for afternoon prayers. Particularly in the afternoon, there were few customers and he was free to chew khat and talk with the other vendors.

Working as a watch vendor brought a decent income, but it was not a prestigious occupation. Working on the street meant that Siraj was exposed to dust, mud, exhaust from cars, and the constant gaze of the public. I never observed this directly, but Siraj claimed that he was sometimes insulted by pedestrians. They would call him a "thief" as they passed by. Although the shouters of these insults were generally not respected individuals, to be insulted in public like this was still extremely unpleasant. Siraj did make an effort to carry himself in a respectable manner. Although he did chew khat in public, this was less of a stigmatized behavior for a Muslim, and he did not smoke cigarettes. He always dressed in neat, clean clothes. For these reasons and because of his close ties with other migrants from Wollo and his active faith in Islam, Siraj had a large social network. He was friendly with a range of wealthier men who sometimes stopped by to visit him. He could also rely on these friends to provide economic aid in times of need.

Kassahun: Street-Side Shop Owner

Kassahun impressed me as a natural businessman who was always interested in discussing trade and profits. He began his working life at age thirteen by selling fruit at his school. Kassahun also shined shoes and performed a number of other small jobs until he was able to purchase a small portable shop. When I met him in 2003, he had been operating the shop for around two years. The shop was similar in size to a wardrobe, and he positioned it in front of an abandoned storefront in the Ferenj Arada neighborhood. Kassahun also owned three bicycles that he rented. Although Kassahun needed permission from the surrounding businesses to operate, he did not pay any rent. When I began my research, Kassahun's shop was near the post office, but after around six months, the post office moved, and the foot traffic on the street greatly decreased, especially during the day. The main street in Ferenj Arada was a popular place for walks in the evening, but during the rest of the day, the traffic was limited to people traveling to and from their homes. In 2005 Kassahun received assistance from the government to open a larger kiosk-style shop in a busy area of the city. It appeared that he was doing well at this location, but the data that I have for him are based on his original portable shop.

Kassahun worked six days a week, taking Sundays off to attend church and relax with his girlfriend. He generally opened his shop early, around 7:00 A.M. Although customers were steady, he still had plenty of time to socialize with friends or other young men working in the area. Kassahun did not chew khat and left his shop only to take a break for lunch. During most of the time that I was conducting research, Kassahun was attending evening classes in the electronics program at the vocational school. He was absent from work during these hours, but he usually reopened the shop upon returning and stayed until around 10:00 P.M. During the month that I monitored his income, he profited 460 birr (around 55 U.S. dollars). Kassahun lived with his mother, but he covered his own expenses for meals and school fees. I do not know the amount of his savings, but he was able to purchase all of the supplies necessary to open a new, larger shop, and this must have cost at least a thousand birr.

Most of Kassahun's customers were from the neighborhood, and he was able to develop a good relationship with them. Although haggling was still common, prices were generally known and it was usually a friendly process. Kassahun's main difficulty in relation to work was renting bicycles. On multiple occasions during the course of my research, he had a bicycle stolen. Each time he did manage to retrieve the bicycle, but in some cases this took months, causing him to lose time and income. After moving to the larger shop, Kassahun eventually stopped renting bicycles.

Kassahun did work on the street, and there was definitely some stigma attached to this. However, particularly in the community in which he worked, Kassahun was well liked and respected. He took a great deal of care in his appearance and always wore clean, fashionable clothes. His ownership of the shop and bicycles made him far wealthier than other young men. He was also a member of an *iqub* (savings organization) made up of other small-business owners in the neighborhood. Members of the *iqub* contribute equal amounts of money, and once a month a different member receives an amount based on the size of the total group contribution. Kassahun's effort in continuing his education also brought him a certain amount of admiration. He finished the two-year program at the vocational school near the end of my research and planned to pursue a diploma in electronics in the future.

Occupation and Values

The case studies of working youth described here demonstrate that social and spatial distance from normative values concerning occupational status and *yiluññta* are key in enabling young men to choose to work. Each of these case studies is also closely connected to the internal and external dynamics of status that I discussed at the beginning of this chapter in relation to Jennifer Johnson-Hanks (2006). Johnson-Hanks's notion of external dimensions of status as both "a sculptor and an indicator of internal honor" has an interesting relationship with these cases. The practices of working young men produce low status through their position within social relationships and the manner in which others evaluate them. For the most part, this external dimension of status does not, however, appear to affect working young men's economic behavior, pride, or internal sense of status. The case at hand reveals that disconnections between external and internal dimensions of status are often the source of diverse cultural and economic practices.

To varying degrees Afwerk, Getanet, Siraj, and Kassahun had low statuses because of their occupation. While Afwerk's lifestyle certainly decreased his status, many people perceived this behavior as being an intrinsic part of working in a lower occupation. Regardless of their actual behavior, many Jimma residents thought that people performing menial labor on the street were likely to chew khat, drink excessively, and generally be dirty. In Chapter 2 I argue that all young men could potentially be classified as duriye. Low-level workers were even more likely to be given this label. Even young women who did not adopt any of the other practices associated with duriye sometimes faced this label because of their occupational status. A good example of this is a young woman who was part of a team of women who worked as shoeshines. By all accounts these were the first women in Jimma ever to work as shoeshines. Although their occupations were unprecedented, by local moral standards their behavior was exemplary. All were religious and polite and used their income to support their families. However, this woman still complained that in her neighborhood people called her a duriye after she began shining shoes. Her occupation determined her character regardless of behavior, and to an extent this was true of all low-level workers.

Although their occupations certainly brought them low status, in interviews most working young men claimed that they did not experience significant mental distress because of their employment. For working young men, there was a disjuncture between the internal and external dimensions of status. Their self-perception was distanced from the community judgments that caused so many young men to avoid low-status work. Working young men acknowledged that it was common for others to perceive their occupations negatively, but they claimed that this did not significantly impact their self-perceptions. This was partially because of the working young men's construction of a set of values concerning occupation that were distinct from their community.

In the case of Afwerk, he had separated himself from his community at a young age, and social norms and judgments had little importance for him. Afwerk dropped out of school in the seventh grade. After briefly attempting woodwork, in his own words he became a duriye.[4] He left home and for the next three years he lived on the streets or in hotels, traveling through the small towns surrounding Jimma and making money through theft. He stole small items from vendors at markets and then resold them elsewhere. "Thief" is one of the worst insults in Ethiopia. Although a known thief may not necessarily be physically removed from a community, that person will lose any sense of belonging. After living the life of a duriye for three years, Afwerk returned to his mother's house and began working as a shoeshine before engaging in bicycle repair. It was difficult for him to reestablish his relationship with his family and neighbors in the community. Eventually people observed him working and that his behavior was changing. At that time he did not stay out at night or drink heavily. People were surprised to see him acting like this, and trust was built slowly. Although people may no longer have viewed him as a criminal, it was impossible for him to ever fully reintegrate himself into the community.

To some extent Afwerk no longer belonged to the society in which he lived, and this allowed him to engage in a number of unique activities. Drinking in public was one. Afwerk also took his dog for walks, shared cigarettes with madmen, and wore some of the strangest haircuts I have ever seen. In one case, when he shaved off everything except for a square of hair on the back of his head (a style he claimed to have found in a book of "African" haircuts), a passing police officer took him to a barber and forced him to shave his head completely.[5] Afwerk had little regard for what others thought of him, as long as he was able to earn enough money to enjoy his life. He developed his own standards of evaluation that were often an inverse of commonly held notions of prestige. He was critical of unemployed young men and mocked the pride they took in their clean clothing. He described how they all owned one outfit that they washed once a week and then took care not to soil. Afwerk argued that this sort of person does not look like he wants to work, and no opportunities will come his way. The cleanliness that was a source of prestige for others was negatively evaluated by Afwerk. For Afwerk, the stigma that accompanied his occupation and lifestyle was not an issue because it did not prevent him from working and doing the things he enjoyed. Afwerk was certainly impacted by the same external dimensions of status as his unemployed peers, and his actions prevented him from developing certain types of relationships. However, because of Afwerk's distinctive understanding of status, the cyclical relationship between internal and external was decoupled, and this facilitated his deviant behavior.

A different form of deviancy came from youth like Getanet, who took a leading role in developing what might be called "urban youth culture." On one occasion when I visited Getanet, he had his hair styled into an elevated peak with a large orange stripe running down the middle. He was wearing a gray suit with oversized lapels that set off his hair nicely. Getanet always had the latest European soccer jerseys that were very popular among young men. His devotion to European soccer was so great that he named his son Henri after the famous French player. Getanet's fashion and dedication to soccer definitely separated him from the norm. While Afwerk's deviant behavior was seen as crude, particularly among youth Getanet's style was admired and even imitated. Most young people were interested in international soccer, fashion, music, and films but did not pursue this passion to the same degree as Getanet. Cultivating a more pronounced youth style was common among young men who were involved in disseminating international and local popular culture. While these youth did not work in prestigious occupations, at least among other youth there was something to be admired in their lifestyle. Getanet may not have cultivated an identity that brought respect from adults in positions of power, but by referencing valued international symbols he was able to instantaneously win prestige among his peers. He also controlled the distribution of style among other young men through his position at a high-end barbershop. By accessing prestige through a style that referenced international popular culture, some working young men avoided much of the fear and stress experienced by other youth in relation to low-status work.

Urban youth culture was not isolated to working youth, and not all working youth participated in it, but it did provide a realm associated with an alternative set of values that enabled young men to access status regardless of their occupation. Youth culture was not defined only through consumption. Particularly young men who were skilled at performing this culture were said to speak an *arada qwanqwa*. *Qwanqwa* means "language" and *arada* means "something that is elevated or held above others." The *arada qwanqwa* consisted of various words and phrases, many borrowed from Arabic or English, that were mixed into standard Amharic. While some terms such as *arrif*, meaning "cool" (in the Western slang sense), were commonly used and known by many adults, special terms for things like money and food were isolated to young men. Fluency in the *arada qwanqwa* did not necessarily bring prestige, but it helped to mark out a social sphere in which a particular set of values persisted.

Weiss (2009) also describes an urban youth culture in Tanzania that surrounded institutions like barbershops. While Weiss does not examine the economic implications of this culture, it appears to be similar to the Ethiopian case in that it provides an alternative source of value and prestige. Young men in Jimma did not appear to immerse themselves in international youth culture to the same degree as young men in Arusha. Weiss describes young men adopting identities and attitudes through the consumption of popular Western rap music. Ethiopian youth were also interested in Western media, but they did not generally appropriate narratives from them in order to conceptualize their own life. Young men did not valorize the identity of a duriye that adults often associated with youth culture and did not see themselves as engaged in a "thug life" that was associated with "the streets." Young men like Getanet were able to access status within youth culture, but there was no attempt to construct this culture as oppositional to society as a whole.

Kassahun provides another example of the interrelationship between one's values and engaging in low-status work. Kassahun's decision to devote his life to business came at a young age. The economic success of Kassahun's siblings meant that working was not an economic necessity, but he had a love for profits and selling. The narrative of starting small and gradually reinvesting one's profits until reaching a position of wealth and power was extremely attractive for him. In discussing his life, he portrayed each decision as a step toward something bigger and better. He started by selling fruit at school, and he used his profits to buy a young goat. He sold the goat after it was fattened and used that money to buy the supplies necessary to start shining shoes. He also earned money from doing contract work for the government and combined this with his shoeshine profits to purchase and stock his portable shop. In contrast to youth who prioritized the relationships surrounding a particular occupation, Kassahun always gave the result priority over the means by which it was achieved. Any unpleasantness associated with work was worth the cost, if it resulted in the growth of his business. When I asked Kassahun about other youth who would never work as a shoeshine or sell small items on the street for fear of what others might say about them, he acknowledged that this attitude was common. However, he argued that these youth would never amount to anything. Maybe he would hire them someday to open the gates to his compound when he drove up in his car. Kassahun's ability to set the past behind him and enjoy his current status was apparent. Although he had been a shoeshine just three years before, when I met him he would never shine another person's shoes. In fact it was common for him to have his expensive leather boots shined while he sat waiting for customers. By constructing a narrative surrounding work that focused on the future instead of the present, Kassahun was able to endure the social stress that often accompanied working in a lower occupation.

Siraj lacked the distinct value system that I have described in relation to Afwerk, Getanet, and Kassahun. Instead, he used migration as a strategy for coping with the low status of his work. This was a common strategy among working young men, and many young men from Jimma moved to Addis Ababa or other large cities to find work. Siraj did not decide to move to Jimma because he could not find work in his hometown of Kombulcha but because he did not feel comfortable working there. In addition to the discomfort of being seen in a low-status position by friends and family, he had less of an incentive to work because he could always rely on his family for support. "In Jimma I have to work. There is no choice. If I do not work, how will I eat? For me it is better here," he explained. By separating himself from his family he was able to force himself into the working life, and once that transition had been made there was no turning back. Although Siraj admitted that if he had stayed at home he would probably be unemployed, he was still critical of youth who made this decision. "They are just boasting," he argued. "They don't want to work on the street." Working with a group of young men who shared a similar background and choices regarding occupation also made it easier for Siraj to ignore the stigma that was attached to his work.

Unlike the attitudes of the others, Siraj's attitude about employment did not involve a different set of values. Siraj still adhered to basic social standards of morality in terms of dress, religion, and general behavior. His only aberration was his choice of occupation. As detailed in Chapter 3, Siraj was still attached to local notions of success and progress, and he applied these to his own life. External and internal dimensions of status were closely connected for Siraj. His adherence to communal values caused him to evaluate his own life in negative terms, probably more so than many of the other working young men in my study. That he felt the need to leave home in order to work reveals that Siraj was strongly motivated by *yiluññta*, or fear of the judgment of others. Spatial distance from his primary community in Wollo helped alleviate this fear, but it was clear that he still felt the stigma of his occupation. He was sensitive to the occasional insult and the way he was viewed by others. Although his acceptance of these social standards helped him conform in other ways, it also instilled in him a degree of anxiety with which he struggled daily.

While fears concerning the social implications of engaging in low-status employment prevented many young men from working, there were clearly exceptions to this dynamic. Kassahun, Siraj, Getanet, and Afwerk reveal the variation in how young men experienced low-status employment. In some cases, like that of Siraj, the low status of his work brought on a considerable amount of distress and forced him to migrate a long distance from his family in order to work. For Afwerk and others like him, low status was not a daily cause of worry. However this social distance also meant that Afwerk had fewer people to call on if he needed significant help. For different reasons, Kassahun and Getanet also seemed relatively immune from a fear of what others might think of them. Although the values of working young men cannot be summarized with neat categories, they all deviate from social norms defining good and bad work. This deviation represents a disjuncture between internal and external dimensions of status, and it is the key to these young men's ability to work in low-status occupations without complaining of mental stress.

Conclusion

There was not necessarily a direct causal relationship between occupational choice and values concerning occupation and status. The values of youth "fit" with their occupation in a way that stabilized the relationship between economic behavior and its consequent status implications. The social evaluation attached to unemployment and lower forms of work caused some young men to experience mental distress. Working young men separated themselves from communal status evaluations and created a counterdiscourse that valued different combinations of economic independence, urban youth style, and progress. This enhanced their ability to work in a low-status occupation and earn an income without suffering large degrees of mental stress. Unemployed youth were invested in more communal notions of status and therefore feared working in lower occupations. These values encouraged them to remain unemployed and prevented them from accessing money through work.

I have argued that particular types of economic behavior are associated with systems of value. This type of argument is sometimes problematic in that it may be overly deterministic and leave little room for change. Values and economic behavior fit so closely that they appear to endlessly reproduce each other. The detailed descriptions of working young men that I have offered are important because they reveal the variation in values that exists within a given space and time. Much of the variation in economic behavior was based not on class but in values concerning status. Working youth had similar class backgrounds to most unemployed young men, but they differed in terms of their evaluations of the social relations surrounding different forms of work. This variation is important because it provides the stimulus necessary to account for change over time.

In relation to economic change, Pierre Bourdieu argues that "everything suggests that an abrupt slump in objective chances relative to subjective aspirations is likely to produce a break in the tacit acceptance which the dominated classes—now abruptly excluded from the race, objectively, and subjectively— previously granted to the dominant goals, and so to make possible a genuine inversion of the table of values" (1984: 168). I have argued that "objective chances" for youth to fulfill their aspirations had decreased because of the proliferation of education and reduction in public sector employment. It would seem that in the case of urban Ethiopia, there has been no "inversion of the table of values." Youth continue to value the relationships and qualities associated with government employment and aspire to membership in a middle class. The divergent values of working youth are not necessarily related to changes in the opportunity structure and appear to be based primarily on their particular life histories. The lives of working young men demonstrate the potential for variation and change that always exists, even without broader structural shifts.

Regardless of the root causes behind working young men's different values, these values influenced their decisions about employment and affected their position within class and status hierarchies. In Chapter 5, I continue exploring this issue and further examine the contrasting value systems of working and unemployed young men. My analysis of occupational status provides further evidence for a critique of material rationalism that has been well established within anthropology. Although economic behavior is often motivated by values that are not related to maximizing material goods, alternative means of assessing stratification have not been well developed. I work toward this goal in the following chapter by examining the multiple status hierarchies that exist in urban Ethiopia and how stratification may be conceived of in nonmaterial terms.

5

Hopeful Exchanges

Reciprocity and Changing Dimensions of Urban Stratification

Duuring my first few months of living in Jimma and studying unemployed young men, I was continually confronted with an apparent mystery. The spectacle of unemployed young men standing about on the street was everywhere. These young men complained of joblessness and frequently asked me for small amounts of money. The same young men, however, spent much of their time chewing khat and watching films, both activities that require money. How was it, I wondered, that unemployed young men always seemed to have a bit of money in their pockets?

A simple answer to this question gradually became apparent: unemployed young men were heavily dependent on support from others. On a daily basis they received handouts of cash, invitations for coffee, and bundles of khat from parents, friends, brothers and sisters, neighbors, and former classmates. The presence of such high levels of gifting raises a number of other more complex and interesting questions. Why do urban Ethiopians give and receive so many gifts? Why is there such great variation in the level of gifts that individuals give and receive? What kinds of inequalities are produced through processes related to reciprocity? To answer these questions I explored how working and unemployed young men give and receive, both with qualitative interviews and by measuring their incomes from work and gifts for one month. These data revealed significant qualitative and quantitative differences based on employment status and family background in young men's engagement in processes of reciprocity. In this chapter I explore these differences and explain how the case of young men in urban Ethiopia contributes to long-standing debates within anthropology concerning issues of exchange, personhood, and inequality.

My discussion in this chapter is broken into three primary sections. In each section I examine the implications of the Ethiopian case for anthropological discussions of exchange. The first section is an analysis of the relationship between investing in people and things. I discuss reciprocity among working and unemployed young men to demonstrate how investing in social relationships contributes to the accumulation of material wealth, which in turn is often invested in relationships. In the second section, I deconstruct this apparently cyclical relationship between investing in people and things and delineate how differences in control over relationships may constitute a distinct form of inequality. Finally, I examine how the balance between investing in people and things changes over time, particularly in relation to policies associated with neoliberal capitalism.

Exchange in Africa: Accumulating Social Relationships and Material Wealth

Anthropologists working in Africa and elsewhere have long conceived of exchange in terms of a balance between social relationships and material goods, or wealth in things versus wealth in people. Put simply, things may be given to people, who are in turn useful for acquiring more things. Redistributing one's material wealth among others creates access to social support, information, and other opportunities that enable the accumulation of further wealth. The maintenance of material inequalities is therefore inextricable from the ability to control social relationships.

Analyses of exchange in Africa have argued that the relationship between investing in people and things is rooted in processes of production (Fallers 1966; Goody 1976). Historically, in Africa land was plentiful and technology simple. Therefore accumulation through agriculture required access to human labor power rather than capital. Ethiopia has often been held up as the exception to this dynamic because of the presence of the plow (Goody 1976). Even among the plow-farming Amhara of Ethiopia, however, land was generally accessed through social relationships (Hoben 1973). Studies of urban Africa have also demonstrated that access to political support and information through people is essential for the accumulation of wealth, especially in the context of the informal economy (Barnes 1986; Hart 1973, 1975, 1988; Tripp 1997).

This is not to say that the relationship between investing in people and investing in things is not without tension. The history of anthropology in Africa is rich with studies documenting the difficulty of accumulating wealth without undermining the social support on which that accumulation is based. David Parkin's (1972) study of the Giriama of Kenya has become a classic analysis of the balance between social relationships and material accumulation. Parkin argued that Giriama palm growers who wished to accumulate material wealth were faced with a challenging problem. To accumulate capital, palm grow-ers had to distance themselves from community expectations that they would redistribute their wealth in the form of feasts involving large amounts of meat and palm wine. At the same time, access to land depended on social support. For palm growers to accumulate material wealth, they had to avoid redistrib-uting their wealth while maintaining the social ties necessary to ensure their access to land. In Parkin's study, conversion to Islam enabled farmers to solve this problem. Islam prevented men from drinking palm wine and eating meat slaughtered by non-Muslims and allowed them to be more selective about their engagement in relations of reciprocity. Therefore religion provided a jus-tification for refraining from expending one's wealth on shared consumption without being exposed to accusations of selfishness.

In the discussion that follows, I examine how working and unemployed young men in urban Ethiopia developed relationships that contributed to the accumulation of material wealth. In some cases young men were faced with challenges similar to Parkin's palm growers. The ability to accumulate wealth depended on relationships with people, but a continual redistribution of one's wealth was necessary to maintain these relationships.

Working Young Men: Material Accumulation through Reciprocity

The case of working young men demonstrates how investing in people facili-tated the accumulation of capital in urban Ethiopia. In both the short and long term, *zemed* relationships were very important for working youth. *Zemed* forms a blurry social category that generally encompassed biological kin and close friends. Donald Levine (1965: 77) defined *zemed* simply as "close ones." *Zemed* implies a closer relationship than a friend (*gwadeñña*). All biological kin with whom one is acquainted are considered zemed. It was sometimes argued that other relationships should not be referred to as zemed, but in popular usage this was common. One of the means by which a "friend" was differentiated from zemed was by the level of support that he or she was willing to provide. For young men, a non-kin zemed was usually someone who could be called on for a gift or a loan of a significant sum of money. For women who gener-ally did not have access to cash, providing help with domestic responsibilities was important. Especially someone who could be counted on to help with the extensive preparation that was required for a celebration or a funeral was con-sidered zemed.

Among working young men, most of their valuable zemed relationships were formed through the process of work. These relationships were generally with other working youth and adults. Two of the working young men in my study were employed at video houses and each had a close zemed relationship with the owner of the house where he was employed. Their relationships were marked by a particularly high level of reciprocity. Yosef worked as an assistant at a video house, selling tickets, making advertisements, and monitoring the audience. He did not receive a regular salary and instead appealed to the owner of the video house, Bekele, whenever he had a particular need for money. Bekele also frequently invited Yosef for coffee, khat, or meals. The lack of regular payment created a dynamic similar to a family business. Both Bekele and Yosef claimed that labor and monetary assistance were exchanged because of a personal relationship and not because of a contract between worker and owner. The presence of a zemed relationship allowed Bekele to invest more trust in Yosef. For example, it would have been easy for Yosef to pocket small amounts of money from ticket sales, but to steal from one's zemed was not likely. Fostering a zemed relationship was one means of creating the trust necessary to run certain types of businesses in the informal economy.

Teddy offers another example of the role of zemed relationships among working youth. Teddy translated Indian films from Hindi to Amharic. A number of youth in Jimma claimed to perform this service but Teddy was known to be the best. After two years of living in Jimma he established a reputation that drew crowds of young customers from neighborhoods throughout the city. Tesfaye, the owner of the video house where Teddy worked, recognized Teddy's value and paid him accordingly. Unlike Bekele and Yosef's arrangement, a regular system of payments was in place, but Tesfaye also solidified his relationship with Teddy by inviting him regularly for meals and khat. Teddy was from Addis Ababa, and Tesfaye provided him with a level of social support that made up for his lack of family in Jimma.

In both cases, zemed relationships were formed through gifting. In an exchange of labor for wages, both sides of the exchange are quantified. For example, Teddy was paid on the basis of the number of films that he translated and the size of the audience. The exchange was quantitative rather than qualitative in the sense that it was not based on a relationship or respective positions within a broader social hierarchy. In previous chapters I have argued that young men working in the informal economy were stigmatized precisely because of their dependence on exchanges that did not conform to valued relations of power. Exchanges associated with wage labor are not connected to a relationship that extends to other areas of life. The meals that Tesfaye purchased for Teddy cannot be quantified on the basis of Teddy's labor—for example, one meal for every film translated. Rather meals are a reflection of a relationship, and engaging in such qualitative exchange is a means of maintaining that relationship.

The economic benefits that both video house owners derived from using gifts to establish zemed relationships were based on the particular nature of the informal urban economy. Trust and loyalty are essential for operating an illegal business that lacks means of regulation such as sales receipts and contracts. In this context capital is invested in relationships, which in turn are effective in generating further capital.

Other youth workers received few gifts, but relationships with zemed were essential for their ability to work. This was particularly true of street workers who lacked a formal right to a place of work. Kassahun and Siraj both depended on permission from shop owners to access the space where they operated their trade. The owner of the café that Siraj sat in front of while selling watches often stopped by to visit, and Siraj was occasionally invited to his home for holidays or other celebrations. Others, like Afwerk, depended on nearby shop owners to watch their equipment while they took breaks. Afwerk also stored his tools in a shop so that he would not have to take them home every night. Street workers also depended on neighboring businesses for continued social and political support. Although it was rarely enforced, working on the streets was technically illegal. Generally if there was no complaint from the surrounding business owners, the violation was overlooked. Business owners could also step in if the police were harassing a street worker and vouch for his character.

Street workers generally reciprocated the nonmaterial aid that they received in a subtle manner. Occasionally they participated in the general upkeep of the property surrounding their workplace. For example, I once paid a visit to Siraj and found him and the other watch vendors putting in concrete in front of the café where they sold watches. Possibly more importantly, the presence of loyal street workers provided a certain level of security for surrounding businesses. Not only were they an additional set of eyes, they generally were also well informed regarding gossip and rumors and could easily identify potential thieves.

The value of receiving social or political support from working youth varied with the individual. Social support from young men like Kassahun or Siraj did have some value. As I detail shortly, workers who demonstrated good business sense and ethics were the most likely candidates for receiving help from other business owners in expanding their business. Although these youth may have been able to offer only limited support at the moment, they had the potential to become valuable allies in the future.

Working youth tended to be on the receiving end of the zemed relationships that surrounded the workplace, but they were sometimes providers for zemed. For example, Getanet, the barber described in the previous chapter, had a brother learning in secondary school in another city. He frequently sent him money and occasionally gave small amounts of money to an uncle who lived in Jimma. This was difficult for him financially, but he felt that he did not have a choice in the matter. It was his responsibility to help his family, and to do otherwise would not feel right to him. Particularly youth like Getanet who had no living parents tried to provide some support for their family. However, the earnings of young workers were generally not adequate to provide significant help to zemed. Typically, working young men were not able to give more than thirty birr per month to their families. Youth like Siraj who did not live near their parents occasionally sent money, but most gifts were reserved for rare trips home. During Siraj's first trip home after three years, he spent two thousand birr he had saved on gifts for friends and family.

Taddesse, a particularly enterprising young man who managed to advance from shining shoes to renting bicycles to owning a small shop in a matter of a few years, was able to provide consistent support for his zemed. His shop did excellent business and he was able to support his mother and three young men that he referred to as "brothers," although only one shared Taddesse's biological parents. Taddesse was also able to provide his brothers with work, and they took over his old business of shining shoes and renting bicycles. While Taddesse's success was rare, it does reveal that given the chance, some young men were eager to reverse the flows of social income between themselves and their zemed. In the last month of my research, when Kassahun followed a path similar to that of Taddesse and moved into a full shop, he also passed on his old business to a young male zemed. Like Taddesse, he continued to receive profits from the business and therefore trust was essential, but he was also providing a chance for a young man with an interest in working to move up the economic ladder. In doing this, Taddesse and Kassahun were spreading their system of values to other youth. They financially rewarded other youth who were willing to do lower jobs such as shining shoes, thus putting their values into practice and encouraging others to pursue their aspirations through difficult manual work.

Both Taddesse and Kassahun were pious Orthodox Christians who did not chew khat and preferred to socialize with other Orthodox youth. In addition to helping youth who shared their interest in business, they supported practicing Orthodox Christians. In the case of working youth, involvement in religion appeared to be an effective means of channeling the redistribution of wealth. Unlike unemployed youth, working youth had regular access to money, and therefore it was useful for them to restrict many relationships while maintaining others. As in Parkin's study of the Giriama, religion enables the maintenance of some contacts while limiting others. The strong piety of Taddesse and Kassahun meant that unemployed youth would never ask them for money for khat or alcohol. In contrast, a person like Afwerk with a known love for honey wine and khat was an easy target for unemployed youth looking for a handout. At the same time that religion closes off some channels of redistribution, it opens others. Religious piety enables the creation of a bond with older, more successful followers of that religion. In the same manner in which Taddesse and Kassahun helped younger men whom they saw as following in their footsteps, they had the potential to appeal to their seniors for assistance. It may not be coincidence that the three working young men who successfully expanded their business during the course of my research were also the most pious individuals in my sample of ten.

The third young man who achieved this success was Siraj. Although he did not have family in Jimma, it was clear that within the Muslim community he had developed a number of useful contacts. In contrast to most other working and unemployed Muslim youth in my study, Siraj wore a beard, which was a sign of piety among Jimma Muslims. He also attended the mosque daily. As I walked down the street with Siraj, he often stopped and greeted older Muslim business owners. This may be contrasted with other working youth, who were generally ignored by their elders. The utility of Siraj's contacts became apparent when he took his business to the next level by purchasing a large amount of clothing and watches and moving to a rural area where goods could be sold at a much higher profit. In order to make this move he had saved money on his own, but he also needed to ask friends for startup capital. All of these friends were Muslim, and they gave him the money that he needed. The value of zemed relationships for working youth is not always reflected in their gift income that I documented with daily journals. Siraj received few gifts during the month that I tracked his income, but when he needed to expand his business he was able to quickly access close to 1,000 birr (around 120 U.S. dollars).

Flows of gifts between working youth and zemed served a number of purposes. For youth like Yosef and Teddy it was a bonus to their salary that implied an obligation to remain loyal to their employer. Youth like Siraj who accessed workspace through zemed relationships were dependent on zemed for their day-to-day ability to work. They could use these same zemed relationships in times of need to obtain capital necessary to expand their business. In the case of Kassahun and Taddesse, supporting zemed who shared similar values enabled them to diversify their business and access income from multiple sources. The common theme in each of these cases is that mutually beneficial relationships were constructed with other entrepreneurs. These relationships followed a "wealth in people/wealth in things" model. By accumulating people (zemed) to aid in their business, Kassahun and Taddesse were increasing their profits. As profits increased, wealth was distributed among their zemed, often in a manner that facilitated the accumulation of further profits. In the same manner, older, more established businessmen were receiving economic benefits through their relationships with working young men, and in turn they often provided support for working young men.

The Dynamics of Reciprocity among Unemployed Young Men

In Chapter 4, I argue that at a basic level, decisions about employment in urban Ethiopia may be conceived of in terms of a balance between maintaining relationships and accumulating material goods. By refusing to take on low-status work, unemployed young men decline to exchange their labor power for money. Their decision is an implicit statement that their position within relations of power in the act of exchange is more important than accessing material goods. The decision to work or not to work can therefore be understood partially in terms of a choice between income and social relations. To work in low-status occupations is to access money but close off certain social relations. To remain unemployed is to forgo an income in favor of preserving social relations. The preceding discussion has problematized this simple dichotomy between work as investing in material wealth and unemployment as investing in social relationships. As I argue in Chapter 4, working in the informal economy continually positions young men within relations of power in a manner that is evaluated negatively. Working young men, however, form numerous zemed relationships that generally conform to normative values concerning exchange and power.

Just as working young men often invested in social relationships, it appears that unemployed young men used people to access material wealth. In this section I describe how unemployed young men gave and received gifts, and in the following section I analyze these patterns in terms of differences in material accumulation based on their access to social relationships. Among the unemployed the most important sharing relationships for accessing income were with one's parents and zemed. For the generation of young men in my study, grandparents were of much less importance. In many cases young men's grandparents lived in rural areas, and they had little contact with them. All but three of the twenty unemployed young men who completed monthlong journals documenting their income and expenses lived with their parents. Parents were at the base of young men's ability to exist without work, because regardless of the parents' wealth, they always provided food and a bed to sleep on. One's parents were often a source of social identity as well that facilitated or constrained potentially valuable economic relationships. Although youth discourse concerning dependence focused primarily on relations with one's parents, it was just as common to receive cash and other gifts from zemed. Zemed potentially provided the additional benefit of access to work, and youth sometimes explained their unemployment by simply saying, "I have no zemed."

Unemployed young men received gift income from parents and zemed in a variety of ways. Some young men appeared to take every opportunity available to accompany zemed to the bus station. Before the bus departed, their zemed gave them a *wichey* (departing gift, given by the person who is leaving), often of five or ten birr. Many young men were able to see off zemed up to twice a week. Visits to the homes of zemed were not as common, but if the host was wealthy it was expected that at the end of the visit he might give the unemployed visitor a small gift of money. Unemployed young men sometimes directly asked their parents for money as well, usually under the pretext of needing cash for an acceptable activity such as watching a soccer match on digital satellite television. Once the money was received, it was spent almost immediately on khat, meals, drinks, or other items that could be shared with friends.

Although young women could potentially access opportunities for work or further education through parents and zemed, it was rare for them to receive money that could be spent at their own discretion. In general young women were encouraged to stay in the home, and therefore there was no need for them to have money that could be used for recreational activities in the city. On the other hand, there was a sense that men need to be active outside the house, and therefore giving a young man five birr to eat breakfast was a means of encouraging him to leave the home and engage with others through the act of shared consumption.

The shared nature of consumption meant that friendship was important for accessing gift income. Many youth were skeptical of befriending those who had "nothing to offer." In some cases this took precedence over similar interests when evaluating an individual's potential for friendship. Young men occasionally explained that they did not want to befriend those who "are like me" because there was nothing of value to be gained from them. A friend should have "use/value" (*tiqem*). This benefit could be the ability to directly give cash, teach a skill, or provide access to work. For example, one young man commented that he would like to befriend a barber because then he would be able to get free haircuts. Although in practice the formation of friendships is generally not this logical, these comments indicate that young men frequently conceptualized friendship in economic terms. As others have argued for more intimate relationships throughout Africa (Cole and Thomas 2009), it is not possible to describe friendships as being based exclusively on affection or material self-interest. Friendship without some form of economic exchange is almost inconceivable. In contrast to the Western cliché that friends and business do not mix, in urban Ethiopia friendship nearly always involves some sort of exchange, and exchange often involves friendship.

Among friends, redistribution of wealth usually took place in the form of invitations. The activities associated with invitations were essential for building positive relationships. With the exception of wealthy university students from Addis Ababa, in Jimma these types of invitations were generally restricted to men. Partially because of a lack of disposable income and partially because of cultural norms regarding spending time in public, it was rare for two young women to visit a café together. In this sense, the relationships that surrounded sharing were particular to young men.

In Chapter 2 I describe the hours of intense conversations and mental traveling associated with chewing khat. More mundane activities such as drinking coffee at a café were also important. A café in urban Ethiopia is an oasis of tranquillity within the chaos and dust of the city. For one or two birr it is possible to escape to a shaded table and enjoy a delicious beverage. On a personal level I have always been struck by how dusty streets littered with trash are also lined with so many well-maintained cafés. In comparison to cities in other countries I have visited in East Africa, the number and quality of cafés serving delicious beverages in urban Ethiopia is striking. To enjoy time with a friend and to be seen by others creates status on multiple levels. At a café conversation is enhanced and a positive relationship is produced. To visit a café or restaurant is also an act of conspicuous consumption. It was not uncommon for young men to linger for more than thirty minutes over an espresso. Seating at cafés is usually within public view, allowing the customer to see and be seen. It was an activity occasionally affordable by even the most cash-strapped young men I knew in Jimma, enabling them to both solidify and demonstrate their friendships.

In theory the distribution of invitations was based on one's ability to give and his friend's need. Depending on one's social network, invitations could be received once or twice a day or less than once in a week. Not sharing what one had contradicted the definition of friendship, and therefore it was clear that one who did not share was not a friend. If one person had money in his pocket today, he bought coffee for his friends. If the same person had money in his pockets tomorrow, he again bought coffee for his friends. Although I argue shortly that class influenced individual access to gift income, the social pressure to share among friends was thought to act as a leveling force.

While giving was generally conceived of as a freely chosen action from which one expected nothing in return, it was highly constrained along lines of gender. When a gift was passed from a man to a woman, young men nearly always expected that both parties were operating on the basis of self-interest. The man provided money and the woman provided intimacy that could take the form of sex, domestic help, or general affection.[1] Most young men did not consider the idea that either party might give freely to the other. Like Jennifer Cole's (2009) analysis of youth in urban Madagascar, men discursively constructed women as necessarily self-interested, whereas men were seen as giving to each other on the basis of real friendship. This expectation, combined with the general inability of women to access shared consumer activities, meant that the process of producing relationships and status through public consumption was highly gendered. Inviting a friend for khat, coffee, or lunch was a masculine activity in that it specifically produced relationships and status between men.

Accessing Material Wealth through Unemployment

I monitored twenty-eight unemployed and working young men's incomes from gifts and work for one month. The quantity of gifts unemployed young men received indicates that they were not necessarily sacrificing material wealth to preserve social relationships. By preserving social relationships through unemployment, young men may have been accessing things, in the manner suggested by the "wealth in people/wealth in things" model. I calculated the monetary value of young men's gifts of cash as well as khat, drinks, meals, and other invitations, and I label this value as gift income. A comparison between total income (including income from gifts, work, and room and board for young men living with their parents) received by working and unemployed youth is quite interesting. During the one-month period that I monitored their income, eleven of twenty unemployed youth received at least 60 percent of the average total income from work and gifts (515 birr/month—about 60 U.S. dollars) of the eight working youth in my study. Four unemployed youth had incomes greater than the monthly average for working youth. My sample of unemployed young men was selected with the intent of including roughly equal numbers of youth with low and high parental incomes. My sample, therefore, overrepresents the number of youth in Jimma with high parental incomes, as most youth are from poor families. However, it does reveal that primarily through gift income, unemployed young men from a particular background were able to acquire material wealth roughly equivalent to that received by working youth. There are certainly important issues with quantifying income from gifts in this manner, and I address those shortly, but first I examine some of the factors that led to such high disparities in gifts received by unemployed young men, both among themselves and relative to working young men.

In my study, four main factors appear to account for differences in gift incomes among the unemployed: head-of-household gender, parental income, the quality and quantity of one's zemed, and neighborhood of residence. To some extent it is possible to argue that differences in young men's gift incomes are based on class background—middle-class youth received more gifts than working-class youth. The importance of neighborhood and head-of-household gender, however, indicate that class alone is not enough to adequately explain stratification in access to gifts. I describe the cases of three young men to illustrate how multiple factors are interconnected, and the importance of relationships for income from gifts.

Ahmed's case demonstrates the manner in which unemployment could be a successful economic strategy for some young men, depending on their family background. At the time of my research, Ahmed was twenty-two years old and had been unemployed for the three years since he had finished secondary school. Although his father is from the distant Wollo region, his mother's family is from the area surrounding Jimma, and his extended family gave Ahmed a great deal of material support. He lived with his parents, who are both employed in relatively well-paid occupations. His father is a secondary school teacher and his mother is a government administrator. Although Ahmed had a driver's license, he had not been successful finding work. He explained that much of the work available to him was not desirable or suitable for someone with a twelfth-grade education. He claimed that in Ethiopia there is a problem of "talk," and he did not want an occupation that would cause others to speak about him negatively.

Ahmed lived in a neighborhood populated by other government workers, similar to his parents. He occasionally worked, usually performing odd jobs for neighbors. As for many young men from privileged backgrounds, the payment that Ahmed received for his work was relatively high. While young men like Berhanu, who is discussed shortly, received eight birr (the equivalent of slightly less than one U.S. dollar at the time of my research) for laying tile all day, Ahmed might get twenty birr for going to the market for his neighbor. More importantly, Ahmed also received a high amount of gifts and cash from family and friends. I tracked Ahmed's income for one month, and he received ninety-three birr from work and the equivalent of four hundred birr in cash gifts or invitations for meals, drinks, and khat. For Ahmed, gifts of five to ten birr from his parents were common, and friends or family sometimes paid for expensive meals such as *kitfo*[2] and beer that would cost more than twenty birr.

Gifts flowed through social relationships. Unemployed young men with access to valuable social relationships and relatively privileged family backgrounds similar to Ahmed's usually had high gift incomes. Ahmed's gift income was on the upper end of the spectrum among the twenty unemployed young men whose incomes I tracked, but his situation was not unique. Access to gift income was not based only on the class background of one's parents. Extended family, the presence of a male household head, and neighborhood of residence were also important.

The case of Berhanu demonstrates how multiple factors interacted to isolate many unemployed young men from the types of relationships that bring gift income. Berhanu was unemployed, and although he lived in the same neighborhood as Ahmed, his gift income was low. Berhanu's parents had moved to Jimma from the distant Amhara region, and except for his brothers he had little extended family in the area. His father was deceased and his mother supported him and his younger siblings by baking and selling *injera*. In terms of parental income, Berhanu was at the low end of my sample.

I was often told that baking *injera* is one of the worst forms of work, but it is also one of the few means that older, single, uneducated women have to support themselves. *Injera* is baked over an open fire, meaning that the work is hot and requires the inhalation of large amounts of smoke. Baking *injera* brings no regular contact with the community, except for the women or children who come to the house to make purchases. Gender roles reinforced the social isolation associated with Berhanu's mother's work. During my walks through the city I frequently encountered the fathers of other unemployed young men, running errands or chatting with friends over coffee. It would not have been appropriate for Berhanu's mother to move this freely through public space. While she often invited women to her house for coffee, they were of a similar economic standing, and these gatherings did not facilitate the development of a social network with individuals wealthier or more politically powerful than herself. Furthermore, her friends were other older women, and it was not possible for these women to have the sort of relationship with Berhanu that Ahmed could have with his father's friends. Most urban Ethiopians would view an older woman inviting a younger man for a meal as inappropriate. In contrast to Ahmed's four hundred birr, during the month I tracked Berhanu's income he received only forty-four birr in gifts or invitations. This disparity was typical of young men with their respective differences in head-of-household gender, extended family, and parental class.

Kebede's situation offers a further point of contrast. Kebede, a young man discussed in other chapters, lived in Mahel Ketema with both of his parents. His father was employed by the government at the city bus station, and his mother occasionally earned money by baking *injera* for other families. Kebede was a practicing Orthodox Christian. His mother was Oromo and his father was Kaffa, and he had a reasonably sized extended family in the area, placing him roughly in the middle of my sample in terms of his zemed network.

His father's job was to help passengers find their bus, load cargo, and generally ensure that the station was running smoothly. It was certainly not a well-paid or powerful position, and it required that Kebede's father perform significant amounts of manual labor. Despite these drawbacks, the job enabled Kebede's father to form social relationships with others. At the time of my research, he had been working at the bus station for nearly thirty years. Buses were the primary means of transportation between cities, and this meant that anyone economically or politically privileged enough to travel passed frequently through the bus station. Kebede's father's position afforded him ample time to meet travelers and gradually form friendships through repeated encounters. He was also able to bestow small favors on travelers. For example, he could reserve the best seats on a bus or advise travelers about which bus was scheduled to leave first. Kebede had five siblings, and aside from meals and a place to sleep he received little from his parents in the way of material support. While he received only 39 birr in cash, he received the equivalent of 205 birr in gifts (excluding room and board). A large amount of his gift income was from friends of his father and reflects the economic value of a social network based in adult men. For example, at one point during the month that I monitored Kebede's income, a friend of his father's visited and purchased multiple meals for Kebede, each valued at five to eight birr. In 2005 Kebede had been unemployed for three years, and his long-term chances of finding desirable employment were unclear. However, at least for the moment, the gender and occupation of the primary wage earner in his household appeared to enable him to engage in desirable sharing relationships.

Neighborhood is an additional factor that affected unemployed young men's access to gift income. The unemployed young men who participated in my study came from five different neighborhoods. These neighborhoods represent three general types: low income with low market activity, mixed income with high market activity, and mixed income with low market activity. I have already provided detailed descriptions of each of these neighborhood types in Chapter 1. Sa'ar Sefer is an example of a low-income, low-market-activity neighborhood; Kulo Berr is an example of a mixed-income, high-market-activity neighborhood; and Qottebe Sefer is an example of a mixed-income, low-market-activity neighborhood.

Neighborhood influenced both the quantity and quality of flows of money among youth. In a neighborhood like Sa'ar Sefer, the lack of trade meant that even the small amount of capital that was present did not tend to change hands often. Although nearly everyone in Kulo Berr was poor, money was constantly circulating in the form of cash or invitations. Mahel Ketema, literally "city center," was a similar neighborhood, and Kebede's residence there most likely contributed to his high gift income. Many of the unemployed young men in neighborhoods like this occasionally earned money from work or knew others who had regular incomes that they were willing to share. In an environment of high trade volumes, profits were quickly earned and lost. Sharing provided a form of security. A young man could not be guaranteed to have money tomorrow, so by sharing with his friends he could ensure that he would at least be able to access small amounts of pocket money. In Qottebe Sefer, many youth had parents who were middle-class government employees and provided them with frequent cash handouts. Unlike the Kulo Berr youth, they did not depend on trade, and parental salaries provided a dependable source of income. Therefore wealthy young men in Qottebe Sefer had nothing to gain by sharing with youth from poor families. There was little incentive for someone like Ahmed to share his gift income with Berhanu, and this is an additional reason why young men like Berhanu had low gift incomes relative to their peers in high-market neighborhoods. If sharing of wealth did take place, it was within class groups and therefore did not function as a means of redistribution.

Young men were not unaware of the manner in which class often structured sharing relationships. They explained that sharing was the norm, but problems sometimes occurred when a person felt that others were simply using his friendship for personal gain. As long as it was felt that the friendship was based on a personal bond or genuine affection, then people were happy to give. For this reason, youth sometimes claimed that friendships worked better between youth of the same economic background. A young man who was always being invited by his friends without the ability to return their generosity would "feel something." Youth sometimes argued that the poor did not want to be friends with the rich because they would be unable to invite them in the manner to which they were accustomed. In this sense, class barriers that prevented sharing were justified on the basis of the emotional state of the poor.

The great variance in gift income received by unemployed young men complicates the contrast with working young men that I have outlined. Working and unemployment cannot be conceived of as a simple trade-off between maintaining relationships and accessing income. Many unemployed young men appear to have accomplished both, avoiding low-status work and receiving high gift incomes. On the other hand, depending largely on family background and neighborhood of residence, other unemployed young men were isolated from the relationships that brought gift income. The relationships that young men like Berhanu preserved by avoiding low-status work appear to be of little economic value. In the following section I complicate this situation further by examining contrasts in how unemployed and working young men used income they received from gifts. A closer analysis of gifting among unemployed young men reveals problems with quantifying gift income and indicates that inequality cannot be conceptualized only in terms of differences in material wealth.

Expanding Relationships through Redistribution

The evidence I have offered concerning unequal distribution of gift income among unemployed youth seems to indicate that reciprocity may reproduce class-based inequalities. Although gifting is often explained in terms of altruistic sharing, quantifying gift incomes reveals that high levels of gifts often flow toward those with relatively privileged backgrounds. In Pierre Bourdieu's terms, it appears that a devotion to the accumulation of symbolic capital masks real economic differences in access to gift income. Bourdieu has suggested that economic calculation must be extended to *"all* the goods, material and symbolic, without distinction, that present themselves as *rare* and worthy of being sought after in a particular social formation" (1977: 178). Bourdieu's insight is useful in that evaluating differences in young men's accumulation of social relationships illuminates patterns of stratification. However, I disagree with Bourdieu regarding the necessary interconvertibility of economic and symbolic capital. To insist on converting between social relationships and economic goods obscures the manner in which differences in control over social relationships may function as a distinct source of inequality. This weakness is found in many influential analyses of youth, aspirations, and class. For example, in discussing youth aspirations, Paul Willis (1977) and Jay MacLeod (2009) give great attention to the role of culture in leading young people to make certain choices about their lives and occupational futures. They do not, however, acknowledge that the prestige associated with cultivating different cultural styles may be an intrinsic source of inequality, regardless of its implications for class. Bourdieu's call for an "economy of practices" (1977: 183) is useful, as long as one form of practice is not prioritized over another. Unemployed young men's specific gifting practices complicate materialist analyses of inequality. Differences in access to gift income are certainly important, but their implications for material accumulation are ambiguous, and inequalities are better understood in terms of access to relationships. Gifting is similar to consumption in the sense that how one gives signals a particular identity and places one within a status hierarchy.

Although gifts received by working young men were often invested in their businesses, almost without exception cash and other gifts received by unemployed young men were immediately redistributed among their peers. If Ahmed, for example, received ten birr from a family member, he usually bought a large bundle of khat to consume with his friends. In no case did unemployed young men save gift income to invest it in a small business or pursue a different long-term goal. In interviews the possibility of doing so was not even mentioned. Gift income was always devoted to immediate and shared consumption. This was true of unemployed young men regardless of their class background.

Young men's immediate redistribution of their gift income indicates that it is not a direct source of long-term inequalities in access to material goods. For unemployed young men, gift income was valuable because of its implications for social relationships. To give implied the existence of a relationship, and not to give indicated that a relationship did not exist. The close connection between sharing and relationships among young men is seen in their creative use of the Amharic term *finter*. In its more formal use, *finter* describes the expansion of a spring or a similar item after it has been released. When finter is used informally by young people, it refers to a particular type of gift that is given to friends after one has acquired something good. The size of a finter depends on the level of one's good fortune. If a young man is wearing a new shirt for the first time, it is expected that he will purchase coffee or tea for his close friends; a new bicycle might require a finter of lunch and khat. Just as things that rest on an expanding spring are elevated, friends of an individual who has experienced good luck expect their fortunes to rise as well.

Conflicts often arose when there was a disjuncture between reciprocity and relationships. During the month that I monitored the income of an unemployed young man named Tsehay, he won a small lottery. The lottery was sponsored by Pepsi-Cola and the prize was a bicycle. Well before the prize was received, Tsehay had arranged a buyer for the cycle, and his friends eagerly anticipated their finter. At the time that he won the prize, Tsehay had been unemployed for around five years. He had an extensive social network and was never short on pocket money, but he had not had a considerable amount of cash for a long time and he was looking forward to buying himself new clothes and shoes. He budgeted some of his money for the finter, and purchased lunch and khat for a group of his friends. The problem came when his friend Alemu felt that the finter was too small and refused to accept it. Tsehay and Alemu were good friends, but they did not speak for nearly a week as a result of this conflict. Eventually Tsehay purchased extra khat for Alemu, and although this did not satisfy his demands, he accepted the gift in order to preserve their friendship.

On a much smaller scale, these sorts of interactions took place every day. Continual invitations were necessary to preserve relationships. When it was felt that one had the ability to invite but chose not to, a serious conflict could arise. The movement of goods from one person to another is thought to operate like the laws of physics, in that each force creates an equal and opposite force. To receive good fortune without sharing is like a spring contracting and expanding in isolation—physically impossible. To receive is also to give. In critiquing Tsehay's behavior, his friend Alemu drew attention to gifts that he had given Tsehay in the past as a sign that a relationship existed between them. Alemu was demanding not a particular sum of money but that Tsehay acknowledge their friendship through sharing. The issue of ownership or rights to property was not relevant to this conflict. Instead it was a matter of maintaining relationships.

Stratification in this case is certainly not divorced from material dynamics. Young men were more likely to participate in sharing relationships if they had wealthy parents. However, these differences are best conceived of not as long-term inequalities in access to economic goods but in terms of access to relationships. The situation faced by young men in urban Ethiopia resembles Marilyn Strathern's analysis of gift exchange in Melanesia. Strathern (1988) argued that in the Melanesian context, social relations are intrinsically desirable, not simply for their utility in accessing material goods. She explains that "in a gift economy, we might argue that those who dominate are those who determine the connections and disconnections created by the circulation of objects" (1988: 167). The same dynamic appears to be at work in urban Ethiopia, where unemployed young men from particular backgrounds have a greater ability to create relationships with others through giving and receiving gifts. The fact that these gifts are immediately invested in other relationships indicates that the value of relationships cannot solely be assessed in terms of their implications for facilitating access to material wealth. Relationships are intrinsically valuable and constitute a distinct source of inequality.

Conceptualizing relationships as an intrinsic source of inequality is necessary for two primary reasons. First, as I argued in the previous chapter, among unemployed youth, labor or one's occupation was not necessarily conceived of in terms of production. One's occupation was a means of establishing an identity that influenced the manner in which one related to others. The productive result of labor was not as important as the manner in which the act of working situated one within relations of power and exchange. Second, although unemployed youth sometimes received large amounts of gift income, it does not make sense to analyze this in terms of an appropriation of the surplus labor of others. As Strathern (1988) explains, the problem with materialist perspectives is the assumptions they make regarding the relationship between individuals and property. "As long as things are 'owned' or the 'use value' of labor is enjoyed, the one-to-one relationship between proprietor and product is assumed" (Strathern 1988: 158). Materialist-based notions of inequality rest on the assumption that one has a right to the product of his or her labor. In the case of unemployed young men, gifts were conceived of as the product of social relationships and not individual labor, and these gifts were immediately directed toward communal consumption. Therefore, in giving and receiving young men were not necessarily alienating others or themselves from the product of their labor.

Charles Piot (1999) draws on Strathern's work in his analysis of gift exchange among the Kabre of Togo. Piot deconstructs the tension between the accumulation of material goods and social relationships by arguing that the economically rational individual is often an inappropriate unit of analysis. Theories in which an "individual's interest is seen as opposed to the interest of other individuals" should not be applied to settings in which individuals are not conceived of as distinct from each other (Piot 1999: 16). In contexts such as these, the division between individual and community is not possible. Piot claims that "persons here do not 'have' relations; they 'are' relations" (1999: 18). If individuals are conceived of in terms of relationships rather than discretely acting subjects, then it would appear to be logically impossible to oppose individual accumulation and investment in social relationships. Ultimately, Piot argues that even when Kabre migrant laborers appear to be accumulating material goods, they are in fact investing in relationships (1999: 170–171).

Piot's argument would seem to undermine the contrast I originally constructed between working and unemployed young men. If relationships are the ultimate goal of exchange, then it is nonsensical to argue that some exchanges contribute to the maintenance of relationships while others facilitate material accumulation. Patterns of reciprocity among unemployed young men appear to support this point. In giving a finter, for example, material goods are tools employed to expand relationships, and using these goods to accumulate more commodities or money is not a relevant possibility.

However, unemployed young men's tendency to use gifting to expand relationships should not imply that the notion of an individual subject accumulating material goods is irrelevant in urban Ethiopia. Young men's gifting behavior clearly cannot be interpreted in terms of economic rationalism, but this does not mean that social relationships are never used specifically to accumulate privately owned material goods. In the tension concerning Tsehay's finter discussed earlier, the finter is treated as both a qualitative gift and a quantitative commodity. On one hand the finter was a gift reinforcing a bond among friends. Tsehay purchased khat and lunch for his friends in exchange for their continued support and friendship. On the other hand, to some extent Alemu was clearly evaluating this exchange from a quantitative perspective. Although he was not able to state exactly what the monetary value of Tsehay's finter should be, he was clear that it was not large enough. Alemu was not putting a specific price on his friendship, but he was perhaps making a ballpark estimate. For the most part the finter is best understood as a qualitative exchange, but it certainly had a quantitative dimension as well. In this sense, the maintenance of a strict dichotomy between multiple forms of inequality and exchange is not possible.

In a given time and place the balance between social relationships and material accumulation may be experienced differently by different people, and multiple forms of inequality may exist simultaneously. In the discussion that follows I argue that although relationships and material accumulation are always connected, at various points in time one may be prioritized over another. Shifts in the prioritization of relationships and material goods are also related to changes in the nature of inequality.

Neoliberal Capitalism and Shifting Inequalities

In Chapter 4, I explain that relations among government workers were based in complete dependence. An individual's position was dependent on the person above him. Maintenance of that position depended on a qualitatively positive relationship. The government worker received or gave on the basis of a close relationship that extended beyond the workplace into all areas of life. In contrast, young men working in low-status jobs in the informal economy usually gave their service only in exchange for something predetermined and specific that was confined to the moment of exchange. On the basis of the model associated with government employment, unemployed young men sought to attain their aspirations through social relationships.

Pierre Bourdieu has argued that aspirations often conform to one's objective chances in life. One of the exceptions to this pattern is "given by historical conjunctures of a revolutionary nature in which changes in objective structures are so swift that agents whose mental structures have been molded by these prior structures become obsolete and act inopportunely" (Bourdieu and Wacquant 1992: 130). This appears to be the case for many unemployed youth whose aspirations for government employment have suddenly become nearly impossible to attain.

In avoiding low-status work, unemployed young men were employing economic and social strategies that had been highly effective for their parents' generation. In contrast to the present, in the past this model of behavior allowed one to simultaneously invest in relationships and gain access to material goods. Many of the parents of young men in my study migrated from the countryside surrounding Jimma at a young age. Few of them finished secondary school, but for the most part they were eventually able to secure employment using social connections. For example, the father of an unemployed young woman in my study moved to Jimma in the 1960s from the nearby Dawro region. He explained that he was a "lower person" during the reign of Haile Selassie. His parents were tenant farmers and there was no school near their home. He claimed that even if there had been a school, only children of the Amhara landowners would have attended. He came to Jimma in search of wage labor. After holding a number of temporary jobs, he found work as a guard at the Jimma Agricultural College. When he arrived in Jimma he had little knowledge of Amharic and relied on the help of a few extended family members. He was involved in the Orthodox Christian Church and the neighborhood *iddir*, and these relationships were adequate for securing desirable employment.[3]

For the generation of young men in my study, however, a secondary school degree and numerous family connections were not enough to secure even a low-level government position. The downsizing of the public sector combined with an increase in the number of graduates meant that government jobs were no longer available. Fewer public sector jobs also meant that government employees had a reduced ability to distribute goods and opportunities within their community. For the most part, the model of behavior pursued by unemployed young men was no longer viable for developing relationships and acquiring material goods.[4]

With the previous link between social relationships, government employment, and economic stratification decoupled through the downsizing of the public sector, processes of reciprocity among young men continued to produce inequalities in control over relationships. However, these inequalities are distinct from the past in that they have fewer direct implications for accessing material wealth. As the concept of the finter demonstrates, among unemployed young men, the ability to give and receive is valued for its power in causing the self to expand and contract through social relationships. This is an intrinsic source of inequality. It is not that control over social relationships was never an independent source of inequality in the past. In the present context, however, the importance of social relationships as a source of inequality is heightened, as they are increasingly independent of materially based differences.

This shift has not been complete. Young men from privileged backgrounds like Ahmed's have a greater ability to participate in relations of reciprocity. Ahmed, for example, eventually took a job at a photo-processing shop. Although this was not his ideal position, the association with technology and lack of manual labor provided a degree of prestige. Ahmed was certainly not unique, and in many cases young men from similar backgrounds eventually attain a desirable job after an extended period of unemployment. My argument is not that one form of inequality replaces another but that the balance between the two shifts.

The decoupling of social relationships and material accumulation functions in a different but related manner for young men working in low-status jobs. In the past, government employment was a source of both status and relatively high income, while entrepreneurial work in the urban informal economy was highly stigmatized and offered little more than a subsistence-level income. Although informal entrepreneurial jobs continue to be stigmatized, limits on the accumulation of wealth appear to have relaxed (Ellison 2006). After the fall of the Marxist "Derg" regime in 1991, the downsizing of the public sector coincided with an increase in opportunities for workers in the informal economy to expand their businesses.

The example of Siraj, the street-side watch vendor discussed earlier, demonstrates the potential for young men in the informal economy to significantly improve their fortunes. Siraj's ability to expand his business depended on social relationships, indicating that a distinct split between relationships and material accumulation has not occurred. However, despite Siraj's reliance on a small number of zemed relationships, more broadly his work was highly stigmatized. Siraj was not the only participant in my research to dramatically change his economic fortunes over the course of a couple of years. Others established small shops or became taxi drivers. Participation in the informal economy was not a guarantee of economic success, but for many it provided working young men with a significant source of income despite the low status that was generally associated with their occupations.

Conclusion

In this chapter I have examined relations of reciprocity among unemployed and working young men to develop a number of different points of analysis. I began by arguing that for both unemployed and working young men, people and things are inextricable. Both groups of young men use relationships to access things. There are, however, important differences in how young men dispose of the things they have accumulated through relationships. Working young men generally invest in their businesses, thus converting people into things that are then used to accumulate more things. In contrast, unemployed young men immediately redistribute gifts among their peers. In this sense, relationships are used to access things that are then converted into more relationships. Based on the gifting practices of unemployed young men, I have argued that materialist conceptions of inequality must be complemented with a notion of relationships as an intrinsic source of inequality. Finally, I have discussed changes in the balance between investing in relationships and material wealth with the passage of time. Anthropologists have critiqued linear notions of change in which engagement with a market economy causes individual accumulation of wealth to be prioritized over social relationships. Although critiques of linear social change are useful, it is still important to examine shifts in the balance between relationships and things that occur over time. In the case of urban Ethiopia, I have argued that policies associated with neoliberal capitalism have decoupled social relationships from material accumulation. This disconnection is not complete, but the close connection between relationships and material accumulation that existed in the past is no longer present.

Returning to the issue of hope, this chapter demonstrates that different strategies for attaining hope produce particular forms of inequality. In previous chapters I examined the importance of young men's values and notions of what it means to be modern for the construction of hope. Here and in the previous chapter it has become apparent that these notions of modernity are related to specific economic strategies, in terms of both work and reciprocity. The hopes of many young men to experience progress within their social relationships leads them to avoid work in the informal economy and invest heavily in the maintenance of relationships. Young men who are not as concerned with normative conceptions of a progressive good life are more likely to take on low-status jobs and the patterns of accumulating things and people that accompany these positions.

Strategies for attaining hope are also linked with the reproduction and subversion of class-based stratification. In striving for progress in their social relationships, young men are enacting what has historically been a middle-class strategy that is associated with education and government employment. For those who already have middle-class social networks and access to wealth, these hopes are attainable—if not immediately, perhaps after a few years of unemployment. For those without these resources, the downsizing of the public sector means that investing heavily in relationships is no longer a viable strategy for class mobility. On the other hand, young men from working-class backgrounds have demonstrated some ability to rapidly increase their wealth through working in stigmatized occupations. It remains to be seen if these young men will be able to translate their material wealth into the high status that has historically accompanied wealth in Ethiopia. It is, however, clear that the economic success of some entrepreneurs in the informal economy indicates that while class hierarchies are not completely destabilized, certain ruptures and possibilities for change have been created.

Finally, without taking away from the importance of class in this case, my analysis should also make clear that class alone is not an adequate concept for understanding the reproduction of material inequality. In the Ethiopian case, neighborhood of residence and head of household gender have significant impacts on young men's gift incomes. These factors certainly do have a relationship with class, but they are in many ways distinct as well. They point to the importance of gender and spatial dynamics in influencing young men's opportunities to accumulate both material wealth and social relationships.

6

Spatial Fixes to Temporal Problems

Migration, Social Relationships, and Work

I n previous chapters I describe how young men experienced unemployment as a problem of time. Many young men believed that their temporal problems could be addressed with spatial solutions, particularly international migration, preferably to the United States or Europe. In the narratives of young men, time was experienced differently outside Ethiopia. As Alemu, an unemployed young man in his late twenties, put it, "I can do more in six months in America [the United States] than I can in five years in Ethiopia. In America there is progress." In this chapter, I describe the variable ways that migration was conceived of as a solution to problems of time. In both discourse and practice, international migration, particularly to the United States, was a key strategy that young men used to move toward their hopes for the future.

That migration is conceived of as a solution to problems faced by urban young men at the turn of the twenty-first century should not imply that it is a new phenomenon in Ethiopia, where men and women, rural and urban, have historically been highly mobile (Baker 1986). An extensive literature exists describing the importance of migration in Africa for accumulating the resources necessary to take on the role of an adult, usually in relation to accessing urban wage labor. For example, in Sharon Hutchinson's (1996) study of the Nuer, she describes young men performing urban wage labor to accumulate the cash necessary to return home, expand their cattle herd, and start a family. Others have argued that accessing modern qualities of space are as important for motivating migration as differences in economic opportunity (Newell 2005). Accumulating wealth and accessing modernity are both important motivations for Ethiopian young men's desires to migrate. The Ethiopian case is distinct, however, because it is not only differences in access to material goods or qualities associated with modernity that motivate migration. Rather, young men seek to leave Ethiopia partially because of differences in the way individuals are thought to interact in different spaces. People of all ages in Jimma construct spatial difference through bounded notions of culture, particularly as it relates to social relationships. I argue that the connection between social relationships and migration supports a rethinking of space. Just as I argue that time is measured in terms of changes in social relationships, spatial movement repositions oneself in relation to others, and this allows space to function as a solution to problems of time.

Being and Becoming through the Diversity Visa Lottery

The rise of the Diversity Visa (DV) lottery as a means of experiencing change or progress represents the transition from temporal to spatial strategies for attaining one's aspirations. Although few U.S.-born citizens know about the annual DV lottery, it is eagerly anticipated in much of the world. The opportunity of using the DV lottery to migrate partially explains the prominent role of the United States in youth discourse concerning international migration. The history of Ethiopian migration to the United States, particularly as political asylum seekers during the Marxist Derg regime, has also created extensive networks of Ethiopian Americans that provide support for new migrants.

Every year fifty thousand winners from countries around the world are selected through the DV lottery to receive a U.S. visa. To be a DV applicant, one must be a secondary school graduate, have a sponsor in the United States (someone who will provide initial support), and a job skill. Many Ethiopians who entered the United States in the 1990s and 2000s had a family member with a Diversity Visa or won a lottery themselves. Although Ethiopia receives a relatively high number of Diversity Visas,[1] the roughly four thousand winners who migrate to the United States every year via the lottery are a small fraction of those who enter the lottery. For most, the lottery is a dream that takes the place of working locally and participating in a temporal narrative of becoming.

Winning the DV lottery does not fit into a larger narrative of progress. Unlike with education, a person does not win the DV lottery because he or she has followed a set of rules for development or passed through a series of stages. It simply happens or it does not, according to chance. Access to technology, wealth, and the prestige of living in the United States is acquired not through the self-discipline necessary to advance from education to employment but through good luck. In the absence of a temporal process of *becoming*, the DV Lottery is a spatial strategy that instantly allows one to *be* modern.

Jane Guyer argues that within the temporal reorientations of the twenty-first century, time is conceived of in terms of particular dates that are qualitatively distinct in their potential to change one's life (2007: 416). The DV Lottery exemplifies the condition of waiting for a significant event. In Jimma the DV lottery was more of a season of activity than a specific day. Prior to the acceptance of applications, advertisements are posted at Internet cafés, and a sense of excitement gradually builds. Applicants needing assistance with the online process crowd the Internet cafés, and then a period of waiting begins. The possibility of receiving an acceptance letter causes visits to the post office to be charged with excitement. Rumors regarding the identities of successful applicants quickly sweep through the city.

Vincent Crapanzano (2003) has argued that a key distinction between hope and desire is that one's hopes are ultimately in the hands of fate. One may actively pursue desire, but in the case of hope a degree of passive waiting is required. In urban Ethiopia the DV lottery combines passive hope with active desire. Entering the lottery certainly requires a specific set of actions aimed at changing one's relationship to his future. As I explained in Chapter 2, the active day-to-day construction of narratives in which one is able to travel abroad is also important for this process. On the other hand, the narrative of attaining a desirable future through the lottery is ultimately based on faith and hope. Actually winning a Diversity Visa relies on intervention from a distant and abstract entity—the U.S. government.[2] The DV lottery is so pervasive as a "myth-dream"[3] because it is based on specific actions that occur at regular intervals of time that have been proven to generate desired results. Every year a new batch of DV winners provides young men with evidence of the potential for success.

The nature of the DV lottery amplifies the possibility for sudden and complete transformation that is a general aspect of migration. The disconnection between the present and the future can be overcome, not by a particular series of steps but through a life-changing event. Youth narratives often constructed migration as facilitating a transformation of identity. The notion that migration and the appropriation of stylistic practices (particularly fashion) may allow a recreation of one's identity has been effectively explored in other studies of urban youth in Africa (De Boeck 1999; Friedman 1994; Hansen 2000; Gondola 1999; MacGaffey and Bazenguissa-Ganga 2000; Newell 2005). In relation to the Congolese subculture of La Sape, Gondola (1999) writes that "popular culture allows African urban youth to build a dreamlike order, otherwise unreachable" (24), and "the sapeur does not dress like a CEO to imitate the CEO. He is a CEO" (32). Newell (2005) extends this analysis of popular culture and argues that migration is also a form of consumption. Migration is in part a symbolic process that allows the traveler to accumulate cultural capital through an association with "modern" or "developed" world areas. In conceiving of migration as a symbolic act, one's identity is transformed through association with place without personally undergoing a temporal process of becoming.

During an afternoon that I spent with Habtamu and his friends as they chewed khat and talked, Habtamu told me about a dream he had the night before: "I was in New York City at an amazing club. We were dancing and drinking, and it was wonderful. Jennifer [Lopez] was singing. You were there too. I didn't want to wake up." "Dreaming" about life in America was also a common activity among young men during the day as they chewed khat and talked. Hours were spent talking about different cities, speculating about life there and the possibility of meeting different celebrities. From Ethiopia this lifestyle can only be dreamed of, but if one wins the DV lottery, the dream becomes a reality.

Young men believed that actually moving to this world that was usually accessed only through dreams caused a complete transformation. That same afternoon one of Habtamu's friends showed me "before and after" photographs of his brother—one before his departure for America and one after. The difference was not immediately apparent to me, but he explained, "Of course, he has become fat, but the really beautiful thing is his skin. His skin glows. Before he was old and starving, but now in America he is young and healthy." According to these young men, America is a land where there are no beggars, everyone is fat, and people pay the equivalent of half a month's salary for a low-level Ethiopian government worker to have their dogs washed. In response to my attempts to provide a more complete picture of life in the United States, Habtamu shouted, "Listen, Danny, the life of a dog in America is better than a human in Ethiopia!"

In discussing Western pop culture and comparing Ethiopia to the United States, young men were defining their own lives in terms of absence—the absence of entertainment, the absence of health, and the absence of modernity. These narratives are similar to Charles Piot's (2005) notion of "living in exile" within one's own country, or the "second-hand" relationship to modernity that Craig Jeffrey (2010) describes among young men in northern India. To migrate was to transform oneself completely and access the life that one deserved. Like the statement "we live like chickens," the comparison with the life of a dog implies that something is not quite human about life in Ethiopia. One cannot really be a full person without leaving the country.

In seeking to migrate to America, young men were attempting to access qualities of place associated with an imagined lifestyle. The United States had certain symbolic qualities, and young men sought *being*, or instant transformation, through association with those qualities. To solve problem of overaccumulation within the context of late capitalism, signs are produced in a manner that generates qualitatively different opportunities to consume (Baudrillard 1982; Harvey 1990: 287). Like Newell's discussion of youth in Cote d'Ivoire (2005), the semiotic processes on which some Ethiopian youth narratives of migration depended function in a similar manner to the consumption of symbols that is associated with a late capitalist economy. To migrate or to appropriate Western goods was to reference place in a way that allowed one to instantly be modern.

In their discussion of the symbolic manipulations of the spectacular subculture of La Sape, MacGaffey and Bazenguissa-Ganga draw attention to the potential for subverting power relationships that exists in relation to these practices. "They [sapeurs] have created their own world with its own status and value system and its own scale of achievement and satisfaction, and they have rejected the values of a system that has excluded and marginalized them" (2000: 157). In other words, referencing other places through stylistic practices enables youth to transgress the economic constraints that they face, thus reconstructing relations of power. Although a specific argument regarding power relations is not necessarily made, other discussions of consumer practices among African youth have argued that identities constructed through consumption place youth in a different and perhaps better world (Masquelier 2005; Weiss 2002). I do not dispute the transformative potential of discourses and practices that are associated with consumption and referencing other places. Analyses of these practices reveal that they are potentially liberating for dominated groups and individuals. However, this type of analysis does not address power relations associated with lived social relationships and economic stratification. Knowing that youth create their own world does not bring us any closer to understanding the inequalities that may exist in that world. James Ferguson (2006) offers a similar critique of alternative or local modernities. Ferguson explains that anthropological analyses of modernity have tended to examine locally specific modernities that emerge within different spaces. While Ferguson acknowledges the insights that these analyses provide, he also notes that they are "a happy story about plurality and non-ranked cultural difference" that neglects "relatively fixed global statuses and a detemporalized world socioeconomic hierarchy" (2006: 192). In other words, although sapeurs may employ stylistic practices to excel in a specifically urban Congolese form of modernity, this does not change their subjugated position within a global economic hierarchy.

Ferguson makes the same argument that I have developed in relation to the DV lottery: that when economic changes, like rising unemployment, prevent progress or development through time, difference is mapped onto space. This spatial difference becomes more or less fixed, meaning that individuals may access progress only through moving from one place to another. While I believe Ferguson offers a powerful argument for giving more attention to global socioeconomic hierarchies in relation to analyses of modernity, in Jimma I did not find that young people saw themselves "not as 'less developed' but simply as less" (Ferguson 2006: 189). While young men clearly felt that Ethiopia was "backward" (hwalaker), they did not transpose this evaluation onto themselves. As the narratives surrounding migration described in this chapter indicate, young men believed that one's personal relationship to modernity could be overcome with spatial movement.

My research indicates that the problem of experiencing progress through time was closely related to local values surrounding occupation and status. In the sections that follow, I describe the importance of migration for repositioning oneself within social relations. Like space and time, social relations and their relative importance for economic stratification are key for understanding the place of urban Ethiopia within a global economy.

Progressing within Social Relationships through Migration

While narratives surrounding migration did reflect a desire to transform one-self through symbolic association with particular qualities of place, they were also concerned with repositioning oneself in relation to family and community. During the course of my research, Solomon, the unemployed young man dis-cussed in Chapter 3, became so frustrated with his inability to progress that he left Jimma to go to the Gambella region, near the Sudan border, where it was rumored that well-paid work could be had on a Chinese oil-drilling project. Although Gambella was unstable at the time and outbreaks of violence were common, Solomon explained that it was better to die there than to wait for death in Jimma. This way at least a good story would be told about him, but staying in Jimma would be to continue a life that lacked meaning.

Solomon's case reflects the manner in which the aspirations and conse-quent economic behavior of young men were related to a desire to reposition themselves socially. Solomon had some practical experience and technical edu-cation, and he was capable of working in a garage. However, as he explained, marriage, supporting a family, and experiencing progress required far more money then he could access through this type of work. Therefore, he chose to migrate in order to transform his life from simply passing day after day without change to moving toward improvement in his relationship with his parents and community. Solomon's example is perhaps a little extreme in that he chose to leave Jimma in search of work. While most men did not actually leave, in their narratives migration was often a solution to the problem of fulfilling their aspirations regarding family and community. The desire to leave Ethiopia was nearly universal, and the plan to return was almost as common. Youth spoke about sending money home while they were abroad and then eventually return-ing with enough resources to raise a family and start a business or development project that would benefit the community. Young men claimed that before mar-riage they first needed to help their parents and siblings. Once their immedi-ate family was in a good situation, they could start a family of their own. This aspiration may be contrasted with the actual situation in which young men depended on parents and family members for meals, spending money, and a place to sleep.

The notion that migration enabled young men to access the resources nec-essary to change their relationship with the community was based largely on almost mythic stories about Ethiopians living abroad. One such story comes from an unemployed young man who had completed secondary school but failed the matriculation exam to advance to the postsecondary level. During the Marxist Derg regime, a friend of his family received a low exam result and was not able to advance to the university. A friend in the United States wrote letters and did everything necessary to get him a visa. In the United States he worked at small jobs and took classes on piloting airplanes. In time he was able to get a pilot's license, return to Ethiopia, and buy two airplanes. He currently runs a successful business in Ethiopia and supports his entire family. The young storyteller emphasized that travel to the United States was essential for this man's success. There is no opportunity to study airplanes in Ethiopia. In Ethiopia failing one's matriculation exam closed off all possibilities for a successful future, but migration enabled opportunity and success that could eventually be brought home.

In contrast to being modern through the symbolic transformation just described, in narratives like this one spatial movement allowed young men to reenter linear processes of progress through time. Instead of taking the place of a temporal process, spatial movement facilitates progress. Migration enables one to engage in the process of education and reposition oneself within local social relationships. The narrative of progress that was fractured with the failure to find employment after leaving school is reconstructed.

These stories were reinforced by the easily observed accomplishments of those who had left the country. In 2007 an Ethiopian American completed construction on a hotel that at four stories was the tallest building in Jimma outside the university. I sometimes pushed youth on the notion that progress could be accessed only abroad and brought up examples of successful businessmen in Jimma who had begun as shoeshines. They acknowledged that this had been possible in the past but claimed that today working at small jobs no longer brought the opportunity for progress. Quite simply, progress could not be had without spatial change.

This attitude was based partially on a conception of the West as a place that was far more open in terms of opportunity and partially on a raw economic calculus. Ahmed, an unemployed young man described in previous chapters, once explained to me that if he had thirty thousand birr, he would not invest it in a business in Ethiopia. Instead he would use the money to travel abroad. Once he was abroad he would work sixteen hours a day at different jobs and quickly reap a great profit from the money he had invested in migration. Young people were quite aware of the exchange rate between dollars and birr (around 8.5 birr to one dollar at the time of my research), and that in America workers are paid by the hour, not by the day. Youth frequently said that they wanted to work two jobs or simply "twenty-four hours a day" once they were out of Ethiopia.

Both the narratives and practices of changing social relationships through migration were highly gendered. In practice, young women were far more likely to leave Ethiopia than any other population group. Most of these young women traveled to the Middle East,[4] where they worked primarily as domestic servants. Salaries for domestic servants were generally a standard one hundred U.S. dollars per month plus room and board. Although workers sometimes had to pay their employers back for the price of transportation, in most cases they were able to consistently send money home. In some cases young women returned home after completing a two-year contract, and in others they continually renewed their contract, with the apparent intention to stay in the Middle East indefinitely.

Unlike travel to the United States or Europe, working in the Middle East was a realistic possibility for many urban young women. Young women on the spatial or economic periphery of the city had more difficulty contacting potential employers, but with persistence it was likely that they could find work. More opportunities were available for Muslim women, but Christians could certainly find work as well. The primary factor preventing young women from seeking work in the Middle East was the potential for abusive (sexually, physically, and mentally) relationships with their employers. Some women reported positive relationships with their employers, but one never knew the character of the family one would be working for until arrival, and abuse was always a serious risk.

Domestic work in the Middle East had a very different role than travel to the United States or Europe in terms of reconstructing the social position of young people. The money earned provided a significant amount of support for a young woman's family while she was abroad, and I knew of a number of unemployed young men who were supported by their sisters. Together with the household work that women freely provided at home, support from those who worked internationally meant that unemployed young women were essential for the survival of the household. However, money earned as a domestic worker was generally not adequate for saving, and after returning to their families, many young women entered a state of extended unemployment. Temporarily earning an income and supporting one's family provided a sense of independence that made unemployment particularly difficult.

In contrast to young men, young women were frequently able to use migration to shift their position within social relations. In Chapter 3 I argue that young men conceptualize progress in terms of moving from a position of dependence to providing material support to others. Young men's notions of progress fit with local values concerning masculinity, in which a key aspect of being a man is taking on the role of the patron in hierarchical patron/client relations. Through migration to the Middle East, young women were repositioning themselves within relations of reciprocity that have historically been highly gendered. They were taking on the valued masculine role of providing material support to others.

I often asked young men why they did not pursue work in the Middle East. They explained that differences between men and women made it impossible. Workers in the Middle East were expected to be submissive and work within the house, and men are not capable of doing this. It was explained to me that men need to "move around," and this would not be permitted. The low income earned by workers in the Middle East was also a factor. Although one hundred U.S. dollars per month was more than men with only a secondary education were likely to earn in Ethiopia, it was still not adequate for accessing the types of change they hoped migration would bring them. Even among pious Muslims, whose cultural and spiritual centers were found in the Middle East, migration to the West was desirable for economic reasons.

Young men often remarked that it would be shameful for them to be financially dependent on a wife or girlfriend. However, this did not prevent them from relying on remittances from their sisters working abroad. I did not observe tensions created by this shift in gendered patterns of reciprocity. It appears that gendered norms regarding giving and receiving can be disrupted when they are accompanied by spatial distance. For the most part, women were able to take on the masculine role of the patron only if they lived outside Ethiopia. This shift in relations of power did not enter into everyday interactions between young men and women living in Ethiopia. In this sense, migration displaced gendered norms governing social relationships.

Young men constructed a loose hierarchy of space based on the potential for shifting one's social position. They sought out spaces that would allow them to fulfill local notions of what it means to be an adult. Although the personal transformation into a modern individual described in the preceding section was an important element of youth narratives, it was secondary to the reconstruction of one's social position. Young men were not simply attempting to reference a lifestyle. They sought to solve their temporal problem of becoming, or progressing, with the spatial solution of migration. In this situation the qualities of space and the experience of time were embedded in social relationships. Young men were using the distinctive qualities of space to navigate through a shattered temporal process in order to reach a goal that was determined largely by relationships with family and community.

Migrating for Work, International Development, and the Life Course

When I conducted the bulk of my research between 2003 and 2005, Solomon was one of the few young men I knew who migrated locally for work. When I returned to Jimma for the first time in three years in 2008, I was surprised to learn that many young men had followed Solomon's path and left town to search out work on different international projects, usually related to infrastructural development. A World Bank–financed hydroelectric project, run by an Italian company, was the most common destination for young men in Jimma. Others worked on a Chinese road construction project. Of the young men I was able to locate in Jimma, many had returned from these projects and were waiting on work with a Korean road construction project that was scheduled to begin soon. The Korean project promised better wages, and the work camp was only a few hours from Jimma.

Although it is unclear what impact these large infrastructural development projects will have on life in Ethiopia more generally (Mains, forthcoming, "Blackouts and Progress"), as a source of work they have significant implications for the lives of young men. Kebede, a young man discussed throughout this book, was one of the men I found back in Jimma waiting for work with the new project. In 2005, after around three years of unemployment, Kebede traveled to the work site for the Chinese road construction project. He used money from his family and kin networks to sustain himself while waiting for work. After about one month, he was offered a job doing low-skill manual labor. Kebede explained that although the job did not pay well, his expenses were also low. Equally important, working on the project instantly placed him within a valuable network of workers from Jimma, many of them earning substantial incomes as drivers or skilled workers. These other workers often invited him for meals or gave him small cash gifts.

After a few months of work, Kebede was able to begin sending small amounts of money home to his parents in Jimma. Although these amounts were not enough to support his family, they marked a symbolic shift in Kebede's status. He had moved from a dependent to a provider. At least for the moment, Kebede was taking on some of the responsibilities associated with adult males. This transition was not permanent. After almost two years of work, Kebede quit and returned to Jimma. He had saved enough money to obtain a driver's license, and he felt that this would significantly increase his pay grade and perhaps provide him with the resources necessary to marry and raise children.

During the few weeks that I spent with Kebede in 2008, his lifestyle appeared to be unchanged from when I had last seen him in 2005. He lived with his parents and spent most of his time at church or playing soccer. He had little money and was once again reliant on friends and family for daily hand-outs. In terms of his economic relationships, Kebede was once again a youth. However, he was confident that his current state of dependence would be over soon. He anticipated beginning work on the Korean project within two months and believed that this would provide a significant change in his life.

When I met with Kebede in 2009, he had followed through on his plans and was working as a foreman on the Korean road construction project. He was earning close to three thousand birr per month (around three hundred U.S. dollars at that time) in addition to an allowance for food and lodging. He was able to send significant sums of money to his family, purchase food for friends who were looking for work, and save money for the future. Although Kebede's current economic situation was quite good, he acknowledged that work for the Korean company would not extend beyond two or three years, and it is highly uncertain whether an opportunity to work with a similar project will be available after that. Ultimately he hoped to find work doing construction in the Middle East.

Kebede's path is typical of the many young men in Jimma who have found work with international projects. Through work they temporarily change their positions within relations of reciprocity and take on roles associated with adult men. The support Kebede received from older and more experienced workers on the Chinese project and later gave to others indicates that many men are able to develop networks of dependents that extend beyond their immediate kin. However, when the work is finished these men often become dependents themselves. I knew many young men in Jimma who had previously earned significant incomes working on the Italian hydroelectric project but were once again living with their parents.

A letter from Solomon sums up the fluctuating nature of life for many young men. Solomon is the best letter writer of the youths who participated in my research, and for some time I was fortunate to receive regular reports from him. After moving to Gambella, he spent a month waiting for work at a Chinese-run oil-drilling project. Once again dealing with the problem of excessive time, but with no friends to provide companionship, he described long days of anxiously waiting for something that might not arrive. Eventually Solomon was hired as a guard, a dangerous job in the politically unstable territory surrounding the Sudan/Ethiopia border. The work was temporary, and when the job finished, he returned to Jimma. If the money he earned had changed his standing locally, he did not mention it in his letters. Solomon writes, in English,

> Here in Jimma the things are going to the same ways. Young people just like me who are jobless, each day, morning and afternoon chewing khat at every small coffee or tea shop. In this ceremony someone thinks about himself, "how to get the job," another one thinks about "how to get satisfaction in my life," and somebody else is doing another investigation about his country, "why is our country backward? How to develop?" In my side everything is difficult for the future because I have no job. So always chewing khat. Maybe I will go to Gambella. If the company calls for me I will go there. If they do not call I don't know what I will do.

The case of mobile young workers from Jimma supports a rethinking of the social category of youth. Clearly, as others have argued, the notion of youth as a period of linear change from childhood to adulthood does not makes sense in this context. Young men and women are not becoming adults in a normative sense, and there is no reason to believe that this condition will change in the near future. There is, however, an important relationship between transition and age-based social categories. Youth does involve transition, and the ideal endpoints of adulthood and childhood provide a useful framework for understanding this process. Young men in Jimma take on varying positions within relations of reciprocity. With the movement between employment and unemployment, young men shift between being a provider and a dependent. At times they are adults and at other times they are youth. In this case, age-based social categories are useful for tracking one's position with relations of reciprocity.

The human life course has often been used as a model for economic development, and as a metaphor it continues to be useful. Just as individual lives move in different and unexpected directions, so do economies. Changes may be cyclical, or follow new and unexpected branches, or occasionally move in a linear manner that is associated with progressive growth. Regardless of the direction of change, young men in urban Ethiopia conceived of movement through time in terms of their position within relationships. Again, this same logic must be applied to development. Rather than conceiving of economic change in terms of growth or another quantifiable indicator, it is necessary to consider development as qualitative changes in relationships. Economic change is the process through which people relate to each other differently.

Development, Culture, and Social Relationships

Young men believed that spatial movement enabled the accumulation of wealth and the reconstruction of one's relationship with family and community, but migration and progress were intertwined with social relationships in an additional and possibly more powerful manner. I noted earlier that migration caused a displacement of norms governing gendered relations of power. Similarly, by physically separating themselves from their community, youth believed that migration allowed a temporary escape from stigmas associated with occupation and normative values concerning the balance between social relationships and material wealth. In this sense migration provided the mental freedom necessary to work. In general the West, and the United States in particular, was conceived of as a space in which social freedom exists. One vocational student with a particularly strong interest in travel abroad explained, "In Ethiopia there is *yiluññta*. We are not free here. In America I would do so many things. I like to play sports, but in Ethiopia I cannot wear shorts. People will talk and insult me. In America I could wear shorts. I would be free to do whatever I wanted."

Statements like this emerge out of broader discussions concerning culture, space, and progress. In Jimma, people of all ages frequently debated how Ethiopia could experience progress at the national level. In these discussions I often encountered critiques of "Ethiopian culture" (*Habesha bahil*).[5] Men and women, young and old, from a variety of class backgrounds sometimes argued that a "bad culture" is preventing desirable economic change, but this discourse was particularly common among students at the vocational school.[6] The following comment from a group of vocational students is typical of these critiques of culture:

> The old culture is useless. Simply visiting friends and celebrating holidays will never lead to change. The hospital, the university, the hotels—everything good in Jimma was built by the Italians. This is why South Africa is so far ahead of us. Now the new generation is beginning to improve things, but the old generation has given us no foundation. Of course, there is less time for friends when there is more work. People say the new generation is selfish, but this is only because we are working and we have more money but less time. Today's generation is for itself. When people work with their own strength, they do not want

to share what they have earned. This culture of always inviting others will disappear. Today people want different things. They don't want to wear the same clothes for a year. They want new clothes every month. They want to look around and see different things. They don't want to eat *injera* every day. If they want all of these things, they have to work.

The vocational students' statement, and critiques of bad culture in general, are based on underlying assumptions that have been widely dismissed by cultural anthropologists, and yet the ideas expressed here provide important insights into issues of space, culture, and migration. Ethiopian critiques of culture assume that distinct and unified Ethiopian and Western cultures exist and that economic growth in Ethiopia can be attained through the adoption of Western culture. For example, the claim that the brief Italian occupation of Ethiopia (1936–1941) is responsible for the presence of all useful local infrastructure implies that Western influence is necessary for economic growth. The students assume that with the passage of time, Ethiopian culture will take on supposedly Western characteristics such as greater individualism, and this will facilitate desirable change. Critiques such as this echo W. W. Rostow's (1971) stages of economic growth and theories of a "culture of poverty." They imply that differences in economic development are a result of culture rather than factors such as imbalanced international trade, policies of structural adjustment, geography, and political corruption. Culture is constructed as bounded, homogenous, and static.

Perspectives like this have been soundly critiqued by social scientists. I want to be absolutely clear that I am not claiming that culture is responsible for poverty in Ethiopia. To speak of an "Ethiopian culture" does not make sense in a nation with such geographic, ethnic, and religious diversity. This is particularly true given the engagement that young Ethiopians have with international cultural products like films and music. Furthermore, as I detail in Chapter 1, the economic situation in Ethiopia has changed significantly, often for the worse, as a result of shifts in national and international economic policy intended to create free markets.

Although Ethiopian critiques of "bad culture" are not particularly helpful in understanding economic development, they are quite useful as reminders of the importance of spatial variation in tensions between social relationships and individual accumulation. The primary theme that emerges in these critical everyday conversations is that the heightened importance of social relationships in Ethiopia prevents economic development. This argument is based on the construction of Ethiopia and the West as places with distinct values concerning the balance between maintaining social relationships and accumulating material goods. A friend who moved from Jimma to Oakland, California, after receiving a Diversity Visa in 2005 once explained to me that the exchange rate works for both dollars and visits with friends. For one U.S. dollar you can get nearly nine Ethiopian birr (this was the exchange rate at the time), and for one meeting with friends in the United States you would see them nine times in Ethiopia. Based on a spatially bounded notion of culture, Ethiopia is thought to be rich in social interaction while the United States is rich in money. In discussions among youth it was common to contrast social life and economic development. During a discussion I observed among unemployed young men, they argued that as economic development increases, social relations decrease. They cited the continuum from rural Ethiopia to Jimma to Addis Ababa to the United States as evidence. With each step, technology and economic activity increases, and it is less likely that a person would know his neighbors or spend time talking and socializing. They concluded that if economic development is impeded by time devoted to social interaction, then social life must be reduced in order to foster development.

Religious holidays and funerals were two cultural institutions that were singled out as standing in the way of economic development. For both Muslims and Christians in Ethiopia, mourning after a death lasts for seven days. Mourners gather in a tent outside the home of the deceased. Some mourners stay all day, while others only stop by for a short visit. There is a high degree of social pressure on friends, family, and neighbors to at least visit the mourning tent during one of the seven days, and ideally one should visit every day. The family of the deceased is generally expected to provide food and drinks for the mourners, and this can be a significant economic burden. Most Ethiopian families are members of at least one *iddir*, a burial association in which members pay a monthly fee and then receive financial support and help with food preparation after the death of a family member (De Weerdt et al. 2007). *Iddir* members are expected to visit the mourning tent when another member dies, and they are fined when they fail to do this. I often heard the argument that all of the time and resources invested in funerals were preventing development.

A similar claim was made about religious holidays. Especially among Orthodox Christians, holidays are numerous, as each day of the month is linked to a particular saint and can be used as an excuse for feasting. Although no one celebrates every saint's day, especially among devout Orthodox Christians a significant amount of time is generally spent at church on the days devoted to major saints. Many Orthodox Christians are also members of religious *mahabers*. A religious *mahaber* is an association devoted to honoring a particular saint. *Mahaber* members generally take turns hosting a celebration at their home on the monthly saint's day. These celebrations vary with the wealth of the *mahaber* members, but a significant outlay of time and resources on the part of the host is always expected. Urban Ethiopians do not necessarily see religious holidays and funerals as "bad culture," but they consistently argue that these cultural institutions oppose economic development. It was common for people to argue that holidays and funerals are important for strengthening social life but also prevent work and the accumulation of material wealth.

Government workers were thought to be particularly guilty of prioritizing social life over work. On multiple occasions I was told about a study that had been conducted at an Ethiopian university. The researcher monitored the time use of government workers and discovered that they use less than thirty hours a year for actual work. The rest of their time is spent attending funerals and holiday celebrations and taking coffee breaks. I was never able to locate this study and I suspect it is an urban myth, but it certainly reveals a widespread belief that government employees spend their time on social rather than economic activities.

The contrast between social life and economic development was sometimes conceived of in terms of a generation gap. This idea was especially common among vocational students who were learning trades such as carpentry and metalworking that have been traditionally stigmatized. The students quoted previously emphasized that "the old culture is useless" and "today's generation is for itself." In this narrative, "today's generation" is contrasted with the past. The association between education and a rejection of tradition is not new to Ethiopia (Levine 1965; Zewde 2002b). However, this narrative is distinctive in making an explicit division between social relationships and economic advancement. Associated with this way of thinking is the notion that money earned from work is private. The students assumed that government employees are not really working for their money. They are paid to drink coffee and socialize, and therefore they are happy to share their incomes with others. In contrast to dominant values concerning social relationships and material wealth, real work for the vocational students was associated with accomplishing something tangible, particularly through physical exertion. Wages earned in this manner could justifiably be spent as one wished, even if this is deemed selfish.

The arguments I have developed in previous chapters demonstrate the flaws in the assumption that economic development corresponds with a decrease in the value of social relationships. Empirically, economic development and engagement with market economies often coincide with an increase in the importance of social relationships (Ferguson 1985; Piot 1999). Indeed, for many young Ethiopians a desire to invest in social relationships was an incentive to work. Furthermore, young men in rural Ethiopia spent far more time working than their counterparts in more developed urban areas. Although there is little evidence to support a simple correlation between a lack of economic development and placing great value on social relationships, the perception of such a relationship is important, particularly when it maps onto spatial difference.

Moving between Social Spaces

Many young men conceived of spatial movement as the only means of escaping from a culture of prioritizing relationships over economic gain. The notion that

migrants left Ethiopia in part to escape stigmas surrounding particular occupations was common. A popular Amharic newspaper published a weekly article
titled "Our People in America." An Ethiopian journalist wrote the article based
on his travels in the United States and interviews with Ethiopian Americans.
One of the common themes in these interviews was that Ethiopian Americans
do not want to speak about their occupation, and it is considered impolite to
ask. The anonymity of urban America made it possible to work without concern for social relationships. The newspaper article was widely read by educated urban Ethiopians, and there was a general understanding that Ethiopian
Americans work in occupations that are stigmatized at home, but spatial distance prevents local stigmas from becoming an issue.

In practice, the relationship between migration to the United States and
social pressure is complicated and deserves further research. In a different
conversation with the friend discussed earlier who moved to Oakland through
the DV lottery, I asked him if there is *yiluññta* in the United States, and he
quickly responded that there is not. I then asked him if he would walk down
the street eating a sandwich in the United States. In Ethiopia, people frequently explained their aversion to eating in public by claiming that *yiluññta* makes
this impossible. In his response to my question, my friend explained that it
would obviously be impossible to eat in public in the United States because
his "culture" does not permit him to do this. Despite these ambiguities regarding the actual effects of migration in alleviating social pressure, the following
quotations reveal that many young men believed that migration would provide
them with the social freedom to work. The first is from a vocational student,
and the dialogue is from a group of other vocational students.

> Everyone wants to leave Ethiopia. This is because work is not appre-
> ciated here (*sira yinakal*). A person who does street work like shining
> shoes and washing cars will be insulted, especially if they are educated.
> They won't be accepted by society. My father has a friend who works in
> South Africa selling socks on the street. He is an adult with a good edu-
> cation. Someone like him would never do this in Ethiopia. Of course,
> he can make more money in South Africa, but also there is no *yiluññta*
> there. An educated person like my father's friend will be insulted here,
> and he may have to fight.

> STUDENT 1: The best reason for leaving Ethiopia is to work and make
>   money, but *yiluññta* is also important. A shoeshine can make fifteen
>   or twenty birr a day. This is good money, but they will be insulted. If
>   I have to do this kind of work, I would have to go to a new city first.
> STUDENT 2: I want to work part time while I am a student, but there
>   is *yiluññta*. Even if they don't insult you, they won't respect you;
>   they will order you around, and no one wants to be known as a
>   shoeshine.

STUDENT 3: I've seen in movies that comedians make money telling jokes on the street in America, but you can't do this in Ethiopia.

Migration within Ethiopia was also common. Siraj, the watch vendor, left his home in Kombulcha largely because he knew that occupational stigmas would prevent him from ever working near his family. Choosing to live without the support of family or friends was no small sacrifice to make. A different young man from the Wollo region left his rural home and worked as a waiter in Jimma. He explained that he had moved so far (two to three days by bus) in order to avoid shaming himself in front of family and friends. Unlike Siraj, he did not have even a minimal social support structure in Jimma. At one point the room he rented was robbed, he lost all of his possessions, and he had no one to turn to for help. Despite these hardships, he felt he had made the right decision by leaving his home. The possibility of migrating within Ethiopia indicates that separation from family and friends was also important for displacing social relationships. Migrating locally and internationally both provided a means to escape social relationships, but international migration was perceived as being more powerful, partially because of the way that social relations were thought to function differently in different spaces.

The shame of working in a low-status occupation was entirely social. Young men claimed that if they are surrounded by strangers they will forget the stress of *yiluññta*. I have argued that the choice to migrate instead of working locally was motivated by a desire to experience progress in one's social relationships, but that is only a partial explanation. In some cases, working locally would have been an option for achieving one's goals, but social pressure prevented youth from doing so. In this sense, the utility of spatial movement as a solution to problems of time was embedded in local values concerning occupation. Young men experienced local cultural norms as barriers to their aspirations for progress, and only by temporarily escaping those norms could they return and reenter their community with a different and more desirable social position. Factors such as the rise of education combined with a decline in government employment were also important in preventing young men from achieving aspirations, but these factors were inseparable from *yiluññta*. It was not simply a difference in the qualities of space in relation to being modern that motivated migration but a difference in the types of social relationships that were thought to exist within those spaces.

Youth discourse about migration and *yiluññta* indicates that a fundamental quality that allows spatial movement to solve problems of time is a shift in the manner in which productive activity is evaluated. Within Ethiopia, work is evaluated primarily in terms of how it allows one to interact with others. Outside Ethiopia, work is essentially seen as the exchange of one's labor power and time for wages. For unemployed young men, progress in terms of one's position within relationships at home is achieved by moving to a space in which work is not assessed in terms of relationships. The choice to work as a taxi driver in the United States is based not on the interactions that are associated with that occupation but on the possibility of earning money. This is not to say that working outside Ethiopia is divorced from *yiluññta* and social relationships. Money earned elsewhere is usually invested in Ethiopia, and work and time in Ethiopia continue to be evaluated in terms of relationships. However, the government employment that previously allowed one to simultaneously work and engage in positive relations is no longer a realistic possibility within Ethiopia. This has led young men to conceive of the construction of desirable relationships as being possible only through movement to a space where work and time function differently.

Conclusion

There is a seeming contradiction between some of the arguments I have developed here and in previous chapters. On one hand, young men hierarchically rank places based on the balance between economic development and social relationships. In statements that appear to echo classic modernization theory, young men claim that free markets and material accumulation are increasingly prioritized over social relationships as one ascends this hierarchy of development. On the other hand, young men conceive of progress as social relationships—progress consists of linear changes in one's relations of dependence with others. The tension between these perspectives is highly productive, in the sense that it offers a means of conceptualizing the relationship between space, time, and social relationships that I have been exploring throughout this book.

In the Ethiopian case, experiencing progress as it is defined locally necessitates movement to a cultural space in which the relevance of social relationships is decreased. Although this can be achieved by moving within Ethiopia, international migration is more effective, and facilitates temporal movement in two different ways. First, it situates one within a place that is conceived as modern in terms of economic development and culture. Second, temporarily working in this space that is seemingly free of *yiluññta* allows young men to progress within their social relationships in Ethiopia. In other words, young men access modern spaces to simultaneously become adults and actualize local notions of progress. In both cases, the implications of spatial movement for social relationships allow it to effectively impact temporal experiences.

A spatially bounded notion of culture, like that present in Ethiopian discourse on development and relationships, has been rightly critiqued by anthropologists, but there is clearly still value in recognizing the presence of culturally distinct places. For certain types of analysis it is useful to stress spatial differences in practices and values, even if they are never coherent and static. Movement between distinct places allows young people to grapple with their temporal problems. I have argued that development must be conceived of in terms of social relationships, but this does not mean that shifts in social relationships are divorced from more standard understandings of development as economic and infrastructural growth. In the Ethiopian case, working on infrastructural projects or moving to larger economies often allows young men to accomplish their goal of achieving progress by repositioning themselves within relations of reciprocity.

The same social relations that young men sought to escape were in some ways intensified through migration. Migrants from Ethiopia to the United States are under great pressure to send remittances to their friends and family in Ethiopia. As individuals move across borders and gifts travel across greater distances, relationships also expand. If, as Charles Piot (1999) argues, the self is relationships, then the migrant self stretches between different spatial locations. A young man living in the United States does not truly escape social relationships, but he is repositioned within them. He becomes a giver of gifts rather than a receiver, a source of support rather than a dependent. In this sense, spatial distance does not eliminate relationships but significantly transforms them.

Conclusion

Sustaining Hope in the Present and the Future

When I returned to Jimma in 2008, after being away for three years, I quickly noticed that the street corners were not nearly as crowded with young men as they had been in years past. Certainly idle young men could still be seen passing their time in the shade, but a definite change had taken place. One of my first stops was at Haile's house. The atmosphere at Haile's house was also different from before. Haile sat in the same place as usual, on a wooden stool on the veranda, but that day he was joined by just one friend. They were chewing khat, but the *chewata* (play/conversation) was gone. Three small tape deck/radios had been opened up. Batteries were strewn on the ground, and wires were connected or disconnected in an arrangement that made no sense to me. Haile put a Kenny Rogers cassette into the open face of one of the tape decks. It seemed that the Kenny Rogers was selected for my benefit. The volume was uncomfortably loud. At first I could not locate the speaker, and then I realized that it was connected by a wire and lying on the ground. Haile and his friend struggled to open another radio. Eventually they pulled the thing apart and stared at the insides. I asked what the problem was, and Haile's friend told me, "It doesn't work." Haile did little to engage me in conversation. He was immersed in the task of figuring out this stereo. I asked about all the young men from the neighborhood, and Haile gradually told me where they had gone. Many had left Jimma in search of work or education. I remarked that everyone had left, and Haile responded in the third person, "Haile is here."

For how long can hope be sustained in the lives of young people in urban Ethiopia? Hope connects the present to the future. Hopelessness results from the cutting of that connection and an inability to move through time toward a desirable future. The preceding chapters have examined how young men in urban Ethiopia imagine hopeful futures and struggle to actualize their desires. To the extent that young men are able to conceive of ways of moving beyond the present, they are involved in the production of hope. Despite claims that they were simply sitting with no possibility for change in the future, with a few exceptions like Haile, when I returned to Jimma in 2008 and 2009, I did not find the young men who had participated in my research where I had left them. For better or for worse, they had continued their struggle for hope. In this final chapter, I examine changes in the lives of some of the young men who were involved in my research in order to explore the long-term possibilities for the reproduction of hope among young men in urban Ethiopia as well as in relation to social theory more generally.

My discussion involves explorations into what I call the economic and discursive sustainability of hope. By *economic sustainability* I refer to the economic means by which lives are reproduced from one day to the next. *Discursive sustainability* refers to the possibility of constructing narratives in which movement through time toward a desirable future appears possible. I examine changes in the lives of young men between 2005 and 2009 to explore how young men repositioned themselves in relation to the future in a context of economic change. Education and migration continue to be major themes in the narratives that young men construct for themselves.

I am also interested in hope as it relates to conceptions of Africa and social theory more generally. A primary theme throughout this book has been the importance of social relationships. I have argued that in urban Ethiopia, work, time, and space are all conceived of in terms of their importance for one's position within relationships. Everyday events such as inviting a friend for coffee and then sitting at a café and discussing the DV lottery have major implications for social relationships. The importance of relationships for the Ethiopian case suggests a return to the issues of hope, social theory, and capitalism that I briefly discussed in the introductory chapter. I have argued that despite their engagement with processes associated with neoliberal capitalism, the lives of young men in urban Ethiopia are often guided by social relationships rather than the logic of the market. I return to this argument here and seek to demonstrate that this is a hopeful form of knowledge. Like Hirokazu Miyazaki (2004, 2006), I am interested in building on Richard Rorty's pragmatic philosophy of hope and knowledge. I examine Rorty together with J. K. Gibson-Graham's (1996, 2006) critique of totalizing theories of capitalism. I argue that an analysis that acknowledges economic diversity and the importance of social relationships opens up space for imagining and attaining new hopeful possibilities.

The concrete realities of young men's lives are evidence of indeterminate possibilities. That we cannot know the future does not suggest inaction in the present. Rather I wish to replace an overly pessimistic conception of Africa with movement toward analyses of specific practices and places.

A Return to Education and Discursive Sustainability

Habtamu, a young man I have discussed at various points in this book, demonstrates both the value and limits of relations of reciprocity for quality of life. Some of his family members received Diversity Visas, and this transformed Habtamu's life. Unlike many young men, access to small amounts of money was never an issue for Habtamu. His family in the United States sent regular remittances to his older sister, who lived with Habtamu in Jimma. This money trickled down to Habtamu in the form of small handouts. In addition to gifts from his family, Habtamu received substantial invitations from his friends. One Sunday during the month that I tracked Habtamu's income from gifts, friends invited him for raw beef and wine (a common Sunday morning ritual among relatively wealthy men). In the afternoon he chewed khat, and then in the evening a different friend invited him for beers. By the end of the day Habtamu had consumed around fifty-eight birr of in-kind gifts, more than some other young men received in the entire month that I tracked their income. This was a particularly good day for Habtamu, but it was rare for a day to pass without him receiving at least a small gift from family and friends.

Although Habtamu did not struggle to live comfortably, he did face challenges in constructing narratives in which he was moving toward a hopeful future. Habtamu lamented a life without progress or change. Like other participants in my research, Habtamu completed forms documenting his daily activities, income, and expenses. He found this to be an interesting exercise and requested that I give him blank copies of the forms so that he could continue documenting his life. He explained that he was able to see clearly that each day was the same. Every day he spent the morning talking with friends or drinking coffee with his family, and every afternoon he chewed khat. In discussing these patterns, Habtamu asked me, "For how long will I live this way?" Economic sustainability was not enough; like most young men, Habtamu sought to construct a narrative in which he could access a future that was different from and better than the present. Progressive narratives connecting the present to the future were the basis for hope. Accessing economic goods through gifts or work allows one to move from one day to the next, but it does not necessarily provide a connection with the future. Economic sustainability alone simply allows one to live like a chicken—eating and sleeping. A "good life" requires qualitative improvement over time, and many young men argued that this cannot be accessed through gifts or available forms of work. As I explain in Chapter 3, progress was conceived of in terms of moving from a position of dependence to providing support for others. This transition was part of taking on the normative responsibilities of an adult, and without it a person would remain a youth indefinitely.

Like many young men, for Habtamu the solution to maintaining a connection between the present and the future was education and international migration. In our many interviews and conversations between 2003 and 2005, he stressed that leaving the country was his primary goal. He sought to join his brothers and sisters in the United States. As I argued in Chapter 6, young men seek out a "spatial fix" for their problems of time. In young men's day-to-day discussions, international migration facilitates the construction of a modern self, access to high-wage jobs, and an escape from local values concerning occupational status.

When I returned to Jimma in 2008, Habtamu invited me to the house he shared with his older sister. We sat on overstuffed sofas, sipping strong cups of coffee, gossiping about other young men from the neighborhood, and discussing his plans for the future. Although he was still interested in moving to the United States, he did not appear to be as fixated with this plan as in years past. When I mentioned the possibility of using his siblings to make it to the United States, Habtamu argued that this was unlikely and that he was more interested in finishing his education and finding work in Ethiopia. His siblings had begun paying for him to study toward his bachelor's degree in Jimma University's engineering program. He was currently in his third year of the six-year evening study program, and he was confident of finding employment at the government telecommunications center after graduation. I did not get the impression that he was in a hurry to complete the program. Returning to school seemed to provide Habtamu with a sense of satisfaction and focus that he previously lacked. He still chewed khat in the afternoons, but now studying in the afternoon and classes in the evening provided him with a focus for his mental energy. Habtamu was moving toward a clear and socially approved goal. Education is a model of progressive linear change, and Habtamu was immersed in this process. By using resources from his family, Habtamu was able to reenter the progressive narrative of education, and for the moment this allowed him to see a path leading from the present to a desirable future. If Habtamu struggled with the maintenance of hope in the past, he now seemed confident that through education his future would be better and more desirable than the present. When I saw him again in 2009, our conversations continued to focus on education. Now Habtamu claimed that he would not be satisfied with a bachelor's degree but hoped to pursue a master's degree. This would qualify him to teach at the university level and enable him to continue his involvement in education for the foreseeable future.

The maintenance of hope through education was not limited to those, like Habtamu, who had access to significant economic resources. Many unemployed young men whom I knew chose to reenter the education system, and for the most part they lacked Habtamu's wealthy family. For young men without the test scores and economic resources to take evening classes at the university, the primary option was to reenroll in secondary school and eventually retake the school leaving examination. This involved a degree of deception because it is technically not permitted for students to retake the exam, but apparently it was not too difficult to get around this barrier. For example, Kifle, an unemployed young man from Sa'ar Sefer, chose to reenroll in ninth grade although he had already completed tenth grade some years earlier. Kifle hoped that after retaking ninth and tenth grades he would receive an exam result that would allow him to advance to the preparatory school, attend the university, and eventually become an English teacher. Kifle was from a very poor family. He had tried joining the army and working as a day laborer in construction, but he believed that returning to education was far more promising. He was retracing a path that had provided him with hope in the past. Once again he was able to envision himself in the future, completing his education and being employed as a government teacher. If failing their school leaving exam caused hope to be cut for young men, hope was at least temporarily reconstructed through reenrollment. In Kifle's case, at least the first stage in this journey was successful. In 2009 I learned that he had passed his tenth-grade exam and advanced to the preparatory school, from where it is highly likely that he will eventually earn a postsecondary degree and perhaps achieve his goal of becoming an English teacher.

The apparent success of Habtamu and Kifle should not imply that reengaging in education was an easy process. Young men who reenroll in education face high odds. A small percentage of students receive a result that allows them to pass on to university education. For those who reenroll in education, there is no reason to believe that they will be more successful than they were in the past. They are competing with a high number of students who are equally invested in education as an opportunity to attain their hopes. For those, like Habtamu, who are able to enroll in the university, their chances are greatly improved, but for most who reenter secondary school, it is likely that they will receive a result similar to the past. The situation faced by young women is even more extreme. I worked closely with three young women from Sa'ar Sefer. When I met with them again in 2008, all three had attempted to retake the school leaving exam, and all three failed. With their numerous household responsibilities, reenrolling in school was impossible, and they had little time to study on their own. Interestingly, all of these women planned to retake the exam again in the future.

Although for some youth, education certainly is a means to an economic end, for most it is a way of reconstructing narratives of hope. Habtamu's case demonstrates that a life of comfort and leisure was not enough for many young men; they wanted to experience progress. That the women from Sa'ar Sefer who had failed their school leaving exam hoped to take it again for a third time indicates that this narrative is almost inexhaustible. Like with the Diversity Visa lottery, one can always try the test one more time, and there are always examples of others who succeed. The annual exam becomes a sort of lottery, the difference being that success places one within a temporal narrative of becoming rather than the immediate spatial transformation associated with migration.

Sustaining Hope through Migration, Work, and Discursive Shifts

As important as education continues to be for sustaining hope, it is not necessarily the most common strategy among unemployed young men. In the previous chapter I discussed a young man named Kebede as an example of migrating locally to find work with international companies engaged in large-scale infrastructural development projects. During my visits to Jimma in 2008 and 2009, it became clear that many young men had followed paths similar to Kebede's. These young men experienced not only spatial movement but also, in some cases, a discursive shift in the way they spoke about progress and the future.

As noted in Chapter 3, Kebede had previously explained to me that he would not accept forms of work that were not helpful in allowing him to obtain progress. When we talked in 2008, his vision of progress had not changed. He still aspired to be in a position to help his family, marry, and educate his own children. The difference was in how he conceptualized the realization of these changes in his social relationships. Whereas in the past he spoke of international migration as the primary means of realizing his goals, in 2008 the emphasis was now on work. At one point in our conversation Kebede repeated the phrase in English, "Work, pray, work, pray, work, pray." This was his explanation of how to deal with the problems of excessive amounts of time and hopelessness. Through work and prayer it is possible to avoid stress in the present and move toward a desirable future.

Kebede used the money he earned working in road construction to obtain a driver's license and eventually found well-paid work as a foreman with a Korean-run road construction project. He hoped to save a large amount of money from this project and then travel abroad for work. He had heard that a good income could be earned working in construction in Qatar or South Africa. Working abroad for a few years would give him the financial base to start a family and provide for his children when he returned to Ethiopia. International migration was still a key part of the narrative that allowed Kebede to connect the present to a hopeful future. However, Kebede reconstructed his progressive vision of the future so that migration was a result of working locally. This discursive transformation enabled him to maintain a hopeful vision of the future in the context of rapid economic change.

Holyfield was one of the young men whom I could always find on a corner near the house I rented when I lived in Jimma between 2003 and 2005. He was well built with a broad muscular back, and he took his nickname from the American boxer whom his friends thought he resembled. Although he was unemployed and his family was certainly not wealthy, he always managed to be dressed in fashionable soccer jerseys and jeans, and others occasionally teased him about the efforts he took to keep himself clean. When I returned to Jimma in 2008, Holyfield was not around. After a few years of unemployment, he had left Jimma to find work with an Italian company, Salini, on the second phase of the Gibe River hydroelectric project (Gibe II). He worked on a project that involves a series of underground tunnels intended to channel water and generate power. He was doing hard manual labor inside the caves, where the heat could be extremely intense. Most of Holyfield's money went for food, but he was able to send a little back to his parents. Eventually the project slowed down, and Holyfield returned to Jimma, hoping to find work with the Korean road construction project.

When we met again in 2009, Holyfield was wearing a brilliant yellow track suit with *Brazil* printed across the front and dark wraparound shades that took on a rainbow sheen when they reflected the sun. Although it was clear that Holyfield still strove to be on the cutting edge of youth fashion, he told me that he was a different person from when we last spent time together in 2005. He explained that the work he did on the hydroelectric project was "working for *injera*" and "living hand to mouth." As noted in Chapter 3, in 2005 young men had used these exact phrases to explain why they were not interested in doing construction work and other menial jobs. But now Holyfield argued, "If you don't work, you can't live. Even if there is little profit, working is better than simply sitting." As with Kebede, Holyfield's words appear to represent a discursive shift in the way young men relate to work and the future. Work for the sake of work is now valued. Some young men argue that only by taking on available jobs is progress within social relationships possible. Certainly not all young men adopted this perspective, and I talked to many who lamented the impossibility of experiencing progress through work. However, it is quite striking that young men like Kebede and Holyfield changed their outlook on work and progress so rapidly.

This change in young men's discourses and practices concerning work occurred within the context of a dramatic increase in the cost of living. In the first half of 2008, the food inflation rate was nearly 35 percent compared to just 3.4 percent in 2004 (Ulimwengu, Workneh, and Paulos 2009). In Jimma friends told me that a bag of teff, the grain used in the production of *injera*, Ethiopia's staple food, was nearly three times the price it had been in 2005. It was becoming increasingly common for families to skip meals to cut down on expenses. Feeding a family had never been an easy task in Ethiopia, but in 2008 it was especially difficult. Many of the practices that I described in previous chapters such as relying on parents for financial support, avoiding certain types of work because of status concerns, and receiving numerous gifts and invitations from zemed were no longer economically feasible. In this context young men claimed that patterns of reciprocity had changed significantly, and unemployment was no longer an option. As one unemployed young man put it, "Now there are no more invitations [gifts]." In Holyfield's neighborhood, young men from wealthier families gossiped that Holyfield's father had kicked him out of the house and forced him to work because of the rising cost of life.

In the cases of Kebede and Holyfield, the complex relationship between historical change and accumulating material goods and social relationships is apparent. I have argued that young men avoid certain forms of work in the interest of preserving social relationships. Decisions about work are not based on a simple calculus of the potential for earning an income. Rather young men seek to position themselves within valued relations of exchange and power, in both the present and the future. Although I do not wish to draw firm conclusions, based on brief return visits to Jimma it appears that Kebede and Holyfield responded to the decreasing economic sustainability of their lifestyles with a discursive shift in their connection to hope. The ultimate goal of repositioning oneself within social relationships remains, but there is a change in how this is accomplished. Work in the present is desirable even if it does no more than sustain a person from one day to the next. Day-to-day sustenance has become necessary, and youth incorporate this work into progressive narratives of hope. In other words, changes in economic context lead to shifts in how young men maintain discursive sustainability.

Sustaining Hope through Entrepreneurial Individualism

"From death or America nothing will remain." A friend of mine in Jimma shared this observation with me, explaining that it was common for young men to interject this comment into conversations. It expresses the idea that because of disease, famine, and migration, Ethiopia will soon become devoid of life. Such a viewpoint is increasingly expressed in journalistic accounts of the future of Africa, most notably in Robert Kaplan's *The Coming Anarchy* (2000; Besteman 2005; Richards 1996). For most who study Africa, it is difficult to avoid sliding into this pessimism. I often get questions from friends and family about the possibility of hope for Africa, and I have a difficult time constructing an answer in the affirmative.

The concrete realities of young men's lives are so important because they are the first step in replacing this pessimism, if not with hope then with a sense of realism about the lives that are constantly playing out in neighborhoods in Jimma and a myriad of other places on the African continent. Although much is uncertain about Ethiopia's future, it is clear that the pessimism present in claims like "from death or America nothing will remain" is not grounded in reality. In fact, to my knowledge none of the young men involved in my research have died or traveled to the United States. Hope may often be cut, but young men's lives continue to be filled with unexpected twists and turns. As social conditions change, young men continue to live and create new economic and discursive means of connecting the present and future.

Death has taken both of Kifle's parents and America has taken Habtamu's siblings, but together with millions of other young people in urban Ethiopia, Kifle and Habtamu remain. Habtamu waits on remittances from his family, buys khat and meals for his friends, sometimes passes the time with conversations about a future life in the United States, and ultimately returns to education as a means for moving from the present to a desirable future. Despite the loss of his parents and failing the school leaving examination, Kifle once again invests in the narrative of attaining a desirable future through education. Kebede initially refused to take on work that did not support his localized conception of progress, but then he reevaluated how progress may be obtained. He puts his faith in both work and religion and believes that any form of employment may provide the basis for future growth. None of these young men has developed a definite solution that will allow him to transition out of the social category of youth. To varying degrees they continue to depend on others, and the possibility of starting a family of their own is still not yet within reach.

These young men remain intently focused on the future. Hope depends on faith in the existence of a future that is distinct from the present, and to the extent that young men continually imagine such futures, the possibility of hope remains. Young men engage with the progressive process of education while dreaming of the possibility of instant transformation through migration. One involves incremental change while the other involves a sudden and complete shift, but both are focused on the future.

The lives of young entrepreneurs in the informal economy provide the sharpest rebuttal to the pessimism that is often directed toward Africa. In Chapter 3, I recount the success of Siraj (the watch salesman) and Kassahun (the shop owner) in expanding their businesses. Although it is not hard to find such tales of economic success, perhaps more important are the young men who grow their families instead of their businesses. Desta was a young man who worked as a bicycle mechanic in the same neighborhood as Afwerk. One of my happiest memories of fieldwork comes from the evening Desta invited my partner and me over to his house to meet his newborn son. His wife brewed strong coffee, and we laughed as his son smiled for my camera. In 2008, Desta was living in a new house. It was located farther from the city center, but Desta was no longer renting. It was with great pride that he again invited me to his house to introduce me to his newest son. Significantly, he had also purchased a television and DVD player, and neighbors gathered at his home to watch videos in the evening. Again in 2009 I was fortunate to visit Desta's home and once again had the delight of meeting another family member, this time an infant daughter. Certainly Desta did not lead the progressive life to which many young men aspired. He still worked as a street-side bicycle repairman, and he will most likely struggle to provide his children with a life that is better than his own. On the other hand, Desta's status as a father and a husband generated a certain degree of respect. He lived, and his family lived. They ate *injera* and *shuro* (chickpea paste), drank coffee, played with their neighbors, and worked hard.

Desta's family's life would surely be made easier by better access to running water, health care, education, and nutritious food. However, the simple fact of Desta's expanding family is grounds for hope. He represents the diversity of possible life courses that are not encompassed with tropes of today's youth as a "lost generation" or "in crisis." Quite simply, Desta and the other young men I have discussed represent unknown possibility. Throughout this book I have placed my discussions of individual youth within a context of political and economic structure. The cutting of hope for young men is related to policies such as the downsizing of the public sector or the Ethiopian state's crushing of opposition political parties. However, a close examination of changes in young men's lives clearly indicates the limits of structural determinism. Desta, Habtamu, and Kebede are not simple products of the economic and political structure in which they live. When Desta has his third child and Kebede finds work on a Korean road construction project, we see the contingencies of history and personality. To the extent that these lives are not structurally determined, they may be a source of hope. The future is not known, and therefore change is possible. In the final section, I seek to move to a more abstract level and examine the potential for hope in social theory and politics. I argue that diverse and indeterminate possibilities provide hope and should motivate action.

Capitalism, Social Relationships, and Knowledge as Hope

Throughout this book I have argued that the lives of young men in Jimma are embedded within processes associated with neoliberal capitalism, but social relationships are often a more important guide for behavior than the rationalizing logic of the market. I have argued for a perspective in which the accumulation of capital is not the ultimate determinant of social life. In this final section, I explore hope from a different perspective. I am interested in the potential for my argument to function as a basis for hope. I continue to present evidence from urban Ethiopia that demonstrates the limits of the neoliberal logic of the market in order to demonstrate how this perspective may be a hopeful form of knowledge.

In the introduction to his collection of essays titled *Philosophy and Social Hope*, Richard Rorty claims, "There is no point in asking whether a belief represents reality, either mental reality or physical reality, accurately. That is, for pragmatists, not only a bad question, but the root of much wasted philosophical energy. The right question to ask is, 'For what purposes would it be useful to hold that belief'" (1999: xxiv). Rorty argues that for pragmatists, a belief is justified if it is useful in attaining a desired end. In this sense, hope takes the place of knowledge. From Rorty's perspective, knowledge consists of beliefs that are useful in reaching individual and collective hopes.

In Chapter 2, I describe how young men in Jimma generated new beliefs about the world through consumption of khat and film. Young men experienced time as a problem because they felt that they had little chance of attaining their hopes for the future. Khat and videos enabled young men to reposition themselves in relation to the future and imagine possibilities in which their hopes could be attained. Richard Rorty writes, "To say that one should replace knowledge with hope is to say . . . that one should stop worrying about whether what one believes is well grounded and start worrying about whether one has been imaginative enough to think up interesting alternatives to one's present beliefs" (1999: 34). From this perspective, the consumption of khat and film was a successful strategy for young men in generating new and useful knowledge. This gives new meaning to the claims of young men that they "learn" from watching videos. From the pragmatist position developed by Rorty, learning need not be understood as accumulating factual knowledge about the world but may be conceptualized as a process in which imagining alternatives to the present becomes possible. In the urban Ethiopian context, spaces such as khat houses and video houses are like universities and think tanks in the sense that they offer fertile environments for the imagination of hopeful possibilities.

It is not clear, however, whether the imaginings of young men as they watched videos and chewed khat enabled them to attain their hopes for the future. Certainly the simple act of imagining a hopeful possibility is a step toward attainment. To believe that an alternative to the present is possible and to posit a strategy for reaching that alternative are both necessary in order to move toward a future that is different from the present. This act of imagination in itself, however, provides little assurance that the strategies that one has imagined will be successful. My interest in exploring the notion of knowledge as hope is not to assess the utility of young men's imaginings for attaining their aspirations. Rather, I seek to move from the concrete discussion of hope among young men in Jimma toward an examination of the more abstract issues of hope and analyses of capitalism.

The position that Rorty develops in *Philosophy and Social Hope* can be frustrating because although he explains pragmatism in the context of a political agenda, he also deconstructs the link between politics and philosophy. He argues that a particular philosophical position can give rise to multiple contradictory political ideals (1999: 23–24). In critiquing the potential of philosophy to function as the basis for a politics of hope, Rorty explains, "The appropriate intellectual background to political deliberation is historical narrative rather than philosophical or quasi-philosophical theory. More specifically, it is the kind of historical narrative which segues into a utopian scenario about how we can get from the present to a better future" (1999: 231). As I noted in the introductory chapter, the historical narrative that Rorty calls for has begun to take shape in critical analyses of neoliberal capitalism. Anthropologists studying Africa have increasingly analyzed local cultural practices in terms of a context shaped by neoliberal capitalism. I am interested in the degree to which analyses of neoliberalism are a hopeful form of knowledge.

Historical narrative and utopian scenarios both have a strong presence in the work of David Harvey.[1] Harvey's *Spaces of Hope* is particularly relevant for a discussion of hope and utopian narratives. Harvey argues for the imaginative construction of utopias and demonstrates the complexities of utopian thought from the perspective of historical materialism (2000: 203–205). For Harvey, imagination is rooted in political and economic conditions that are defined by neoliberal capitalism. This is a "free-market utopianism" in which "a secularized and more open spatiotemporality had to be imposed upon the world at a variety of scales (urban and regional as well as international), within which capital investments could more easily flow, along with movements of information, people, commodities, cultural forms, and the like" (2000: 192). In other words, neoliberal capitalism restructures conceptions of space and time at a number of different levels.

Harvey's analysis of the spatial and temporal dynamics of capitalism is insightful and has certainly influenced my work. However, I believe that he extends his analysis of capitalism too far and in a manner that is antithetical to hope. The evidence from urban Ethiopia does not support Harvey's vision of capitalism as a singular global system. J. K. Gibson-Graham's (1996) observation that capitalism is not a unified structure and coexists with other forms of economic exchange is certainly well supported by the discussion I have offered in the preceding chapters. There should be no doubt that processes associated with neoliberal capitalism influence life in urban Ethiopia. The downsizing of the public sector, economic dependency on the global coffee market, and the import of cheap Chinese manufactured clothing are all associated with neoliberal processes. That said, the same individuals who are embedded in these processes do not exclusively participate in relationships that can be described as capitalist. In previous chapters I discussed Siraj, a petty trader who sold Chinese-made watches for a living. The fact that he worked in the informal economy rather than as a government employee and that he sold Chinese rather than Ethiopian-made goods are both at least partially related to policies intended to encourage global exchange and downsize the public sector. However, Siraj's ability to do business was made possible by relationships that have been formed on the basis of a common religion, birthplace, and ethnicity. Siraj is an Oromo Muslim from Wollo (northeastern Ethiopia). Most of the other young men who sat with him selling watches were from a similar background. If Siraj needed to borrow money, he relied on these young men. They shared with him because they had the same homeland and practiced the same religion with a similar degree of piety. In 2005 Siraj used these relationships to pull together a large amount of money that he used to start a business selling Chinese-made clothing in a remote area near a gold mine. Siraj's business was highly profitable, and he returned to Jimma with gifts for his friends, including honey and mangoes for me. In the Ethiopian case, neoliberal policies clearly do not cause all relationships to function on the basis of the market. Rather, policies associated with the creation of markets necessitate economically irrational relationships. The expansion of the informal economy that is partially a result of structural adjustment means that young men like Siraj are increasingly reliant on friendships, trust, and gifting to do business. Capitalist processes do not inevitably transform all of the hidden pockets of nonmarket social relations. Rather, uneven global economic development often produces nonmarket relations.

I have discussed how young men experience time and space. Like their economic activities, young men's temporal and spatial experiences were influenced but not determined by capitalism. These young men did not experience something like time-space compression; rather, time expanded for them as the possibility of attaining their aspirations seemed well beyond the foreseeable future. The downsizing of the public sector was certainly important in creating the widespread unemployment that influenced their experiences of time and space. This did not, however, cause their day-to-day lives to be increasingly defined through the market. For young men, time and space were not evaluated in terms of their potential for maximizing material goods. Instead they were conceived of in terms of social relationships. The struggle to experience progress and the desire to migrate abroad were both based on a desire to reposition themselves within social relationships.

When I visited Siraj in 2008, he was proud to tell me that he had continued to progress in his relationships with others. In a recent phone conversation, his mother told him that he should stop sending money and that he should focus on his own life. Siraj's business activities had continued to expand, and he was driving a minibus in an area where lucrative contracts were common. The owner of the minibus was a source of loans and gifts, and, like previous benefactors, he shared Siraj's birthplace, ethnicity, and religion. Siraj noted that his ethical behavior was also highly important for securing this relationship. Siraj regularly sent large sums of money to his family. He was particularly proud that he had paid approximately five thousand birr (around five hundred U.S. dollars at the time) for his sister to travel to Beirut to work as a domestic servant, thus providing a long-term source of income for his family. With the passage of time Siraj had become a significant source of support for his extended family, and now further progress could be made. He was capable of starting his own family and thus transforming his position within social relationships once again. For Siraj, work and spatial movement had facilitated a shift in the correspondence between time and relationships. Relationships now moved with time in the progressive manner that Siraj desired.

The Ethiopian case provides clear evidence of the limits of capitalism. J. K. Gibson-Graham does not, however, primarily rely on empirical evidence to support her critique of the notion of capitalism as a unified system. Rather, she appears to be operating on the basis of something like Richard Rorty's notion of knowledge as hope. Gibson-Graham writes, "Understood as a unified system or structure, Capitalism is not ultimately vulnerable to local and partial efforts at transformation" (1996: 256). "The inability of Capitalism to coexist thus produces not only the present impossibility of alternatives but their future unlikelihood" (1996: 258). The truth of this argument is based in part on its relationship with a hopeful future, rather than its correspondence with real practices. An understanding of capitalism as finite and limited has greater justification than an understanding of capitalism as a unified and totalizing economic system, because the former provides more potential for the imagination and attainment of hopeful alternatives.

From the perspective developed by Gibson-Graham, the most important flaw in Harvey's analysis is that it does not provide grounds for hope. Working from the Marxian assumption that ideas and beliefs are closely related to economic context, Harvey argues that the speculative and chaotic nature of capitalism actually supports imaginative production. The sheer immensity of consumer opportunity that exists within a capitalist economy is evidence of the vast potential to imagine new possibilities. Harvey writes, "If such fictitious and imaginary elements surround us at every turn, then the possibility also exists of 'growing' imaginary alternatives within its midst" (2000: 211). Although Harvey's analysis is intended to create hope, it seems that he may be doing exactly the opposite. Economic context certainly influences people's conceptions of the possible, but even in recuperating the possibility for hope, Harvey gives far too much causative power to capitalism. Implicit in Harvey's argument that capitalism provides a ripe environment for speculative imagination is the notion that capitalism is everywhere and all-encompassing. If capitalism truly controls collective consciousness to such a great degree, then any alternative must be just as far reaching and totalizing. The process of change must infiltrate all aspects of day-to-day life. One mode of production must replace another.

Harvey writes that "insurgent political practices must occur in all theaters on this long frontier. A generalized insurgency that changes the shape and direction of social life requires collaborative and coordinating actions in all of them" (2000: 234). This is certainly an ambitious project. It is perhaps no accident that the utopian story that provides a playful finish to Harvey's book is a postapocalyptic narrative in which total collapse is necessary before rebuilding is possible. The concrete realities of economic practices in Ethiopia indicate that the all-encompassing beast that Harvey sees in capitalism is perhaps quite limited in its reach. For this reason an insurgent politics need not occur at multiple levels. Change may occur in specific and isolated sites. These sites are not completely disconnected from capitalist processes, but it would be a mistake to define them as "capitalism." I have described how unemployed young men experience stratification in terms of differences in control over social relationships. This indicates that inequality is not entirely determined by something called capitalism and that relations of inequality may change even while local economic policies remain the same.

I have little hope that humans can develop an alternative to capitalism as Harvey conceives it. I do, however, have great hope for the possibility of imagining desirable futures for a world of diverse economic practices that are embedded in social relationships. Numerous possibilities exist, and we know this because they are already being practiced in places like Jimma, Ethiopia. It is certainly not my claim that because economic policy does not determine social relationships, political activism is not necessary. Rather, I believe that the continuing importance of social relationships and the indeterminate nature of young men's lives encourages action on multiple fronts. As the examples discussed here indicate, in contrast to images of young men as emasculated and "simply sitting" or as dangerous explosives, young men continually act strategically to balance interrelated material and social aspirations. Youth in Ethiopia face enormous barriers to attaining their aspirations, and yet hope is never completely cut. Youth struggle for friendships, money, marriage, and jobs. At times they wait and invest their hope in particular events such as the DV lottery or a national election, but when these events pass, young people return to their daily struggles for a better life. In a similar manner, I believe my analysis supports working toward specific political changes. Rather than adopting the pessimistic perspective advanced in many journalistic accounts that improving quality of life in Africa is impossible, there must be acknowledgment that the future is unknown. For Jimma residents, this may mean working for political change at a local level rather than waiting for a regime change in Addis Ababa. Ethiopians also resist inequality by crossing national borders, illegally or legally, and implicitly demanding that access to resources and opportunities should not be determined by nationality. Acts of resistance and solidarity are also possible elsewhere. In the United States, for example, the massive government subsidies paid to U.S. farmers are a continued threat, to the livelihoods of not only Ethiopian farmers but also farmers in much of the global South. In the absence of the generalized insurgency that Harvey calls for, specific actions can be taken to change policies that exacerbate global inequality, and international coalitions may be formed to hold accountable the corporations that work with states to profit from the extraction of resources from Africa. It is possible to simultaneously work for political change while still acknowledging that such changes are made extremely difficult by structural barriers.

If one accepts that neoliberalism does not provide an adequate explanatory principle for the cultural and economic dynamics of urban Africa, then a space is opened for exploring new analytical directions. This perspective offers hope because it undermines the determining power of neoliberal capitalism. It facilitates the imagination of alternative possibilities for the future. In the sense that this analytical space is not predetermined by a single theory or economy, it represents a space of hope.

Notes

INTRODUCION

1. *Tesfa qoretewal* sometimes implies that a person has cut his or her own hope, or that one causes oneself to be hopeless. I do not believe this is the case for Ethiopian youth. I argue that Ethiopian young people simultaneously experience hope and hopelessness, and that these emotions are closely related to structural economic conditions.

2. Mixed religious and ethnic groups were the norm among young male friends, but this was not generally the case for adult men. For the most part, groups of adult male friends that I interacted with tended to be of the same ethnicity and religion. This generational difference may be a result of the economic and political shifts that I describe in Chapter 1.

3. I use *progress* in place of the Amharic *lewt*. In Kenneth Maes's study of health care volunteers in Addis Ababa, *lewt* was also commonly mentioned as an aspiration or goal (Maes 2010). Maes translates *lewt* as "change," and indeed this is the definition offered in many English–Amharic dictionaries (Aklilu 1986: 6). In the narratives of youth involved in my research, however, *lewt* consistently referred to gradual improvement over time, and therefore I translate it as "progress."

4. The convention when citing Ethiopian scholars is often to use the first, rather than the second name. In Ethiopia the father's first name becomes the second name of his children, and people are referred to by their first names. For example, in Ethiopia I am Dr. Daniel, not Dr. Mains. However, many of the Ethiopian scholars that I cite are Ethiopian Americans who have adopted Western naming practices. For the sake of consistency, I adopt the standard Western practice of listing last name first in the bibliography and referring to scholars by their last names. Researchers should, however, keep in mind that in some libraries, particularly in Ethiopia, the works cited in my bibliography will be listed by the author's first name. For example, Bahru Zewde's

important books on the history of modern Ethiopia will be cataloged under *Bahru*, rather than *Zewde*.

5. Anthropologists have gone far beyond Harvey's notion of neoliberalism as a class project. John Clarke (2008) gives a useful description of the various ways that anthropologists and others have employed the concept of neoliberalism.

6. Examples of the isolated extraction of resources described by Ferguson (2006) may be found in the recent exploration of oil drilling possibilities in the Gambella and Ogaden regions of Ethiopia. Perhaps not coincidentally, both of these areas have experienced escalating levels of violence.

7. Partially in reaction to conceptions of a singular neoliberalism, anthropologists have increasingly advocated examinations of locally specific neoliberalisms and how people rework neoliberal discourses in new and surprising ways (Ellison 2009; Kanna 2010; Rudnyckyj 2009). Although there is certainly value in this move, there is also a danger of expanding the category of neoliberalism so far that the term loses analytical utility (Collier 2009; Mains, forthcoming, "Blackouts and Progress"). In these analyses it is often unclear which aspects of neoliberalism are being retained and discarded in the formation of localized neoliberalisms.

8. I refer to J. K. Gibson-Graham in the singular because she is the combined identity of Julie Graham and Katherine Gibson.

CHAPTER 1

1. Electricity, improved phone service, and even the Internet came to Goha Tsion in the early 2000s, but it still would not be considered a city by residents of Addis Ababa.

2. The Oromo are the most populous ethnic group in Ethiopia and include Muslims, Orthodox and Protestant Christians, as well as believers in the sky god, Waaqaa.

3. At the time of my research, Thursday markets still drew the largest crowds.

4. *Ferenj* means "foreigner," and *arada* is something that is elevated or held in higher esteem than others. While the label *ferenj* clearly stems from the Italians' residence in this neighborhood, *arada* implies both that the neighborhood is at a slightly higher elevation than other areas and that the Italians sought to elevate themselves by living separately from Ethiopians. *Mahel Ketema* translates as "city center," and this neighborhood is often referred to as *Shoa Berr* ("the door to the Shoa region"), or *Arab Terra* ("the place of Arabs").

5. In a survey of secondary and college students conducted by Donald Levine, 55 percent were Amhara, 22 percent Tigrayan, 15 percent Oromo, 4 percent Gurage, and 4 percent other (1965: 114).

6. Among urban youth, 37.8 percent of the labor force was unemployed in 1990; and then 59 percent in 1994; and 54.3 percent in 1997 (Krishnan 1998). Based on a different survey conducted in 1994, Serneels (2007) claims that unemployment among urban young men (ages fifteen to thirty; does not include active students) is more than 50 percent. The average length of unemployment was three to four years, and most unemployed were first-time job seekers.

7. Serneels does briefly acknowledge the possibility that notions of "good" and "bad" work may influence youth employment decisions and acknowledges the need for more qualitative research in order to understand why youth make the apparently irrational decision to avoid taking on other forms of work while waiting for an opportunity in the public sector.

CHAPTER 2

1. It is interesting that the same idiomatic terms are used in Amharic and English. I am uncertain about the origins of the expressions *to kill time* and *to pass time* in Amharic. Although the young men with whom I worked did not have adequate experience with English to be aware of these phrases, I did occasionally hear educated adults make statements in both English and Amharic such as, "Today's youth are just killing time." Young men may have adopted the phrase from educated English speakers. The use of these terms may reflect the notion that in contrast to the lives of unemployed young men, time should be used productively.

2. Weiss (2005: 109) notes that both the Swahili and Haya terms for *thought* describe "worries/troubles," and he speculates that this may indicate a "widespread semantic association in East Africa." It is interesting that the Amharic term for *thought* also expresses similar meanings.

3. Opinions were often split regarding Indian films in Ethiopia. On one hand, as in Larkin's study, some young people found them more appropriate for the relatively conservative culture of Muslim and Orthodox Christian Ethiopia. The emphasis on family and the theme of transformation from poverty to wealth were generally appreciated. On the other hand, some youth argued that Indian films are "for children," and they tired of the choreographed dances and songs. In the Ethiopian context, U.S. films were not seen as "ideologically loaded," as they are in Muslim Nigeria, and Western culture was not perceived as something that must be resisted.

4. One of the most striking things about this film is that the woman's family eats only imported packaged foods and never *injera*. The common explanation for this among the Jimma audience was that the owner of an import business had sponsored the film in exchange for numerous product placements.

5. Brian Larkin (2008) describes a similar dynamic in contemporary Hausa films that depict romantic relationships as based on mutual affection between two individuals rather than a relationship between extended families.

6. The future for young men was not conceptualized in concrete temporal terms. Connecting the present with the future implied not that young men knew where they would be in five years but that they had a general sense of confidence that they would experience progress with the passage of time.

7. Italics denote words that were spoken in English.

8. This appears to be partially related to notions of public space in Jimma. To wander around (*mezor*), especially in the afternoon, is associated with being a *duriye* ("delinquent"—described further later in this chapter). To be seen in public like this frequently leads to insults. One of the advantages of khat is that it is chewed in private and it consumes a large amount of time. Although a person may be unemployed, at least the individual's idleness will not be visible if he is hidden away chewing khat. Some of the few unemployed youth who did not chew khat resented the fact that because they spent more of their time in public areas, they were considered duriye.

9. Although khat was perceived by some as increasing one's libido to uncontrollable levels, for others it caused impotence that could sometimes be overcome with heavy drinking.

10. For a detailed discussion of the relationship between khat, sex, and HIV, see Abebe and colleagues (2005).

11. It was not simply the fact that I lived in Atlanta before conducting research that caused these young men to reference the city. Both Habtamu and his friends had family living in the Atlanta area.

12. In contrast to Biaya's (2005) discussion of youth in Addis Ababa, crime was not valorized among young men in Jimma. While Biaya is correct to note that becoming a *shifta* ("bandit") was common among nobility who wished to access power in the nineteenth century, I never observed the term *shifta* being used in a positive manner or to describe young men at all.

13. It is worth noting that one video house escaped harassment. Tesfaye's video house, located in Kulo Berr, continued to operate throughout the shutdown, thus drawing enormous crowds because of the lack of competition. He was also able to hire the best Hindi-to-Amharic translator in Jimma away from another video house. Tesfaye explained that he was able to capitalize on the shutdown because he showed only Indian movies, which were not considered a negative cultural influence. While this may have partially explained the lack of police attention, he later acknowledged that because he grew up in Kulo Berr, most of the police were his friends and he was always generous with them. Whatever the reason, Tesfaye's ability to expand his business during a phase when others were suffering losses meant that his monthly profits were three to four times those of other video houses that I examined. His take-home pay was greater than that earned by a doctor at Jimma University.

14. *Adegeñña* means "dangerous." The dictionary definition of *bozeni* is "lumpen proletariat" (Aklilu 1986). Although it is sometimes used in a similar manner to *duriye*, it is often applied more specifically to young criminals.

15. Also similar to Liechty's study, women usually watched films only when their brothers brought videos home and shared them with the family. In Ethiopia this practice was confined to the relatively small portion of the population who had access to a DVD or videocassette player.

CHAPTER 3

1. Eva Poluha (2004) and Amy Stambach (2000) insightfully examine the day-to-day construction of power relationships through classroom instruction among children in Addis Ababa and Tanzania, respectively.

2. The value of education was not entirely conceived of in terms of its utility for obtaining employment. The symbolic value of completing a particular level of education provides a source of respect that is of intrinsic value. Among teachers, for example, there is a clear hierarchy between those with two-year diplomas and those with four-year degrees. Those with a degree have greater earning potential, but the value of the degree cannot be easily quantified. Particularly among adults, in casual discussions about neighbors and friends, the educational level of the object of discussion is established, and this sets a tone for the rest of the conversation. Fitting with notions of personhood described in early ethnographies of Amhara in northern Ethiopia (Levine 1965; Hoben 1973), educational attainment is often treated as a source of status regardless of other personal attributes. A titled lord commanded respect based on his title, not because of an underlying difference in his cultural practices or lineage. In the same manner, degrees, diplomas, and other signifiers of educational attainment were valued without the assumption that the degree holder was a different quality of person.

3. As in many of the private elementary schools in Addis Ababa, the quality of education at Eldan School in Jimma was excellent, and the price was high. Including transportation, the monthly fee was one hundred birr, nearly half the monthly salary of a day laborer or low-level government worker, but within reach of most urban professionals. Based on observations at Eldan School, I would predict that most of these students are able to advance to postsecondary education and access desirable employment. In this

sense, private education may be drastically changing the class structure in urban Ethiopia as well as the urban/rural divide.

4. *Shuro* is a spicy chickpea paste that is a popular dish with most Ethiopians and generally eaten daily by poor families.

5. Fertility rates in urban Ethiopia have dropped dramatically in recent years, to the point that they are below replacement levels in Addis Ababa (Kinfu 2000). The common explanation for this decline is that increased education and empowerment of women, combined with increased availability of contraceptives, has caused more women to delay marriage and childbirth. Like Bledsoe, Lerner, and Guyer (2000), my study indicates that attention must also be given to the roles of economic decline and the desires of young men surrounding childbirth in order to understand falling fertility rates.

6. Young men often used the Amharic term *debirt* to describe their condition. *Debirt* is close in meaning to "depression." Both the sight of a person suffering from a physical injury and a day spent alone with nothing to do could be described with the adjective form of *debirt*, but the term is more likely to be applied in the case of the latter.

7. Although the term *ferenj* literally translates as "foreigner," in practice it is not used in reference to Africans of a non-Ethiopian nationality. In most cases a *ferenj* is of European or sometimes Asian descent.

CHAPTER 4

1. As the evidence in this chapter indicates, I do not believe young men in Ethiopia are making decisions about unemployment based on economic maximization. That said, there are other flaws with Serneels's argument that unemployment maximizes one's income in the long term. His argument is based on the assumptions that one will eventually obtain public sector employment and that the high wages earned will make up for the time one spent outside the labor force. First, there is little evidence that unemployed young men eventually obtain government employment. Second, their limited education means that young men who do find government jobs generally receive a relatively low government salary, and are lucky to earn higher incomes than they could have accessed in the private sector.

2. Ethiopians who spoke English often explained that *sira yinakal* means that work is underestimated, but I do not feel that *underestimate* adequately captures the power of perceived negative cultural attitudes toward work.

3. The importance of money in social relations was changing. Extremely wealthy individuals were able to access status. However, while working youth often had more access to money than their unemployed peers, their greater purchasing power did not appear to bring them respect at the community level.

4. This is one of the rare situations in which someone referred to himself as a duriye. In this case, by associating past behavior with being a duriye, Afwerk implies that in the present he is not a duriye.

5. Weiss (2005) offers a similar description of hairstyles as a source of conflict between young men and authorities in urban Tanzania.

CHAPTER 5

1. Based on their monthly journals, two of my unemployed primary informants actually received substantial gifts from their girlfriends. Although other young men sometimes claimed that it would be shameful to receive a gift from a woman, in practice both of these men were happy to accept gifts.

2. *Kitfo* is finely chopped beef mixed with butter and spices that is usually served raw or lightly cooked. It is considered a great delicacy and is especially prized by Gurage people.

3. Based on their lack of education, the generation formed by parents of youth in my study were much more flexible in terms of the work they were willing to accept. The model of accessing government employment through relationships was primarily associated with those who had at least reached, if not completed, the secondary level of education.

4. In her study of youth in Madagascar, Jennifer Cole (2009) also claims that affective relationships have increasingly become decoupled from material accumulation as a result of recent economic shifts.

CHAPTER 6

1. For the 2006 DV lottery, 6,995 Ethiopians were finalists, more than in any other country in the world. Of these, approximately two-thirds will actually receive visas. An obsession with the DV lottery is not unique to Ethiopia, and Piot (2010) has described economic networks surrounding brokers arranging false marriages for DV winners in Togo.

2. Piot (2010) describes different active attempts, including prayer and arranging false marriages and adoptions, to influence the outcome of the DV lottery in Togo. False marriage is certainly common in Ethiopia, but the degree and intensity of active intervention in the DV process does not match what Piot describes for Togo.

3. In his exploration of hope, Crapanzano borrows this term from analyses of cargo cults.

4. The Middle East was referred to as *Arab hager* ("Arab country"), and the most common destinations for young women I knew were Saudi Arabia, Dubai, and Lebanon.

5. The term *habesha* brings together the complexities of ethnic, religious, and national identities in Ethiopia (James et al. 2002; Mains 2004). It may refer to all citizens of Ethiopia or specifically reference the Orthodox Christians who trace their ancestry to highland Ethiopia and have historically dominated the Ethiopian state. Many citizens therefore deny the label of *habesha* and prefer to identify themselves in terms of ethnicity or religion. These individuals are often uncomfortable being identified as Ethiopian as well. Those espousing the discourse of bad culture that I encountered in Jimma did not appear to be conscious of these issues concerning national identity. Rather they assumed that descriptions of "Ethiopian culture" could be applied to people like themselves—ethnically and religiously diverse urban dwellers. Rather than explore the intricacies of national identity in this chapter, I assume that discussions of Ethiopian culture are a way of critiquing the practices and beliefs of one's community.

6. The relationship between culture and development was not necessarily a new idea. In 1908 Emperor Menelik issued a proclamation that is worth quoting in full:

> Let those who insult the worker on account of his labour cease to do so. Discrimination is the result of ignorance. God said to Adam: "in the sweat of thy brow shalt thou eat bread." If we do not carry out this injunction, if everyone is idle, there will be neither government nor country. In European countries when people undertake new kinds of work and make cannon, guns, trains, and other things . . . they are praised and given more assistants, not insulted in account of their craft. But you by your insults are going to leave my country without

people who can make the plough; the land will thus become barren and destitute. Hereafter anyone who insults these people is insulting me. From this time forth anyone found insulting another on account of his work will be punished by a year's imprisonment. If Officials find it difficult to imprison such a person for a year let the former be arrested and sent before me. (R. Pankhurst 1968)

CONCLUSION

1. Ironically, given the Marxist roots of David Harvey's arguments, Richard Rorty argues that at the turn of the twenty-first century, Marxist thought has little value for creating the sorts of historical narratives that he calls for. Although I critique Harvey, I also believe that he convincingly demonstrates the continued relevance of Marx for understanding inequality.

References

Abebe, Dawit, Asfaw Debella, Amare Dejene, Ambaye Degefa, Almaz Abebe, Kelbessa Urga, and Lemma Ketema. 2005. "Khat Chewing Habit as a Possible Risk Behavior for HIV Infection: A Case-Control Study." *Ethiopian Journal of Health and Development* 19 (3): 174–181.

Abelti, Gebeyehu, Marco Brazzoduro, and Behailu Gebremedhin. 2001. *Housing Conditions and Demand for Housing in Urban Ethiopia*. Addis Ababa, Ethiopia: Central Statistical Authority.

Abu-Lughod, Lila. 2005. *Dramas of Nationhood: The Politics of Television in Egypt*. Chicago: University of Chicago Press.

Aklilu, Amsalu. 1986. *Amharic–English Dictionary*. Addis Ababa, Ethiopia: Kuraz.

Amit, Vered, and Noel Dyke, eds. n.d. *Young Men in Uncertain Times*. Oxford: Berghahn Books.

Appadurai, Arjun. 1996. *Modernity at Large: Cultural Dimensions of Globalization*. Minneapolis: University of Minnesota Press.

Arrighi, Giovanni. 2002. "The African Crisis: World Systemic and Regional Analysis." *New Left Review* 15:5–36.

Baker, Jonathan. 1986. *The Rural–Urban Dichotomy in the Developing World: A Case Study from Northern Ethiopia*. Oslo: Norwegian University Press.

Balsvik, Randi Ronning. 1985. *Haile Selassie's Students: The Intellectual and Social Background to Revolution, 1952–1977*. East Lansing: Michigan State University.

Barber, Karin. 1997. "The Édá Theatre and *The Secret Is Out*." In *West African Popular Theater*, ed. Karin Barber, John Collins, and Alain Ricard, 183–209. Bloomington: Indiana University Press.

Barnes, Sandra. 1986. *Patrons and Power: Creating a Political Community in Metropolitan Lagos*. Bloomington: Indiana University Press.

Baudrillard, Jean. 1982. *For a Critique of the Political Economy of the Sign*. St. Louis, MO: Telos Press.

Besteman, Catherine. 2005. "Why I Disagree with Robert Kaplan." In *Why America's Top Pundits Are Wrong: Anthropologists Talk Back*, ed. Catherine Besteman and Hugh Gusterson, 83–101. Berkeley: University of California Press.

Biaya, Tshikala. 2005. "Youth and Street Culture in Urban Africa: Addis Ababa, Dakar, and Kinshasa." In *Makers and Breakers: Children and Youth in Postcolonial Africa*, ed. Alcinda Honwana and Filip De Boeck, 215–228. Oxford, England: James Currey.

Bizuneh, Genene, Teshome Adino, Giuseppe Gesano, Antonella Guarneri, and Frank Heins. 2001. *Work Status and Unemployment in Urban Ethiopia*. Addis Ababa, Ethiopia: Central Statistical Authority.

Bjeren, Gunilla. 1985. *Migration to Shashamene: Ethnicity, Gender, and Occupation in Urban Ethiopia*. Uppsala, Sweden: Scandinavian Institute for African Studies.

Bledsoe, Caroline, Susana Lerner, and Jane Guyer, ed. 2000. *Fertility and the Male Life-Cycle in the Era of Fertility Decline*. Oxford, England: Oxford University Press.

Bohannan, Paul. 1959. "The Impact of Money on an African Subsistence Economy." *Journal of Economic History*. 19 (4): 491–503.

Boli, John, Francisco Ramirez, and John Meyer. 1985. "Explaining the Origins and Expansion of Mass Education." *Comparative Education Review* 29 (2): 145–170.

Bourdieu, Pierre. (1963) 1979. *Algeria 1960: The Disenchantment of the World*, trans. Richard Nice. Cambridge, England: Cambridge University Press.

———. 1977. *Outline of a Theory of Practice*. Cambridge, England: Cambridge University Press.

———. 1984. *Distinction: A Social Critique of the Judgment of Taste*. Cambridge, MA: Harvard University Press.

Bourdieu, Pierre, and Loïc J. D. Wacquant. 1992. *An Invitation to Reflexive Sociology*. Chicago: University of Chicago Press.

Bourgois, Philippe. 1995. *In Search of Respect: Selling Crack in Spanish Harlem*. New York: Cambridge University Press.

Buck-Morss, Susan. 2000. *Dreamworld and Catastrophe: The Passing of Mass Utopia in East and West*. Cambridge, MA: MIT Press.

Central Statistical Authority (CSA). 2006. *Statistical Abstract 2005*. Addis Ababa, Ethiopia: Federal Democratic Republic of Ethiopia.

———. 2008. *Statistical Abstract 2007*. Addis Ababa, Ethiopia: Federal Democratic Republic of Ethiopia.

Clarke, John. 2008. "Living With/in and Without Neoliberalism." *Focaal—European Journal of Anthropology* 51:135–147.

Cole, Jennifer. 2004. "Fresh Contact in Tamatave, Madagascar: Sex, Money, and Intergenerational Transformation." *American Ethnologist* 31 (4): 573–588.

———. 2005. "The Jaombilo of Tamatave (Madagascar), 1992–2004: Reflections on Youth and Globalization." *Journal of Social History* 38 (4): 891–914.

———. 2009. "Love, Money, and Economies of Intimacy in Tamatave, Madagascar." In *Love in Africa*, ed. Jennifer Cole and Lynn Thomas, 109–134. Chicago: University of Chicago Press.

Cole, Jennifer, and Lynn Thomas, eds. 2009. *Love in Africa*. Chicago: University of Chicago Press.

Collier, Stephen. 2009. "Topologies of Power: Foucault's Analysis of Political Government Beyond 'Governmentality.'" *Theory, Culture & Society* 26 (6): 78–108.

Comaroff, Jean, and John Comaroff, eds. 1993. *Modernity and Its Malcontents: Ritual and Power in Postcolonial Africa*. Chicago: University of Chicago Press.

Comaroff, Jean, and John Comaroff. 2000. "Millennial Capitalism: First Thoughts on a Second Coming." *Public Culture* 12 (2): 291–343.

———. 2005. "Reflections on Youth: From the Past to the Postcolony." In *Makers and Breakers: Children and Youth in Postcolonial Africa*, ed. Alcinda Honwana and Filip De Boeck, 19–30. Oxford, England: James Currey.

Crapanzano, Vincent. 2003. "Reflections on Hope as a Category for Social and Psychological Analysis." *Cultural Anthropology* 18 (1): 3–32.

Cruise O'Brien, Donal. 1996. "A Lost Generation? Youth Identity and State Decay in West Africa." In *Postcolonial Identities in Africa*, ed. R. Werbner and T. Ranger, 55–74. London: Zed Books.

De Boeck, Filip. 1999. "Domesticating Diamonds and Dollars: Identity, Expenditure and Sharing in Southwestern Zaire (1984–1997)." In *Globalization and Identity: Dialectics of Flow and Closure*, ed. B. Meyer and P. Geschiere, 177–208. Oxford, England: Blackwell.

Demerath, Peter. 2003. "Negotiating Individualist and Collectivist Futures: Emerging Subjectivities and Social Forms in Papua New Guinean High Schools." *Anthropology and Education Quarterly* 34 (2): 136–157.

De Weerdt, Joachim, Stefan Dercon, Tessa Bold, and Alula Pankhurst. 2007. "Membership-Based Indigenous Insurance Organizations in Ethiopia and Tanzania." In *Membership-Based Organizations of the Poor*, ed. Martha Chen, Renana Jhabvala, Ravi Kanbur, and Carol Richards, 157–176. London: Routledge.

Diouf, Mamadou. 2003. "Engaging Postcolonial Cultures: African Youth and Public Space." *African Studies Review* 46 (1): 1–12.

Donham, Donald. 1986. "Old Abyssinia and the New Ethiopian Empire: Themes in Social History." In *The Southern Marches of Imperial Ethiopia: Essays in History and Social Anthropology*, ed. Donald Donham and Wendy James, 3–48. Cambridge, England: Cambridge University Press.

———. 1999a. *History, Power, Ideology: Central Issues in Marxism and Anthropology.* Berkeley: University of California Press.

———. 1999b. *Marxist Modern: An Ethnographic History of the Ethiopian Revolution.* Berkeley: University of California Press.

Dore, R. 1976. *The Diploma Disease: Education, Qualification, and Development.* London: Allen and Unwin.

Ellison, James. 2006. "Everyone Can Do as He Wants": Economic Liberalization and Emergent Forms of Antipathy in Southern Ethiopia." *American Ethnologist* 33 (4): 665–686.

———. 2009. "Governmentality and the Family: Neoliberal Choices and Emergent Kin Relations in Southern Ethiopia." *American Anthropologist* 111 (1): 81–92.

Escobar, Arturo. 1995. *Encountering Development: The Making and Unmaking of the Third World.* Princeton, NJ: Princeton University Press.

Fallers, Lloyd. 1966. "Social Stratification and Economic Processes in Africa." In *Class, Status, and Power: Social Stratification in Comparative Perspective*, ed. R. Bendix and S. M. Lipset, 141–149. New York: Free Press.

Ferguson, James. 1985. "The Bovine Mystique: Power, Property and Livestock in Rural Lesotho." *Man* 20 (4): 647–674.

———.1990. *The Anti-Politics Machine: "Development," Depoliticization, and Bureaucratic Power in Lesotho.* Cambridge, England: Cambridge University Press.

———.1999. *Expectations of Modernity.* Berkeley: University of California Press.

———. 2006. *Global Shadows: Africa in the Neoliberal World Order.* Durham, NC: Duke University Press.

————.2007. "Formalities of Poverty: Thinking about Social Assistance in Neoliberal South Africa." *African Studies Review* 50 (2): 71–86.

Freeman, Carla. 2000. *High Tech and High Heels in the Global Economy: Women, Work, and Pink-Collar Identities in the Caribbean.* Durham, NC: Duke University Press.

Friedman, Jonathan. 1994. *Cultural Identity and Global Processes.* London: Sage.

Fuglesang, Minou. 1994. Veils and Videos: Female Youth Culture on the Kenyan Coast. Stockholm: Stockholm University.

Gebissa, Ezekiel. 2004. *Leaf of Allah: Khat and the Transformation of Agriculture in Harerege, Ethiopia, 1875–1991.* Oxford, England: James Currey.

Gemeda, Guluma. 1984. "The Process of State Formation in the Gibe Region: The Case of Gomma and Jimma." In *Proceedings of the Second Annual Seminar of the Department of History.* Addis Ababa, Ethiopia: Addis Ababa University.

————. 1987. "An Outline of the Early History of Jimma Town." Paper presented at the Fourth Annual Seminar of the Department of History, Addis Ababa University, Awassa, Ethiopia, July 9–11.

Geschiere, Peter. 1997. *The Modernity of Witchcraft: Politics and the Occult in Postcolonial Africa.* Charlottesville: University of Virginia Press.

Gibson-Graham, J. K. 1996. *The End of Capitalism (as We Knew It): A Feminist Critique of Political Economy.* Oxford, England: Blackwell.

————. 2006. *A Postcapitalist Politics.* Minneapolis: University of Minnesota Press.

Gondola, Didier. 1999. "Dream and Drama: The Search for Elegance among Congolese Youth." *African Studies Review* 42 (1): 23–48

Goodstein, Elizabeth. 2005. *Experience without Qualities: Boredom and Modernity.* Stanford, CA: Stanford University Press.

Goody, Jack. 1976. *Production and Reproduction: A Comparative Study of the Domestic Domain.* Cambridge, England: Cambridge University Press.

Gould, W.T.S. 1993. *People and Education in the Third World.* Essex, England: Longman.

Guyer, Jane. 2007. "Prophecy and the Near Future: Thoughts on Macroeconomic, Evangelical, and Punctuated Time." *American Ethnologist* 34 (3): 409–421.

Hansen, Karen Tranberg. 2000. "Gender and Difference: Youth, Bodies, and Clothing in Zambia." In *Gender, Agency, and Change: An Anthropological Perspective*, ed. Victoria Goddard, 32–55 . London: Routledge.

————. 2005. "Getting Stuck in the Compound: Some Odds against Social Adulthood in Lusaka." *Africa Today* 51 (4): 2–17.

Hart, Keith. 1973. "Informal Income Opportunities and Urban Employment in Ghana." *Journal of Modern African Studies* (September): 61–89.

————. 1975. "Swindler or Public Benefactor? The Entrepreneur in His Community." In *Changing Social Structure in Ghana*, ed. J. Goody, 1–35. London: International African Institute.

————. 1988. "Kinship, Contract and Trust: The Economic Organization of Migrants in an African City Slum." In *Trust: Making and Breaking Co-operative Relations*, ed. D. Gambetta, 176–193. Oxford, England: Blackwell.

Harvey, David. 1990. *The Condition of Postmodernity.* Cambridge, England: Blackwell.

————. 2000. *Spaces of Hope.* Berkeley: University of California Press.

————. 2005. *A Brief History of Neoliberalism.* Oxford, England: Oxford University Press.

Hassen, Mohammed. 1990. *The Oromo of Ethiopia: A History 1570–1860.* Cambridge, England: Cambridge University Press.

Hoben, Allan. 1970. "Social Stratification in Traditional Amhara Society." In *Social Stratification in Africa*, ed. Arthur Tuden and Leonard Plotnicov, 187–224. New York: Free Press.

———. 1973. *Land Tenure among the Amhara of Ethiopia*. Chicago: University of Chicago Press.

Hutchinson, Sharon. 1996. *Nuer Dilemmas: Coping with Money, War, and the State*. Berkeley: University of California Press.

Jalata, Asafa. 1993. *Oromia and Ethiopia: State Formation and Ethnonational Conflict, 1886–1992*. Boulder, CO: Rienner.

James, Wendy, Donald Donham, E. Kurimoto, and A. Triulzi, eds. 2002. *Remapping Ethiopia: Socialism and After*. Oxford, England: James Currey.

Jeffrey, Craig. 2008. "'Generation Nowhere': Rethinking Youth through the Lens of Unemployed Young Men." *Progress in Human Geography* 32 (6): 739–758.

———. 2010. *Timepass: Youth, Class, and the Politics of Waiting in India*. Stanford, CA: Stanford University Press.

Jeffrey, Craig, Patricia Jeffery, and Roger Jeffery. 2008. *Degrees without Freedom? Education, Masculinities and Unemployment in North India*. Stanford, CA: Stanford University Press.

Johnson-Hanks, Jennifer. 2006. *Uncertain Honor: Modern Motherhood in an African Crisis*. Chicago: University of Chicago Press.

Kanna, Ahmed. 2010. "Flexible Citizenship in Dubai: Neoliberal Subjectivity in the Emerging 'City-Corporation.'" *Cultural Anthropology* 25 (1): 100–129.

Kaplan, Robert. 2000. *The Coming Anarchy: Shattering Dreams of the Post Cold War*. New York: Random House.

Karp, Ivan. 2002. "Development and Personhood: Tracing the Contours of a Moral Discourse." In *Critically Modern: Alternatives, Alterities, Anthropologies*, ed. Bruce Knauft, 82–104. Bloomington: Indiana University Press.

Katz, Cindi. 2004. *Growing Up Global: Economic Restructuring and Children's Everyday Lives*. Minneapolis: University of Minnesota Press.

Kinfu, Yohannes. 2000. "Below Replacement Fertility in Tropical Africa? Some Evidence from Addis Ababa." *Journal of Population Research* 17 (1): 63–82.

Kingfisher, Catherine, and Jeff Maskovsky. 2008. "Introduction: The Limits of Neoliberalism." *Critique of Anthropology* 28 (2): 115–126.

Kipnis, Andrew. 2008. "Audit Cultures: Neoliberal Governmentality, Socialist Legacy, or Technologies of Governing?" *American Ethnologist* 35 (2): 275–289.

Knauft, Bruce. 2002a. *Critically Modern: Alternatives, Alterities, Anthropologies*. Bloomington: Indiana University Press.

———. 2002b. *Exchanging the Past: A Rainforest World of Before and After*. Chicago: University of Chicago Press.

Kondo, Dorinne. 1990. *Crafting Selves: Power, Gender, and Discourses of Identity in a Japanese Workplace*. Chicago: University of Chicago Press.

Koselleck, Reinhart. (1979) 1985. *Futures Past: On the Semantics of Historical Time*, trans. Keith Tribe. Cambridge, MA: MIT Press.

Krishnan, Pramila. 1998. *The Urban Labour Market During Structural Adjustment: Ethiopia 1990–1997*. Oxford, England: Centre for the Study of African Economies.

Larkin, Brian. 1997. "Indian Films and Nigerian Lovers: Media and the Creation of Parallel Modernities." *Africa* 67 (3): 406–440.

———. 2008. *Signal and Noise: Media, Infrastructure, and Urban Culture in Nigeria*. Durham, NC: Duke University Press.

Levine, Donald. 1965. *Wax and Gold: Tradition and Innovation in Ethiopian Culture.* Chicago: University of Chicago Press.

―――. 1974. *Greater Ethiopia: The Evolution of a Multiethnic Society.* Chicago: University of Chicago Press.

Lewis, Herbert. 1964. "A Reconsideration of the Socio-political System of the Western Galla." *Journal of Semitic Studies* 9 (1): 139–143.

―――. 2001. *Jimma Abba Jifar: An Oromo Monarchy, Ethiopia 1830–1932.* Lawrenceville, NJ: Red Sea Press.

Liechty, Mark. 2003. *Suitably Modern: Making Middle-Class Culture in a New Consumer Society.* Princeton, NJ: Princeton University Press.

Lloyd, Cynthia, ed. 2005. *Growing Up Global: The Changing Transition to Adulthood in Developing Countries.* Washington, DC: National Academies Press.

MacGaffey, Janet, and Remy Bazenguissa-Ganga. 2000. *Congo-Paris: Transnational Traders on the Margins of the Law.* Oxford, England: James Currey.

MacLeod, Jay. 2009. *Ain't No Makin' It: Aspirations and Attainment in a Low-Income Neighborhood.* Boulder, CO: Westview Press.

Maes, Kenneth. 2010. "Examining Social Determinants of Food Insecurity, Common Mental Disorders, and Motivations among AIDS Care Volunteers in Urban Ethiopia during the 2008 Food Crisis." Ph.D. dissertation, Emory University, Atlanta, GA.

Mains, Daniel. 2004. "Drinking, Rumour and Ethnicity in Jimma, Ethiopia." *Africa* 74 (3): 341–360.

―――. 2007. "Neoliberal Times: Progress, Boredom, and Shame among Young Men in Urban Ethiopia." *American Ethnologist* 34 (4): 659–673.

―――. Forthcoming. "Blackouts and Progress: Privatization, Infrastructure, and a Developmentalist State in Jimma, Ethiopia." *Cultural Anthropology* 27 (1).

―――. Forthcoming. "Cynicism and Hope: Urban Youth and Relations of Power during the 2005 Ethiopian National Election." In *Contested Power: Traditional Authorities and Elections in Ethiopia,* ed. Kjetil Tronvoll and Tobias Hagmann, Leiden, Netherlands: Brill.

Mannheim, Karl. 1972. "The Problem of Generations." In *The New Pilgrims: Youth Protest in Transition,* ed. Philip Altbach and R. Laufer, 101–138. New York: David McKay.

Markakis, John. 1974. *Ethiopia: Anatomy of a Traditional Polity.* Oxford, England: Clarendon Press.

Masquelier, Adeline. 2005. "The Scorpion's Sting: Youth, Marriage and the Struggle for Social Maturity in Niger." *Journal of the Royal Anthropological Institute* 11:59–83.

―――. 2009. "Lessons from *Rubí*: Love, Poverty, and the Educational Value of Televised Dramas in Niger." In *Love in Africa,* ed. Jennifer Cole and Lynn Thomas, 204–228. Chicago: University of Chicago Press.

Mitchell, J. Clyde, and A. L. Epstein. 1959. "Occupational Prestige and Social Status among Urban Africans in Northern Rhodesia." *Africa* 29:22–39.

Miyazaki, Hirokazu. 2004. *The Method of Hope: Anthropology, Philosophy, and Fijian Knowledge.* Stanford, CA: Stanford University Press.

―――. 2006. "Economy of Dreams: Hope in Global Capitalism and Its Critiques." *Cultural Anthropology* 21 (2): 147–172.

National Urban Planning Institute. 1997. *Report on the Development Plan of Jimma Town.* Addis Ababa, Ethiopia: National Urban Planning Institute.

Negatu, Deresse. 2004. "Chewing Over Khat Closures." *Fortune* (August 1): 1–3, 21.

Newell, Sasha. 2005. "Migratory Modernity and the Cosmology of Consumption in Cote d'Ivoire." In *Migration and Economy: Global and Local Dynamics*, ed. Lillian Trager, 163–192. Walnut Creek, CA: AltaMira Press.

Pankhurst, Alula. 2001. "Dimensions and Conceptions of Marginalisation." In *Living on the Edge: Marginalised Minorities of Craft Workers and Hunters in Southern Ethiopia*, ed. Dena Freeman and Alula Pankhurst, 1–22. Addis Ababa, Ethiopia: Department of Sociology and Social Administration, Addis Ababa University.

Pankhurst, Alula, and Dena Freeman. 2001. "Change and Development: Lessons from the Twentieth Century." In *Living on the Edge: Marginalised Minorities of Craft Workers and Hunters in Southern Ethiopia*, ed. Dena Freeman and Alula Pankhurst, 331–359. Addis Ababa, Ethiopia: Department of Sociology and Social Administration, Addis Ababa University.

Pankhurst, Richard. 1968. *Economic History of Ethiopia, 1800–1935*. Addis Ababa, Ethiopia: Haile Selassie I University Press.

———. 1985. *History of Ethiopian Towns from the Mid-nineteenth Century to 1935*. Stuttgart, Germany: Steiner.

Parkin, D. 1972. *Palms, Wine and Witnesses: Public Spirit and Private Gain in an African Farming Community*. Cambridge, England: Cambridge University Press

Parry, Jonathan. 1989. "On the Moral Perils of Exchange." In *Money and Morality of Exchange*, ed. J. Parry and M. Bloch, 64–93. Cambridge, England: Cambridge University Press.

Paules, Greta. 1991. *Dishing It Out: Power and Resistance among Waitresses in a New Jersey Restaurant*. Philadelphia: Temple University Press.

Piot, Charles. 1999. *Remotely Global: Village Modernity in West Africa*. Chicago: University of Chicago Press.

———. 2005. "Border Practices: Playing the US Diversity Visa Lottery." Annual meeting of the African Studies Association, Washington, DC, November 17–20.

———. 2010. *Nostalgia for the Future: West Africa after the Cold War*. Chicago: University of Chicago Press.

Poluha, Eva. 2004. *The Power of Continuity: Ethiopia through the Eyes of Its Children*. Uppsala, Sweden: Nordiska Afrikainstitutet.

Postone, Moishe. 1993. *Time, Labor, and Social Domination: A Reinterpretation of Marx's Critical Theory*. Cambridge, England: Cambridge University Press.

Powdermaker, Hortense. 1962. *Copper Town: Changing Africa: The Human Situation on the Rhodesian Copperbelt*. New York: Harper and Row Publishers.

Ralph, Michael. 2008. "Killing Time." *Social Text* 97 26 (4): 1–29.

Richards, Audrey. 1940. *The Political System of the Bemba Tribe—Northern Rhodesia*, ed. M. Fortes and E. E. Evans-Pritchard. London: Oxford University Press.

Richards, Paul. 1996. *Fighting for the Rain Forest: War, Youth, and Resources in Sierra Leone*. Portsmouth, NH: Heinemann.

Richland, Justin. 2009. "On Neoliberalism and Other Social Diseases: The 2008 Sociocultural Anthropology Year in Review." *American Anthropologist* 111 (2): 170–176.

Rofel, Lisa. 1999. *Other Modernities: Gendered Yearnings in China after Socialism*. Berkeley: University of California Press.

Rorty, Richard. 1999. *Philosophy and Social Hope*. New York: Penguin.

Rostow, W. W. 1971. *The Stages of Economic Growth: A Non-Communist Manifesto*. Cambridge, England: Cambridge University Press.

Rudnyckyj, Daromir. 2009. "Spiritual Economies: Islam and Neoliberalism in Contemporary Indonesia." *Cultural Anthropology* 24 (1): 104–141.

Schielke, Samuli. 2008. "Boredom and Despair in Rural Egypt." *Contemporary Islam* 2:251–270.

Serneels, Pieter. 2007. "The Nature of Unemployment among Young Men in Urban Ethiopia." *Review of Development Economics* 11 (1): 170–186.

Silberschmidt, Margrethe. 2004. "Masculinities, Sexuality, and Socio-economic Change in Rural and Urban East Africa." In *Rethinking Sexualities in Africa*, ed. Signe Arnfred, 233–250. Uppsala, Sweden: Nordiska Afrikainstitutet.

Stambach, Amy. 2000. *Lessons from Mount Kilimanjaro: Schooling, Community, and Gender in East Africa*. New York: Routledge.

Stoller, Paul. 2002. *Money Has No Smell: The Africanization of New York City*. Chicago: University of Chicago Press.

Strathern, Marilyn. 1988. *The Gender of the Gift: Problems with Women and Problems with Society in Melanesia*. Berkeley: University of California Press.

Taussig, Michael. 1980. *The Devil and Commodity Fetishism in South America*. Chapel Hill: University of North Carolina Press.

Thompson, E. P. 1967. "Time, Work Discipline, and Industrial Capitalism." *Past and Present* 38:56–97.

Tripp, Aili. 1997. *Changing the Rules: The Politics of Liberalization and the Urban Informal Economy in Tanzania*. Berkeley: University of California Press.

Ulimwengu, John, Sindu Workneh, and Zelekawork Paulos. 2009. *Impacts of Soaring Food Price in Ethiopia: Does Location Matter?* Washington, DC: International Food Policy Research Institute.

Weber, Max. 1978. "Class, Status Groups, and Parties." In *Max Weber: Selections in Translation*, ed. W. G. Runcimou, 43–56. Cambridge, England: Cambridge University Press.

Weiss, Brad. 2002. "Thug Realism: Inhabiting Fantasy in Urban Tanzania." *Cultural Anthropology* 17 (1): 93–124.

———. 2004a. "Contentious Futures: Past and Present." In *Producing African Futures: Ritual and Reproduction in a Neoliberal Age*, ed. Brad Weiss, 1–20. Leiden, Netherlands: Brill.

———. 2004b. "Street Dreams: Inhabiting Masculine Fantasy in Neoliberal Tanzania." In *Producing African Futures: Ritual and Reproduction in a Neoliberal Age*, ed. Brad Weiss, 193–228. Leiden, Netherlands: Brill.

———. 2005. "The Barber in Pain: Consciousness, Affliction, and Alterity in Urban East Africa." In *Makers and Breakers: Children and Youth in Postcolonial Africa*, ed. Alcinda Honwana and Filip De Boeck, 102–120. Oxford, England: James Currey.

———. 2009. *Street Dreams and Hip Hop Barbershops: Global Fantasy in Urban Tanzania*. Bloomington: Indiana University Press.

Willis, Paul. 1977. *Learning to Labour: How Working Class Kids Get Working Class Jobs*. Farnborough, England: Saxon House.

Zewde, Bahru. 2002a. *A History of Modern Ethiopia, 1855–1991*. Oxford, England: James Currey.

———. 2002b. *Pioneers of Change in Ethiopia: The Reformist Intellectuals of the Early Twentieth Century*. Oxford, England: James Currey.

Zournazi, Mary. 2003. *Hope: New Philosophies for Change*. New York: Routledge.

Index

Abba Jifar II, 27–28
Abdul Karim, 30
abjection, 2
Abu-Lughod, Lila, 51, 54
Addis Ababa, 27
adegeñña bozeni (dangerous/criminal unemployed youth), 64
afkala (Oromo traders), 29
Afwerk, 70, 100–108, 111, 117–118, 175n4
Ahmed, 123–124
Alemu, 49, 56–57, 128, 130
Al-Moudi, Mohammed, 34
ambitions. *See* aspirations
Amhara: hierarchy and Orthodox Christianity and, 96; land grants to, 30; occupations among, 28, 31–32; and patron/client relationship, 95–98; unemployment among, 35
Amharic, 33
amro yikefetal (opening of the mind), 56
antisocial accumulation, 98
Appadurai, Arjun, 43, 50
arada qwanqwa (urban slang), 109
arrif (cool), 104, 109
Arusha, 109
aspirations: in African youth generally, 2–3; consumer-based, 69–70; and decreased opportunities, 3–4, 88–89, 112, 131; desires to be modern, 8–10; education and, 33, 67–68, 72–73, 75–76; and expectations of government jobs, 4, 35–36, 75, 131; and imagination, 54–55, 59–60; leading to

frustration, 47, 67; leading to reevaluation of work, 160, 163; and masculine ideals, 88; and social relationships, 13–14, 69, 77–78, 84, 151; spatial strategies to achieve, 10–11, 136, 139, 140, 150–152; among working youth, 71, 118
assab (thought), 46
Ato Bashu, 70–71
Ato Seifu, 63
Ato Uta, 74

baking, 71, 124
barbers, 40, 102–104
bargaining/haggling, 105, 106
Bazenguissa-Ganga, Remy, 138–139
Bekele, 116
Berhanu, 45, 124
Beti, 91
bicycle rentals, 106, 118
bicycle repair, 70, 101–102, 163
bizness (material support), 53
Bjeren, Gunilla, 31
blacksmithing, 29, 92
Bohannan, Paul, 89
Boli, John, 76
Bond, James, 51
boredom, 82–83
Bourdieu, Pierre, 12, 84, 88, 112, 127, 131
brewing, home, 71
buda (evil eye), 29
bus station work, 93, 102, 124–125

cafés, 121–122
Cameroon, 91
capitalism, 15–17, 130–132, 164–169
carpentry, 29, 92
car washing, 150
certificates, exam, 74
Chan, Jackie, 51
chewata (play), 6, 60
chewing. *See* khat
chickens, living like, 67
children, goals of raising, 69, 79–81, 85, 144, 160, 163
Christians: greater opportunities for, 31–33, 41; and hierarchy, 96; and holidays, 148; and khat use, 6, 55; and reciprocity, 118
city, definition of, 26
Clarke, John, 172n5
class: and consumption, 90, 91; and cultures of waiting, 46; and gift income, 123–127, 134; government work as transcending, 95; in Jimma City, 27–32, 36–38; and leisure activities, 6; neoliberalism and, 16; portrayal in Ethiopian film, 53; private education and, 174–175n3; in revolutionary urban Ethiopia, 32–33; self-perpetuation of, 88; and status, 11–13; vs. status, 91, 93–94, 112; and unrealistic aspirations, 88–89; working-class youths, 88
coffee, 6, 30–34, 166
Cole, Jennifer, 3, 65, 122
Comaroff, Jean and John, 2
Coming Anarchy, The (Kaplan), 162
commodity exchange, 98
Congo, 137
cost of living, 161
Côte d'Ivoire, 138
craft workers, 28–29, 92–93, 97. *See also* vocational students
Crapanzano, Vincent, 137
cultural styles and prestige, 109, 127

Dakar, 46
Dawro, 30, 31, 40
day laborers, 40, 41
debirt (depression), 175n6
Demerath, Peter, 73
demibeña relationships, 97–98
Derg regime, 9, 29, 32–33, 41, 76, 132, 136
Desta, 163–164
diploma disease/inflation, 75
disconnection, 2
discursive sustainability of hope, 156
Diversity Visa lottery, 83, 136–139
domestic servants, 40, 41, 141–142, 167

Donham, Donald, 8–9
downsizing of public sector, 34, 131–133, 166–167
duriye, 61–62, 65–66, 109
Dyson, Jane, x

economic maximization, 87, 175n1
economic restructuring, 8
economic sustainability of hope, 156
economy of practices, 127
education: annual exam as lottery, 159; degree as source of status, 174n2; and expectations of progress, 71–77, 157–159; free public, 32–33; homogenizing effects of, 76; inflation of, 71, 75; and job availability, 5, 33; linearity of, 77; private schools, 74, 81, 174–175n3; reenrollment in, 158–159; and unemployment rate, 35
ehjebena (eye-opener/morning khat), 101
elections of 2005 and 2010, 35
Ellison, James, 181
English language, 52, 74
EPRDF (Ethiopian People's Revolutionary Democratic Front) policies, 33–35
ESLCE (Ethiopian School Leaving Certificate Examination), 74–75
Ethiopia: from late 1800s to 1974, 27–32; agriculture in, historically, 114; desires to leave, 150–151; ethnicity and identity in, 176n5; map of, viii; postrevolutionary, 33–36; poverty ranking of, 8; revolutionary, 32–33; views of culture in, 146–147. *See also* Jimma
Ethiopian films, 52–54
ethnic federalism, 35
ethnicity: and education, 5, 9, 32, 42; and employment, 35; and "Ethiopian culture," 176n5; and *iddir* membership, 20; and occupation, 31–32, 35; and religion, 33; and rural youth, 34–35; and socializing, 6, 171n1; and stratification, 31–33
Europe: advent of progress in, 75; and boredom, 82; seen as "civilized," 29, 176n6
Evans-Pritchard, E. E., 85
exchange: in Africa generally, 114–115; between class and status, 13–15; between genders, 54, 122; gift income, 41, 55, 120, 122–127; gift vs. commodity, 98–99; as investment in relationships, 129–131; and occupation, 89–90, 96–100; quantitative vs. qualitative, 116, 130; spheres of, 89–90, 98–99; unemployed youth and, 119–126, 129; and *zemed* relationship, 116. *See also* reciprocity
exile within one's country, 138

families: ability to marry/raise children, 47, 69, 79–81, 85, 144, 160, 163; ability to support parents/siblings, 11, 69, 78–79, 94, 117–118, 142; as alternate form of progress, 163–164; female heads of households, 33, 40, 124; home life, 20, 36–38; portrayal in Ethiopian film, 52–53; size of, 69, 80–81, 175n5 (ch. 3). *See also* gifting

farming, 28, 35, 76

farra (rural/backward), 57

fendata (explosive), 3

ferenj (foreigner), 83, 172n4

Ferenj Arada, 30, 38, 45, 105, 172n4

Ferguson, James, 2; on isolated extraction of resources, 172n6; on modernity, 9, 68, 139; on neoliberal capitalism, 15–17; on point-to-point global connections, 50–51; on pro-/anti-social accumulation, 98; on "rational" choice, 89–90; on spatial strategies, 9, 68, 139

Fiker Siferd ("*Love Verdict*") movie, 53

film. *See* videos

finter (good-fortune gift), 128, 130

food taboos and craft workers, 29

Freeman, Dena, 97

friendships, strategic, 121, 126

funerals, 95, 98, 115, 148

Genu, Qeñazmach Teka, 34, 99–100

Getanet, 102–104, 108–109, 111, 117

getter (countryside), 27

Gibe region, 28

Gibson-Graham, J. K., 17, 156, 166, 167–168

gifting: *finter*, 128, 130; between genders, 122; gift income, 41, 55, 120, 122–127; invitations as, 121–122, 124, 128, 147, 161; and stratification, 14, 126–127, 130, 133; *zemed* relationships through, 116. *See also* exchange; reciprocity

Giriama, 114–115

Goha Tsion (Kare Gowa), 26–27

Gondola, Didier, 137

Goodstein, Elizabeth, 68, 82

government work: all kinds valued equally, 75, 94; benefits of, 94; decrease in, 35, 84, 89, 131; desirability of, 31, 35–36, 77; education as no longer assuring, 34, 72; expectations of getting, 4, 35–36, 75, 131; low-level, 36, 40; occupations, 93–96; as prioritizing social life over work, 149; and relationships, 84, 95; salary/status as not based on production, 84, 98; status of, 94–98; transcending class, 95; unemployment as only alternative to, 75, 77; vocational students' views of, 96

grandparents, 120

Gurage people, 32, 35

Guyer, Jane, 68, 83, 136

gwadeñña (friend), 115

gwilt (right), 28, 31

habesha, 176n5

Habesha bahil (Ethiopian culture), 146–147

habitus, 60, 88

habt (wealth), 72

Habtamu, 6, 56–60, 137–138, 157–162

haggling/bargaining, 105, 106

Haile, 5–8, 45, 155

Haile Selassie, 28, 30–31

Harvey, David, 10, 16, 82, 165–166, 168

hilm (dream), 56

Hirmata market, 27–28, 30

HIV/AIDS, 52–54, 58–60

Hoben, Allan, 31, 95, 96

Holyfield, 160–162

homes and home life, 36–38

honor, 91

Hoolaa Café, 49

hope/hopelessness: ambition/expectations tied to, 3, 71–77; and entrepreneurial individualism, 162–164; and imagination, 43; and khat, 57–58; leaving the present, 155–156; and linear progress, 9; and narratives from film, 54–55; neoliberalism on, 15–17; passivity, 137; simultaneous, 171n1; taking place of knowledge, 164; *tesfa qoretewal*, 1, 171n1; and unstructured time, 44, 54, 160

hotels, 40

Hutchinson, Sharon, 135

hwalaker (backward), 52, 139

iddir (burial association), 20, 71, 79, 131, 148

identity: class, 90; *duriye*, 61–62, 65–66, 109; films examining, 51; flexibility in, 99–100; through gifting, 127; through goods owned/consumed, 12, 90, 139; through migration, 137, 138; separate from community, 90; urban youth culture, 70, 109; through work, 12–13, 84, 90, 95, 129

imagination: and aspirations, 54–55, 59–60, 76, 138, 156; and boredom, 82; enabling hope, 43, 163; as harmful to youths, 64–65; khat and, 48, 50–51, 54–55, 60–61; and neoliberal capitalism, 165, 168; as source of new knowledge, 43–44, 165, 168–169; videos and, 46–47, 60

IMF-mandated reforms, 33–34

inequality: and neoliberal capitalism, 130–132, 168–169; reciprocity and, 127–130; and relationships, 114

injera (bread), 71, 124, 173n4
International Coffee Organization, 34
international symbols, 109
invitations, 121–122, 124, 128, 147, 161
iqub (savings organization), 106
Italian occupation, 30, 146–147

Jeffrey, Craig, 4–5, 46, 71–72, 138
Jimma: from late 1800s to 1974, 27–32; from
    1974 to 1991, 32–33; post-1991, 33–36; city
    map of, 39; classification as urban, 27–28;
    homes, class and status in, 36–38; neighbor-
    hoods, street life, and economic opportunity
    in, 38–42
Jimma University, 34
Johnson-Hanks, Jennifer, 91, 107

Kabre, 129–130
Kaffa, 31, 32, 40
Kambata, 30–31
Kaplan, Robert, 162
Kassahun, 105–106, 109–111, 117–119
Katmandu, 65
Katz, Cindi, 60
Kebede, 80–81, 124–125, 143–144, 160–164
Kenya, 114–115
ketema (city), 26
Kezkaza Welafen ("*Cold Flame*") movie, 52–53
khat, 6; adult disapproval of, 44, 63–66; *ehje-
    bena* (eye-opener), 101; and imagination, 48,
    50–51, 54–55, 60–61; for insight, 56; *mirqa-
    na*, 56–57, 60, 145; rate of consumption of,
    55; and religion, 55; sale of, 41; and sex, 58–
    59; and watching videos, 47–48
khat houses, 48–49
Kifle, 158–159
kindergartens, private, 74
kitfo (beef dish), 124, 176n2
knowledge, as equated with wealth, 72–73
Koselleck, Reinhart, 75, 82
Kulo Berr neighborhood, 40–41, 125–126

land-owning class, 28–32
land rights, 97
Larkin, Brian, 51, 173n5
La Sape, 137, 138–139
Learning to Labour (Willis), 88
Levine, Donald, 72, 74, 75, 96, 115
lewt (progress), 8, 171n3
Liechty, Mark, 11–12, 65, 90
love, concepts of, 53–54

MacGaffey, Janet, 138–139
MacLeod, Jay, 127

Madagascar, 3, 65, 122
Maes, Kenneth, 171n3
mahaber (association to honor saint), 148
Mahel Ketema, 30, 96, 125, 172n4
mango parable, 83–84
Mannheim, Karl, ix
map: of Ethiopia, viii; of Jimma, 39
marriage: and craft workers, 29; men's expecta-
    tions surrounding, 69, 77–79; and raising
    children, 69, 79–81, 85, 144, 160, 163;
    women's expectations surrounding, 79
Marxian social theory, 177n1; on class, 11;
    on culture and economy, 168; on time and
    labor, 69, 84–86
masculine ideals, 2, 12, 81, 88, 142–143
Masquelier, Adeline, 54
material consumption, 70
material wealth: as means to status, 133; rela-
    tionships as means to, 114–119, 129; unem-
    ployment as means to, 122–126
Matric Sefer neighborhood, 39
Melanesia, 128–129
Menelik, Emperor, 176–177n6
mengist sira (government work), 94. *See also*
    government work
merchants, small-scale, 40
metfo (bad), 93
mezor (wander around), 173n8
middle class: attaining through education, 89,
    133; and consumption, 11–12, 90; and gift
    income, 123, 126; standard of living of, 37–
    38
migration: within Ethiopia, 151, 160–161; to
    Middle East, 141–142; reasons for, 71, 110,
    151; social relationships and, 140–143; tem-
    porary jobs and, 144–145; U.S. Diversity Visa
    lottery and, 83, 136–139
minibus driver, 167
mirqana, 56–57, 60, 145
Miyazaki, Hirokazu, 17, 156
modernity, 8–9; and family size, 81; films as
    models of, 53; through migration, 136, 138
modernization narratives, 2, 8
Mohammed, 70–71, 81, 104
multiparty elections, 35
Mulugeta: daily activities of, 45–46; family
    occupations of, 6; and too much time, 46
mulu qen (full day), 57
Muslims: and khat use, 55; and reciprocity,
    118–119

narratives of modernization, 2, 8
narratives of progress, 69–71; in contrast with
    DV lottery, 136; through education, 159;

through raising a family, 163–164; social life decreases, 148; through spatial movement, 141

nationalization of land, 32

neighborhoods, 38–42; as a factor affecting reciprocity, 125–126

neoliberal capitalism, 10, 15–17, 130–132, 164–169

Newell, Sasha, 137, 138

Niger, 2

Nigussie, Dr., 63

Nuer, 85, 135

occupations: government, 93–96; low-status, 92–93, 99, 110–111; and values, 106–112

Oromo: Christian, 41; land grants to, 30; Muslim, 31–32, 40; occupations among, 28–29, 31; seizure of land belonging to, 30

Orthodox Christians. *See* Christians

Outline of a Theory of Practice (Bourdieu), 88

Pankhurst, Alula, 29, 97

Papua New Guinea, 61, 73

parents, 69, 77, 120

Parkin, David, 14, 114–115

Parry, Jonathan, 98

patron/client relationships, 95, 96–97

personhood, notions of, 97

Philosophy and Social Hope (Rorty), 164–165

Piot, Charles, 15, 98, 129–130, 138, 153

plow-farming, 114

political uprisings, 3

Poluha, Eva, 96–97, 174n1

portable shops, 105–106, 110

Postone, Moishe, 84–85

postrevolutionary urban Ethiopia, 33–36

pottery, 29

pragmatism, 164–165

present, as indefinite period, 83

priesthood, 28

private education, 74, 81

progress, 1; and becoming an adult, 77–82; boredom and, 82–83; contrast between generations, 71, 131, 146–147; education and expectations of, 71–77; leaving Ethiopia key to, 8; *lewt*, 8, 171n3; narratives of (*see* narratives of progress); rural-urban migrant perceptions of, 70; and technology, 82

prosocial accumulation, 98

public sector. *See* government work

qoshasha (dirty), 93

Qottebe Corner, 42

Qottebe Sefer neighborhood, 41–42, 126

Ralph, Michael, 46, 84

reciprocity: 2008/2009 changes in, 161; and adulthood, 81; and redistribution of wealth, 127–130; religion and, 118–119; shop owners and, 105, 117, 119, 132; for startup capital, 119, 166; at video houses, 115–116; Western vs. Ethiopian, 147–148; among working youth, 115–119

relationships: expanding through redistribution, 127–130; to family/community, 69, 77–79, 81–82, 84; gift vs. commodity exchanges, 98; as goal of exchange, 130; and government work, 84, 95; hierarchical, 96; identity as, 129–130; as means to material wealth, 114–119; patron/client, 95, 96–97; and views of Western culture, 147–148. *See also* reciprocity

religious holidays, 148

restaurants, 40

revolutionary urban Ethiopia, 32–33

Richards, Paul, 51

Rorty, Richard, 17, 156, 164–165, 177n1

Rostow, W. W., 83

rural youth, 34–35, 65–66

Sa'ar Sefer neighborhood, 39–40, 93, 95–96, 125

sandal maker, 80

sapeurs, 13, 137, 138–139

secondary school: graduates and unemployment, 1, 4–5, 34; private, 5; public, 32–33

second coming of Christ, 83

self-employment, 36

Senegal, 2

Serneels, Pieter, 87

shared consumption, 121

shifta (bandit), 174n12

shoeshines, 93, 100, 107–108, 110, 118, 150

shop owners, 40, 96, 105–106, 118; and reciprocity, 105, 117, 119, 132

shuro (chickpea paste), 80

siblings, 6, 69, 140, 158

Siraj, 70–71, 104–105, 110–111, 117–119, 132, 151, 166–167

sira yinakal (work not respected), 93, 175n2

slaves, 28

socialism, 2. *See also* Derg regime

soldiers, 28

Solomon, 69, 77, 79–81, 140, 143, 145

Spaces of Hope (Harvey), 165

spatial strategies, 136–146

sports and consumption, 108–109

stages of growth, 83

Stambach, Amy, 174n1

status: from alternative youth culture, 70, 109;
   based on relationships, 28, 91–92; flexibility
   in, 99–100; internal and external, 91–92,
   106–111; as less important for parents, 77;
   of occupations, 92–100, 106–111; unemployment as, 46; valued over income, 89; vs.
   class, 91
stigma: toward craft workers, 28–29, 92–93,
   97; and form of exchange, 116; United
   States as freedom from, 146, 150–151
Strathern, Marilyn, 128–129
stratification: historical roots of unemployment,
   25–27; and reciprocity, 128–129; urban,
   31–33, 42
street life, 38–42
street-side shop owner, 105–106
street vendors/workers, 41, 70, 117
sus (addiction), 50
symbolic capital, 127

Taddesse, 118–119
tailoring, 70–71
Tanzania, 109
taxi driver, 151–152
teaching, 74
Teddy, 116
tej (honey wine), 70
tella (home-brewed beer), 39, 71
tesfa qoretewal (hope is cut), 1, 171n1
Tesfaye, 116, 174n13
Teshome, Tewodros, 52
thieves, 108
Thompson, E. P., 85
thought defined as stress/trouble, 46–47, 173n2
time: as independent variable, 85; killing, 10,
   46, 173n1; as relationships, 83–85; and
   space and neoliberalism, 10–11; tasks measured by, 85; unstructured, 44–47, 63, 76,
   85
time, experience of, 68–69; by adults vs. youth,
   63; boredom as, 82–83; as burdensome, 44,
   46–47, 49–50; in different cultures, 82–83;
   during mirqana, 60; while in school, 76
tiqem (use/value), 72, 121
Tiv, 89
Togo, 129–130
translators, 116
Tsehay, 128, 130

uket (knowledge), 72
unemployed youth: and absence of change, 76;
   as chosen lifestyle, 81, 83, 87, 99, 123; depression among, 4; and gift income, 122–126;
   and income vs. social relations, 119–120; and

khat consumption, 60; and reciprocity, 119–
   122; and reenrollment in education, 158–159;
   revisited in 2008/2009, 155, 158–164; rural,
   35; sex and marriage among, 53–54
unemployment rates: as higher among educated, 4, 34; as higher among government-work
   seekers, 36; in Jimma, 1, 172n6 (ch. 1)
United States: conceptualization of time in,
   83; conceptualization of work in, 140–141;
   Diversity Visa lottery, 83, 136–139; dreams
   of, 137–138; migration to, 59–60, 136–138;
   as place of social freedom, 146, 150–151
urban, definitions of, 25–27
urban youth culture, 70, 108–109
utopianism, 165–166, 168

values systems, 106–112
vegetable sellers, 41
vernacular modernisms, 9
video houses: as employment, 62, 115–116;
   raids of, 62–66
videos: consumption of, 47, 50–55, 60–61, 64–
   66; Ethiopian films, 52–54; and imagination,
   46–47, 60; Indian films, 173n3; seen as educational, 51; seen as harmful, 63–64
vocational students, 19–20; avoidance of khat
   by, 57, 58; and concerns about stigma, 92;
   and desires to migrate, 150–151; and negative views of government work, 96, 149; on
   "old culture," 146–147, 149; working, 106;
   working for money and not relationships,
   149

wages, government vs. self-employment, 36,
   149
waiters, 151
waiting, cultures of, 46–47
watch repair and sales, 70, 104–105
wealth in things/people, 114, 119, 121, 122
weaving, 29
Weber, Max, 11–12, 91
weddings, 79–80, 95
Weiss, Brad, 46, 60, 61, 82, 109
welding, 92
wichey (departing gift), 120
Willis, Paul, 12–13, 88, 127
women: as duriye, 107; and education, 5, 159;
   equating employment with equality, 79; generational differences among, 71; gifting to
   boyfriends, 175n1 (ch. 5); household duties
   of, 46, 47; and khat, 48, 49; and migration to
   Middle East, 141–142, 167; not considered
   among "youths," 65; and reciprocity, 115,
   122, 143; as shoeshines, 107; as single heads

of households, 33, 40, 124; supporting families, 142–143; unstructured time among, 46–47, 65; and video houses, 50; and *zemed*, 120

work: 2008/2009 discursive changes toward, 161–162; choosing to, 100–106; Emperor Menelik on, 176–177n6; not considered a valued activity, 93; purposes of, 73, 84

working youth: case studies, 101–106; and reciprocity, 115–119; values of, 106–111

yasallafal (causes to be passed), 46

yasgedal (causes to be killed), 46

Yem, 31, 32

yiluññta (fear of judgment of others), 11–12, 87, 93, 99–100, 111, 146, 150–152

Yonas, 62, 64

Yosef, 116

youth: and becoming an adult, 12, 52, 77–81; concepts of, 2, 64–65; in contrast with parents' generation, 71, 76–77, 131, 146–147; as culturally constructed category, 65–66; education and job prospects of, 5; on Ethiopian culture, 146–147; extension of, 3; and gender, 65; as "historical offspring of modernity," 2; on marriage and children, 79–81; and masculine ideals, 2, 12, 81, 88, 142–143; rural, 34–35, 65–66; urban youth culture, 70, 108–109; and video houses, 50; as voting block, 35. *See also* working youth

Zambia, 2

zemed (close ones) relationships, 115–120

Zewde, Bahru, 28

ziqqiteñña sira (lower, inferior), 93

Zournazi, Mary, 16

Daniel Mains is Wick Cary Assistant Professor of Honors at the University of Oklahoma.